Ancient
Civilizations
Biographies

Ancient
Civilizations
Biographies

Judson Knight

Stacy A. McConnell and
Lawrence W. Baker, Editors

AN IMPRINT OF THE GALE GROUP

DETROIT · SAN FRANCISCO · LONDON
BOSTON · WOODBRIDGE, CT

Ancient Civilizations: Biographies

Judson Knight

Staff

Stacy A. McConnell, Lawrence W. Baker, *U•X•L Editors*
Carol DeKane Nagel, *U•X•L Managing Editor*
Tom Romig, *U•X•L Publisher*

Rita Wimberley, *Senior Buyer*
Evi Seoud, *Assistant Production Manager*
Mary Beth Trimper, *Composition Manager*

Margaret A. Chamberlain, *Permissions Specialist (pictures)*
Martha Schiebold and Michelle DiMercurio, *Senior Cover Art Directors*
Pamela A.E. Galbreath, *Senior Page Art Director*
Cynthia Baldwin, *Product Design Manager*
Barbara J. Yarrow, *Graphic Services Supervisor*

Linda Mahoney, LM Design, *Typesetting*

Front cover: Cleopatra, drawing. Archive Photos. Reproduced by permission.
Back cover: Confucius, drawing. Library of Congress.

Library of Congress Cataloging-in-Publication Data

Knight, Judson

Ancient Civilizations: Biographies / Judson Knight; edited by Stacy A. McConnell and Lawrence W. Baker

p. cm.

Includes biographical references and index

ISBN 0-7876-3985-0

Civilization, Ancient–Juvenile literature. 2. Biography–To 500–Juvenile literature.

[1. Civilization, Ancient–Biography.] I. McConnell, Stacy A. II. Title

CB311 .K595 2000

930–dc21   99-045751
  [B]—DC21   99-20707
                                                                                      CIP

To Tyler, from her ancient daddy;
and to Deidre, from her modern husband.

Contents

Biographies

Akhenaton attempted to completely reshape Egyptian religion. *(Reproduced by permission. Corbis-Bettmann.)*

Advisory Board

Special thanks are due to U•X•L's Ancient Civilizations Reference Library advisors for their invaluable comments and suggestions.

- Jonathan Betz-Zall, Children's Librarian, Sno-Isle Regional Library, Edmonds, Washington

- Nancy Guidry, Young Adult Librarian, Santa Monica Public Library, Santa Monica, California

- Karen Shugrue, Junior High Media Specialist, Agawam Junior High School, Feeding Hills, Massachusetts.

Reader's Guide

Ancient Civilizations: Biographies presents the life stories of thirty-eight individuals who had a great influence on the ancient civilization in which they lived. The biographies span from the beginning of Sumerian civilization in 3500 B.C. to the decline of the Teotihuacán around A.D. 750. Well-known historical figures, such as Greek philosopher Aristotle and Persian emperor Xerxes, are featured, as well as lesser-known figures, such as Celtic queen Boadicea and Egyptian ruler Hatshepsut. More than 50 black-and-white illustrations and photographs enliven the text, while cross references provide easy access to related figures. Sidebars in every entry focus on high-interest topics, and a "For More Information" section guides the researcher to other reference sources. *Ancient Civilizations: Biographies* also features a glossary of terms used throughout the volumes, a timeline containing significant milestones within the lives of the individuals profiled, and an index covering the people, places, and events discussed throughout *Ancient Civilizations: Biographies*.

Comments and Suggestions

We welcome your comments on *Ancient Civilizations: Biographies,* as well as your suggestions for persons to be featured in future editions. Please write, Editors, *Ancient Civilizations: Biographies,* U•X•L, 27500 Drake Rd., Farmington Hills, Michigan, 48331-3535; call toll-free: 1-800-877-4253; fax to (248) 699-8097; or send e-mail via-http://www.galegroup.com.

Words to Know

A

Acropolis: An elevated fortress in Greek cities.

Ancestor: An earlier person in one's line of parentage, usually more distant in time than a grandparent.

Anoint: To pour oil over someone's head as a symbol that God has chosen that person to fill a position of leadership.

Apostle: A religious figure who is sent out to teach, preach, and perform miracles.

Archaeology: The scientific study of past civilizations.

Architect: Someone who designs a building or other structure.

Aristocrat: A very wealthy and/or powerful person.

Assassination: Killing, usually of an important leader, for political reasons.

B

Baptism: To be lowered into water as a symbol of death and rebirth.

Bureaucracy: A network of officials who run a government.

Bust: A sculpture of a human head, neck, and shoulders.

C

Caravan: A company of travelers, usually with pack animals, through a desert or other forbidding region.

Caste system: A system of ranking people into very social groups, which prevailed in India from ancient times to the modern day.

Census: A count of the people living in a country.

Civil servant: Someone who works for the government.

Civil war: A military conflict that occurs when a group of citizens within a nation attempts to break away from the rule of the government.

Commoner: Someone who is not a member of a royal or noble class.

Concubine: A woman whose role toward a man is like that of a wife, but without the social and legal status of a wife.

Constitution: A set of written laws governing a nation.

Contemporary (n.): Someone who lives at the same time as another person.

Cremation: The burning, as opposed to burial, of a dead body.

Crucifixion: A Roman punishment in which the victim was nailed up to a cross until he died.

Cult: A small religious group, most often with highly unusual beliefs.

D

Deify: To turn someone or something into a god.

Deity: A god.

Democracy: A form of government in which the people, usually through elected representatives, rule.

Descendant: Someone who is related to an earlier person, or *ancestor.*

Disciple: A close follower of a religious teacher.

E

Edict: A command.

Epic: A long poem that recounts the adventures of a legendary hero.

Epistle: A letter.

Eunuch: A man who has been castrated, thus making him incapable of sex or sexual desire.

F

Famine: A period when there is not enough food in a region to feed all its people.

Fasting: Deliberately going without food, often but not always for religious reasons.

G

Gentile: Someone who is not a Jew.

H

Hellenic: Greek.

Hellenistic: Influenced by Greece.

Heresy: Something that goes against established religious doctrine.

Hoplite: A heavily armed foot soldier.

I

Islam: A faith that arose in Arabia in the 600s A.D., led by the prophet Muhammad (A.D. 570?–632.)

L

Legacy: Something that is left to a later generation.

Legitimacy: The right of a ruler to hold power.

M

Martyr: Somebody who dies for their faith.

Medieval: Relating to the Middle Ages.

Mercenary: A professional soldier who will fight for whoever pays him.

Middle Ages: The period from the fall of the Roman Empire to the beginning of the Renaissance, roughly 500 to 1500 A.D.

Middle Class: A group in between the rich and the poor, or the rich and the working class.

Millennium: A period of a thousand years.

Mint (v.): To produce currency.

Missionary: Someone who goes to other lands to convert others to their religion.

Moat: A trench, filled with water, which surrounds a castle or city.

Monarch: A king.

Monotheism: Belief in one god.

Muslim: A believer in Islam.

N

Noble: A ruler within a kingdom who has an inherited title and lands, but who is less powerful than the king or queen.

O

Obelisk: A tall, free-standing column of stone.

Oligarchy: A government ruled by a few people.

P

Pagan: Someone who worships many gods; also used as an adjective.

Papyrus: A type of reed from which the Egyptians made the first type of "paper."

Peasant: A farmer who works a small plot of land.

Phalanx: A column of hoplites designed for offensive warfare.

Pharisee: A member of a group of Jewish religious scholars who demanded strict adherence to religious law.

Philosophy: A discipline which seeks to reach a general understanding of values and of reality.

Plague: A disease or other disaster that spreads among a group of people.

Proportion: The size of one thing in relation to something else, and the proper representation of their relationship.

R

Rabbi: A Jewish teacher or priest.

Radical (adj.): Thorough or sweeping changes in society; used as an noun for a person who advocates such changes.

Regent: Someone who governs a country when the monarch is too young, too old, or too sick to lead.

Reincarnation: The idea that people are reborn on earth, and live and die, again and again.

Relief: In sculpture, a carved picture, distinguished from regular sculpture because it is two-dimensional.

Renaissance: A period of renewed interest in learning and the arts which began in Europe in the 1300s and continued to the 1700s.

Revolution: In politics, an armed uprising against the rulers of a nation or area.

S

Sack (v.): To destroy a city.

Satrap: A governor in the Persian Empire.

Scribe: A small and very powerful group in ancient society who knew how to read and write.

Siege: A sustained military attack against a city.

Stele (or stela): A large stone pillar, usually inscribed with a message commemorating a specific event.

Stupa: A dome-shaped Buddhist temple.

T

Theorem: A statement of fact in logic or mathematics, derived from other formulas or propositions.

Totalitarianism: A political system in which the government exerts total, or near-total, control.

U

Usurp: To seize power.

Utopia: A perfect society.

V

Vassal: A ruler who is subject to another ruler.

Vineyard: A place where grapes are grown for making wine.

Vizier: A chief minister.

W

West (cap.): The cultures and civilizations influenced by ancient Greece and Rome.

Z

Ziggurat: A Mesopotamian temple tower.

Timeline

c. **3500** B.C.: Beginnings of Sumerian civilization.

c. **3100** B.C.: Pharaoh Menes unites the kingdoms of Upper and Lower Egypt.

c. **3000** B.C.: Babylon established.

c. **2920** B.C.: First Dynasty begins in Egypt.

c. **2800** B.C.: Mycenaeans leave the Black Sea area, moving toward Greece.

2750 B.C.: Early Dynastic Period begins in Sumer.

c. **2650** B.C.: Beginning of Old Kingdom in Egypt.

c. **2650** B.C.: Step Pyramid of Saqqara, designed by **Imhotep**, built under reign of pharaoh Zoser.

c. **2550** B.C.: Great Pyramid of Cheops built in Egypt.

c. **2500** B.C.: Indus Valley civilization begins in India.

c. **2334** B.C.: **Sargon of Akkad**, first great Mesopotamian ruler and founder of Akkadian empire, born.

c. **2300** B.C.: Early Dynastic Period ends in Sumer; Akkadian Empire established.

c. 2200 B.C.: Hsia, semi-legendary first dynasty of China, begins.

2150 B.C.: End of Old Kingdom in Egypt; beginning of First Intermediate Period.

c. 2150 B.C.: Akkadian Empire ends with Gutian invasion of Mesopotamia; rise of Ur.

c. 2000 B.C.: Hurrians invade northern Mesopotamia, establish kingdom of Mitanni.

c. 2000 B.C.: Origins of Gilgamesh Epic in Sumer.

c. 2000 B.C.: Phoenician civilization established.

c. 2000 B.C.: Lung-shan culture develops in northern China.

c. 2000 B.C: Beginnings of Mayan civilization in Mesoamerica.

c. 2000 B.C.: Establishment of Kushite civilization in Africa.

c. 2000 B.C.: Beginnings of Minoan civilization in Crete.

1813 B.C.: Shamshi-Adad, first important Assyrian ruler, takes throne.

1792 B.C.: End of Old Babylonia in Mesopotamia; Hammurabi, who later establishes first legal code in history, takes throne.

1766 B.C.: Shang Dynasty, first historic line of Chinese kings, begins.

1759 B.C.: Middle Kingdom ends in Egypt; beginning of Second Intermediate Period.

c. 1750 B.C.: Beginning of Hittite civilization, establishment of capital at Hattush in Asia Minor.

c. 1700 B.C.: Crete experiences earthquake; later the Minoans rebuild their palaces at Knossos and other sites.

c. 1700–1500 B.C.: Phoenicians develop the world's first alphabet.

c. 1650 B.C.: Beginnings of Mycenaean civilization in Greece.

c. 1500 B.C.: Indo-Europeans invade India; beginning of Vedic Age.

c. 1500 B.C.: Formative or Preclassic Period begins in the Americas.

c. 1500 B.C.: Thebes founded on Greek mainland.

c. 1500–c. 1300 B.C.: Kingdom of Mitanni flourishes in Mesopotamia.

1473 B.C.: Pharaoh **Hatshepsut** assumes sole power in Egypt; first significant female ruler in history.

c. 1450 B.C.: Minoan civilization in Crete comes to an end, probably as a result of volcanic eruption on Thera.

1363 B.C.: Ashur-uballit, who establishes the first Assyrian empire, begins reign.

1352 B.C.: Pharaoh Amenhotep IV begins his reign in Egypt.

c. 1347: Amenhotep IV changes his name to **Akhenaton** and introduces sweeping religious reforms.

1323 B.C.: Death of Tutankhamen in Egypt; power struggle follows, along with effort to erase memory of Akhenaton.

c. 1300 B.C.: City of San Lorenzo established in Mesoamerica.

1279 B.C.: Beginning of Pharaoh Ramses II's reign in Egypt.

c. 1200 B.C.: Sea Peoples bring an end to Hittite civilization in Asia Minor.

c. 1200 B.C.: Aramaeans, after briefly controlling Babylonia, conquer Syria.

c. 1200 B.C.: Olmec civilization established in what is now Mexico.

c. 1200 B.C.: Bantu peoples migrate southward from what is now Nigeria.

c. 1200 B.C.: Trojan War.

c. 1200 B.C.: Etruscans settle on Italian peninsula.

c. 1200–900 B.C.: Carving of giant heads by Olmec in Mesoamerica.

c. 1140 B.C.: Macedonians move southward, displacing the Dorians from northern Greece.

c. 1100 B.C.: Dorians bring an end to Mycenaean civilization; beginning of Dark Ages in Greece, which last for four centuries.

1070 B.C.: End of New Kingdom in Egypt; Third Intermediate Period Begins.

1027 B.C.: Revolt led by Prince Wu Wang brings an end to Shang Dynasty, and establishment of Chou Dynasty, in China.

c. 1020 B.C.: Beginning of Saul's reign in Israel.

c. 1000 B.C.: Saul killed; **David** becomes ruler of Israel.

c. 1000 B.C.: End of Vedic Age, beginning of Epic Age, in India.

c. 1000 B.C.: Beginnings of Chavín civilization in South America.

c. 1000 B.C.: Celts begin to spread from Gaul throughout Europe.

c. 960 B.C.: David dies; Solomon becomes ruler of Israel.

922 B.C.: End of Solomon's reign, and of unified kingdom of Israel.

800s B.C.: Dorians establish Sparta.

883 B.C.: Ashurnasirpal II assumes throne in Assyria, establishes Neo-Assyrian Empire.

879 B.C.: Beginning of King Ben-Hadad II's reign in Syria.

c. 850 B.C.: Greeks start trading with other peoples; beginning of the end of the Dark Ages.

c. 800 B.C.: Carthage established by Phoenicians.

c. 800 B.C.: Poets Homer and Hesiod flourish in Greece.

700s B.C.: Scythians drive Cimmerians out of the Black Sea region; Cimmerians spread to Asia Minor and Assyria.

776 B.C.: First Olympic Games held.

771 B.C.: Invasion by nomads from the north forces Chou Dynasty of China to move capital eastward; end of Western Chou period.

753 B.C.: Traditional date of Rome's founding; Romulus first of seven legendary kings.

c. 751 B.C.: **Piankhi** takes throne in Kush.

745 B.C.: Tiglath-Pileser III begins reign in Assyria.

722 B.C.: Spring and Autumn Period, a time of widespread unrest, begins in China.

735 B.C.: Spartans begin twenty-year war with Messenia.

c. 732 B.C.: Assyrians gain control of Syria.

c. 725 B.C.: King Mita, probable source of the Midas legend, unites the Phrygians.

721 B.C.: Sargon II of Assyria conquers Israel and carries off its people, who become known as the Ten Lost Tribes of Israel.

715 B.C.: End of war with Messenia brings a rise to Spartan militarism.

712 B.C.: Kushites under Shabaka invade Egypt, establish Twenty-Fifth Dynasty.

712 B.C.: End of Third Intermediate Period, and beginning of Late Period, in Egypt.

c. 700 B.C.: End of Dark Ages, beginning of two-century Archaic Age, in Greece.

c. 700 B.C.: City-state of Athens, established centuries before, dominates Attica region in Greece.

600s B.C.: State of Magadha develops in eastern India.

600s B.C.: Important developments in Greek architecture: establishment of Doric order, first structures of stone rather than wood.

689 B.C.: Assyrians sack Babylon.

c. 685 B.C.: Gyges founds Mermnad dynasty in Lydia.

672 B.C.: Assyrians first drive Kushites out of Egypt, install Necho I as pharaoh.

669 B.C.: Beginning of Ashurbanipal's reign; last great Assyrian king.

667 B.C.: Assyrian troops under Ashurbanipal complete conquest of Egypt from Kushites.

Mid–600s B.C.: Meröe Period begins when Kushites, removed from power in Egypt, move their capital southward.

Mid–600s B.C.: Establishment of Ionian Greek trading colony at Naucratis in Egypt.

Mid–600s B.C.: Age of tyrants begins in Greece.

653 B.C.: Scythians overrun Iran.

652 B.C.: Shamash-shuma-ukin, ruler of Babylonia, leads revolt against his brother Ashurbanipal, king of Assyria.

c. 650 B.C.: Scribes in Egypt develop demotic script.

c. 650 B.C.: Macedonian dynasty begins in northern Greece.

648 B.C.: Ashurbanipal of Assyria subdues Babylonian revolt; his brother Shamash-shuma-ukin reportedly commits suicide.

625 B.C.: Thales, first Western philosopher, born in Ionian Greece.

627 B.C.: Ashurbanipal of Assyria dies.

625 B.C.: Nabopolassar establishes Chaldean (Neo-Babylonian) Empire.

621 B.C.: Draco appointed by Athenian oligarchs; creates a set of extremely harsh laws.

616 B.C.: Power-sharing of Sabines and Latins in Rome ends with Etruscan takeover under legendary king Tarquinius Priscus.

613 B.C.: First recorded sighting of Halley's Comet by Chinese astronomers.

612 B.C.: Babylonians and Medes destroy Nineveh; end of Neo-Assyrian Empire.

610s B.C.: Babylonia and Media divide the Middle East between them.

c. 610–c. 580 B.C.: Female poet Sappho flourishes in Greece.

c. 600 B.C.: Pharaoh Necho II of Egypt sends a group of Carthaginian mariners on voyage around African continent.

c. 600 B.C.: End of the Horse Period, beginning of the Camel Period, in the Sahara Desert.

c. 600 B.C.: **Nebuchadnezzar II** builds Hanging Gardens in Babylon, one of the Seven Wonders of the Ancient World.

Late 600s, early 500s B.C.: Romans wage series of wars against Sabines, Latins, and Etruscans.

500s B.C.: Armenia arises in region formerly known as Urartu.

500s B.C.: Career of Lao-tzu, Chinese philosopher.

500s B.C.: High point of Etruscan civilization in Italy.

586 B.C.: **Nebuchadnezzar II** destroys Israelites' capital at Jerusalem; beginning of Babylonian Captivity for Israelites.

c. 560 B.C.: Beginning of Croesus's reign in Lydia.

559 B.C.: Cyrus the Great of Persia takes the throne.

550 B.C.: Cyrus the Great of Persia defeats the Medes, establishes Persian Empire.

c. 550 B.C.: King Croesus of Lydia conquers Greek city-states of Ionia.

c. 550 B.C.: Temple of Artemis at Ephesus, one of the Seven Wonders of the Ancient World, built.

546 B.C.: Persian armies under Cyrus the Great depose King Croesus and take over Lydia.

546 B.C.: Cyrus the Great of Persia conquers Ionian city-states of Greece.

538 B.C.: Persians conquer Babylonia; end of Chaldean (Neo-Babylonian) Empire, and of Israelites' Babylonian Captivity.

c. 528 B.C.: In India, Gautama Siddartha experiences his enlightenment; becomes known as the **Buddha**.

521 B.C.: Darius the Great of Persia conquers Punjab region of western India.

510 B.C.: Athenians remove Hippias from power.

505 B.C.: Founding of Roman Republic.

c. 500 B.C.: End of Epic Age in India.

c. 500 B.C.: Kingdom of Aksum established in Africa.

c. 500 B.C.: End of Archaic Age, beginning of Classical Age, in Greece.

c. 500 B.C.: Celts (Gauls) enter northern Italy.

c. 500 B.C.: Various Celtic tribes settle in Britain.

500 B.C.: Chinese philosopher **Confucius** accepts a series of official appointments from Duke Ting.

485 B.C.: Persians under **Xerxes** suppress revolt in Egypt.

481 B.C.: End of Spring and Autumn Period of Chou Dynasty in China.

480 B.C.: **Xerxes** burns Athens.

479 B.C.: Golden Age of Greece begins.

478 B.C.: Delian League founded in Greece, with Athens as its leading city-state.

474 B.C.: Carthaginians end Etruscan dreams of empire with defeat at Cumae; Etruscan civilization begins to decline.

460 B.C.: **Pericles** becomes sole archon of Athens, beginning the splendid Age of Pericles.

453 B.C.: Warring States Period begins in China, only ending when Ch'in Dynasty replaces Chou in 221 B.C.

451 B.C.: The "Twelve Tables," first Roman legal code, established.

449 B.C.: Persian Wars officially come to an end.

c. 440 B.C.: Parthenon built in Athens.

c. 440 B.C.: **Phidias** sculpts Statue of Zeus at Olympia, one of the Seven Wonders of the Ancient World.

431 B.C.: Peloponnesian War between Athens and Sparta begins in Greece.

430 B.C.: **Herodotus** begins publishing *The History*.

429 B.C.: Plague breaks out in war-torn Athens.

420 B.C.: Because it broke Olympic truce by attacking Athens, Sparta keeps it athletes out of the Olympic Games.

404 B.C.: Athens surrenders to Sparta, ending Peloponnesian War.

404 B.C.: Golden Age of Classical Greece comes to an end.

c. 400 B.C.: Tres Zapotes replaces La Venta as principal Olmec ceremonial center.

c. 400 B.C.: Decline of Chavín civilization in South America.

300s B.C.: Ch'in state emerges in western China.

Mid–390s B.C.: **Plato** travels throughout Mediterranean world, begins writings.

390 B.C.: Beginnings of Roman military buildup after expulsion of Gauls.

Mid–380s B.C.: Plato establishes Academy in Athens.

Mid–300s B.C.: Mausoleum at Halicarnassus, one of the Seven Wonders of the Ancient World, built.

359 B.C.: Philip II takes throne in Macedon, and five years later begins conquest of Balkan peninsula.

c. 350 B.C.: Aristotle writes constitution for Athens.

343 B.C.: Aristotle becomes tutor of young Macedonian prince Alexander (Alexander the Great).

338 B.C.: Macedonian forces under Philip II defeat Greek city-states at Charonea; Macedonia now controls Greece.

336 B.C.: Philip II assassinated; 20-year-old Alexander III (**Alexander the Great**) becomes king of Macedon.

335 B.C.: Alexander consolidates his power, dealing with rebellions in Macedon and Greek city-states.

335 B.C.: Aristotle establishes Lyceum, school in Athens.

334 B.C.: Alexander begins his conquests by entering Asia Minor.

334 B.C.: Beginning now and for the last 12 years of his life, **Aristotle** writes most of his works.

332 B.C.: End of Late Period in Egypt; country will not be ruled by Egyptians again for some 1,500 years.

331 B.C.: Alexander establishes city of Alexandria in Egypt.

330 B.C.: Persepolis, capital of the Persian Empire, falls to Alexander the Great.

324 B.C.: Chandragupta Maurya, founder of Mauryan dynasty, takes the throne of Magadha in eastern India.

323 B.C.: Beginning of Hellenistic Age, as Greek culture takes root over the next two centuries in lands conquered by Alexander.

312 B.C.: Seleucid empire established over Persia, Mesopotamia, and much of the southwestern Asia.

c. 300 B.C.: Sarmatians drive the Scythians back to the Caucasus, and begin occupation of Black Sea region.

c. 300 B.C.: Composition of *Mahabharata,* India epic, begins; writing will continue for the next six centuries.

c. 300 B.C.: Hinduism develops from the Vedic religion brought to India by the Aryans.

c. 300 B.C.: Kushites develop Merotic script.

290 B.C.: Romans defeat Samnites, establish control over much of southern Italy.

282 B.C.: Colossus of Rhodes, one of the Seven Wonders of the Ancient World, completed; destroyed in earthquake 54 years later.

c. 280 B.C.: Lighthouse of Alexandria, last of the Seven Wonders of the Ancient World, built.

279 B.C.: Celts invade Greece, but are driven out by Antigonus Gonatas.

272 B.C.: Bindusara, ruler of Mauryan dynasty of India, dies; his son **Asoka**, greatest Mauryan ruler, later takes throne.

264 B.C.: First Punic War between Rome and Carthage begins.

257 B.C.: King **Asoka** of India appoints "inspectors of morality" to ensure that his subjects are well-treated.

247 B.C.: Beginning of Parthian dynasty in Iran.

246 B.C.: End of Shang Dynasty in China.

241 B.C.: First Punic War ends with Roman defeat of Carthage; Rome controls Sicily, Corsica, and Sardinia.

223 B.C.: Antiochus the Great, most powerful Seleucid ruler, begins reign in Syria.

221 B.C.: Chinese under **Ch'in Shih Huang Ti** begin building Great Wall.

218 B.C.: **Hannibal** of Carthage launches Second Punic War against Romans, marching from Spain, over Alps, and into Italy.

213 B.C.: Emperor **Ch'in Shih Huang Ti** calls for burning of most books in China.

207 B.C.: End of shortlived Ch'in Dynasty in China; power struggle follows.

202 B.C.: Having defeated Hsiang Yü, Liu Pang (Han Kao-tzu) becomes emperor, establishes Han Dynasty in China.

197 B.C.: Romans defeat Macedonian forces under Philip V at Cynocephalae; beginning of end of Macedonian rule in Greece.

186 B.C.: Mauryan Empire of India collapses.

170s B.C.: Parthians begin half-century of conquests, ultimately replacing Seleucids as dominant power in Iran and southwest Asia.

165 B.C.: Nomadic Yüeh-Chih tribes, driven out of China, arrive in Bactria; later, Kushans emerge as dominant tribe.

c. 150 B.C.: Greco-Bactrians under Menander invade India.

149 B.C.: Romans launch Third Punic War against Carthage.

146 B.C.: Romans completely destroy Carthage, ending Third Punic War.

141 B.C.: Emperor **Han Wu Ti** takes throne in China.

133 B.C.: Chinese emperor Han Wu-ti launches four decades of war which greatly expand Chinese territory.

c. 130 B.C.: Kushans begin a century-long series of conquests, ultimately absorbing Greco-Bactrian kingdom.

c. 120 B.C.: Chang Chi'en, on a mission for Emperor **Han Wu Ti**, makes first Chinese contact with Greek influenced areas.

88 B.C.: Social War ends; Rome extends citizenship to non-Roman Italians.

88 B.C.: Sulla, rival of Roman consul Marius, becomes commander of forces against Mithradates the Great of Pontus in Asia Minor.

77 B.C.: Roman general Pompey sent to crush uprising in Spain.

60 B.C.: **Julius Caesar**, Pompey, and Crassus form First Triumvirate.

51 B.C.: After death of her father, Ptolemy XII, **Cleopatra** becomes co-ruler of Egypt with her brother and husband.

49 B.C.: Pompey orders Caesar to return from Rome; Caesar crosses the River Rubicon with his army.

44 B.C.: On March 15, a group of conspirators assassinates **Julius Caesar** in the chambers of the Roman senate.

44 B.C.: Octavian, Mark Antony, and Lepidus form Second Triumvirate.

37 B.C.: Mark Antony leaves his wife, Octavian's sister, and joins **Cleopatra**; launches military campaigns in southwest Asia.

37 B.C.: Herod the Great becomes vassal king in Roman-controlled Judea.

31 B.C.: Beginning of Octavian's sole control of Rome, end of a century of unrest.

31 B.C.: Beginning of *Pax Romana,* or "Roman Peace," which prevails throughout Roman world for two centuries.

27 B.C.: Octavian declared Emperor Caesar Augustus by Roman senate; Roman Empire effectively established.

24 B.C.: Romans attempt unsuccessfully to conquer southwestern Arabia.

17 B.C.: **Vergil's** *Aeneid* published.

c. 6 B.C.: **Jesus Christ** born.

9 A.D.: Wang Mang usurps throne of Han Dynasty in China, establishing Hsin Dynasty.

9 A.D.: Forces of Augustus defeated by Germans, ending Roman expansion to the north.

14 A.D.: Augustus dies; his stepson Tiberius becomes emperor, marking official establishment of Roman Empire.

23 A.D.: Han Dynasty regains control of China; beginning of the Later Han Period.

c. 30 A.D.: **Jesus Christ** dies.

35 A.D.: Seleucia, former capital of Seleucid Empire, attempts to break away from Parthian rule and establish Hellenistic kingdom.

c. 36 A.D.: Saul has vision on road to Damascus which leads him to embrace Christianity; becomes most important apostle.

41 A.D.: Caligula killed by Roman military; Claudius becomes emperor.

43 A.D.: Rome launches last major conquest, in Britain.

44 A.D.: Judea becomes Roman province.

47 A.D.: Victorious in Britain, Romans demand that all Britons surrender their weapons.

49 A.D.: Council of Jerusalem, early meeting of Christians attended by Apostle **Paul,** is held.

c. 50 A.D.: Josephus, Jewish historian whose work is one of the few non-biblical sources regarding Jesus, flourishes.

60 A.D.: After the Romans attack her family, **Boadicea,** queen of the Iceni people in Britain, leads revolt.

64 A.D.: Rebuilding of Temple in Jerusalem, begun by Herod the Great in 20 B.C., completed.

64 A.D.: Nero blames Christians for fire in Rome, beginning first major wave of persecutions.

69 A.D.: Vespasian becomes Roman emperor, begins establishing order throughout empire.

70 A.D.: Future Roman emperor Titus, son of Vespasian, destroys Jerusalem and its temple.

c. 78 A.D.: Kaniska, greatest Kushan ruler, takes throne; later extends Buddhism to China.

79 A.D.: Titus becomes Roman emperor.

79 A.D.: Mount Vesuvius erupts, destroying the city of Pompeii in Italy.

81 A.D.: Death of Titus; his brother, the tyrannical Domitian, becomes Roman emperor.

c. 90 A.D.: John writes Revelation, last book in the Bible.

98 A.D.: Roman historian Tacitus publishes *Germania,* one of the few contemporary accounts of German tribes and Britons.

100 A.D.: The Sakas, a Scythian tribe, take over Kushan lands in what is now Afghanistan.

c. 100 A.D.: Taoism, based on the ideas of Lao-tzu six centuries before, becomes a formal religion in China.

c. 100 A.D.: Establishment of Teotihuacán, greatest city of ancient America.

c. 100 A.D.: Old Silk Road, trade route between East and West, established.

135 A.D.: Roman emperor Hadrian banishes Jews from Jerusalem.

c. 150 A.D.: Nomadic Hsien-Pei tribe of China briefly conquers a large empire.

161 A.D.: Greek physician **Galen** goes to Rome; later becomes physician to Marcus Aurelius and other emperors.

174 A.D.: Roman troops under **Marcus Aurelius** defeat Germans.

184 A.D.: Yellow Turbans lead revolt against Han Dynasty emperor of China; revolt is crushed five years later by Ts'ao Ts'ao.

c. 200 A.D.: Germanic tribes conquer Sarmatians, ending their control over Black Sea area.

c. 200 A.D.: Zapotec people establish Monte Albán, first true city in Mesoamerica.

c. 200 A.D.: Anasazi tribe appears in what is now the southwestern United States.

200s A.D.: Diogenes Laertius writes *Lives of the Eminent Philosophers,* primary information source on Greek philosophers.

220 A.D.: Later Han Dynasty of China ends.

221 A.D.: Three Kingdoms period in China begins.

c. 226 A.D.: Sassanian dynasty begins in Persia.

265 A.D.: Three Kingdoms period in China ends.

300s A.D.: Buddhism enters China.

300s A.D.: Books of the Bible compiled; some—the so-called Apocryphal Books—are rejected by early Christian bishops.

c. 300 A.D.: End of Formative or Preclassic Period, beginning of Classic Period, in Americas.

301 A.D.: Armenia becomes first nation to officially adopt Christianity.

317 A.D.: Eastern Chin Dynasty established in China.

c. 320 A.D.: Candra Gupta establishes Gupta Empire in India.

325 A.D.: Council of Nicaea adopts Nicene Creed, Christian statement of faith; declares Arianism a heresy.

330 A.D.: Constantine renames Greek city of Byzantium; as Constantinople, it becomes eastern capital of Roman Empire.

c. 335 A.D.: Candra Gupta dies; his son Samudra Gupta takes throne, and later conquers most of Indian subcontinent.

350s A.D.: Sassanian dynasty of Persia faces invasion by Huns.

376 A.D.: Samudra Gupta, ruler of Gupta Empire in India, dies; Candra Gupta II, greatest Gupta ruler, takes throne.

383 A.D.: At Fei Shui, an Eastern Chin force prevents nomads from overrunning all of China.

386 A.D.: Toba nomads invade northern China and establish Toba Wei Dynasty.

394 A.D.: Roman emperor Theodosius I brings an end to ancient Olympic Games.

late 300s A.D.: Sakas lose control of the Punjab region in western India.

c. 400 A.D.: End of Kushite kingdom in Africa.

410 A.D.: Visigoths under Alaric sack Rome on August 24, hastening fall of western empire.

420 A.D.: End of Eastern Chin Dynasty in China.

428 A.D.: Parthian rule of Armenia ends.

448 A.D.: Huns, under Attila, move into western Europe.

c. 450 A.D.: Hunas (Huns or Hsiung-Nu) invade Gupta Empire in India.

451 A.D.: Huns under Attila invade Gaul; defeated at Châlons–sur–Marne.

500s A.D.: African kingdom of Aksum establishes control over "incense states" of southern Arabia.

c. 500 A.D.: Hunas invade India again, hastening downfall of Gupta Empire.

c. 500 A.D.: Japanese adopt Chinese system of writing; beginnings of Japanese history.

c. 500 A.D.: Bantu peoples control most of southern Africa.

c. 540 A.D.: End of Gupta Empire in India.

554 A.D.: End of Toba Wei Dynasty in northern China.

575 A.D.: Sassanid Persians gain control over Arabian peninsula.

581 A.D.: Establishment of Sui Dynasty, and reunification of China.

600s A.D.: Three kingdoms emerge as Korea establishes independence from China.

c. 600 A.D.: African kingdom of Aksum declines.

618 A.D.: End of Sui Dynasty, beginning of T'ang Dynasty, in China.

622 A.D.: Mohammed and his followers escape from Mecca (the *Hegira*); beginning of Muslim calendar.

642 A.D.: Founding of Cairo, Egypt.

672 A.D.: Muslims conquer Egypt.

c. 750 A.D.: Decline of Teotihuacán in Mesoamerica.

1300s A.D.: Lighthouse of Alexandria destroyed in earthquake.

1687 A.D.: Parthenon damaged by explosion during war.

1776–88 A.D.: British historian Edward Gibbon publishes *The History of the Decline and Fall of the Roman Empire.*

1799 A.D.: Rosetta Stone discovered by French troops in Egypt.

1800s A.D.: Gilgamesh Epic of Mesopotamia recovered by scholars.

1800s A.D.: Linguists discover link between Indo-European languages of India, Iran, and Europe.

1813 A.D.: French publication of *Description of Egypt,* first significant modern work about Egyptian civilization.

1821 A.D.: Champollion deciphers Rosetta Stone, enabling first translation of Egyptian hieroglyphs.

1860 A.D.: First discovery of colossal stone heads carved by Olmec in Mexico.

1871 A.D.: Heinrich Schliemann begins excavations at Hissarlik in Turkey, leading to discovery of ancient Troy.

1876–78 A.D.: Schliemann discovers ruins of Mycenae in Greece.

1894 A.D.: Pierre de Coubertin establishes modern Olympic Games; first Games held in Athens two years later.

Late 1800s A.D.: Archaeologists discover first evidence, outside of the Bible, of Hittite civilization in Asia Minor.

1922 A.D.: British archaeologist Howard Carter discovers tomb of Egyptian pharaoh Tutankhamen.

1947–1950s A.D.: Dead Sea scrolls discovered in Palestine.

1952 A.D.: Mycenaean Linear B script deciphered.

1960s A.D.: Archaeologists discover evidence of volcanic eruption on Greek island of Thera c. 1500 B.C.

Ancient
Civilizations
Biographies

Akhenaton

Born c. 1370 B.C.
Died 1336 B.C.

Egyptian pharaoh, religious reformer

It takes a truly remarkable person to inspire controversy more than 3,000 years after his death, but the Egyptian pharaoh Akhenaton was just such a figure. He attempted a thorough reform of Egypt's religion, banning the worship of all gods except Aton, a deity represented by a sun-disk. He is often credited as the originator of monotheism, or the worship of a single god. His reign also saw enormous developments in Egyptian art, which up to that time had been stiff and unrealistic.

Akhenaton's religious reformation ultimately failed, however. The Egyptians, horrified by what they considered his disrespect for the gods, would remove his name from their historical record. But was he truly the villain his successors believed him to be, or was he a heroic figure, as he has often been regarded in modern times? Were his religious beliefs sincere, or were they, as some historians have suggested, directed more by circumstances than by heartfelt convictions? It is a measure of Akhenaton's complex character that these questions are still being asked.

Thou art in my heart; there is none other who knows thee, save thy son Akhenaton; thou hast made him wise in thy plans and thy power.

"Psalm to the Blessed Aton," *attributed to Akhenaton*

Corbis-Bettmann. Reproduced by permission.

"Amon is pleased"

It is ironic that the pharaoh who later changed his name to Akhenaton (ahk-NAH-tuhn), or "Servant of Aton," should have been born with the name Amenhotep (ah-mehn-HOH-tehp; sometimes rendered as Amenophis), meaning "Amon is pleased." Amon (AH-muhn) had once been worshiped as a separate god in Upper Egypt, but eventually the god's identity merged with that of Ra, a deity of Lower Egypt.

Akhenaton no doubt grew up worshiping Amon-Ra, along with a host of lesser deities. He was raised in the royal court, first at Memphis in Lower Egypt, and later at Thebes (THEEBZ) in Upper Egypt. Both cities served as capitals at different times and represented the two Egyptian kingdoms united almost 2,000 years before Akhenaton's time.

Akhenaton was born the son of Amenhotep III and Queen Tiy (TEE). His mother, unlike most Egyptian queens, was a *commoner*—that is, someone not of royal blood. She exerted considerable influence over her husband; thus it was perhaps fitting that Akhenaton's own wife would become one of the most visible Egyptian queens [see sidebar]. At the time of his birth, Akhenaton's parents did not expect him to become king. He had an older brother, Thutmose (TUHT-mohz). But his brother died at a young age; therefore, Akhenaton became pharaoh when he was eighteen years old.

A new religion

In the year he became pharaoh, Akhenaton married the princess Nefertiti (neh-fehr-TEE-tee). It is possible he ruled jointly with his father for some time, a common practice in Egypt. For the first four years of his reign, Akhenaton ruled under the title Amenhotep IV. In the fifth year, however, he changed his name, which is sometimes cited as Akhenaten, Akhnaten, Akhnaton, or Ikhnaton.

The year of the name change—perhaps 1347 B.C.—marked the beginning of a religious revolution that would rock the foundations of Egyptian life. Akhenaton declared that Aton was supreme above all gods and renamed himself "servant of Aton." He also declared that Nefertiti would become Nefer-nefru-aton (NEH-fehr NEH-froo AH-tuhn), or "exquisite [nearly perfect] beauty of Aton."

Nefertiti

Nefertiti (neh-fehr-TEE-tee) was the most famous queen of Egypt other than Hatshepsut (see entry). Unlike Hatshepsut, she did not actually rule the country. As the wife of Akhenaton, however, she took part in the radical reforms he tried to bring about in the Egyptians' religion. She may, in the view of some scholars, actually have been the driving force behind those reforms.

Some historians speculate that Nefertiti came from the nation of Mitanni in Mesopotamia, with which Egypt had close relations; however, her name, meaning "the beautiful one is come," is Egyptian. Certainly Nefertiti was beautiful, as can be seen in a well-known *bust* of her, in direct contrast to her unusual-looking husband.

Nefertiti (polychromed bust), illustration.
Archive Photos/Hirz. Reproduced by permission.

Because the royal couple allowed artists to depict them realistically, presenting them as ordinary people, historians know more about their home life than they do that of most pharaohs. One *relief* carving shows the couple with their little daughters gathered around them. One child sits on Nefertiti's lap and another on her shoulder, while Akhenaton kisses a third daughter.

Even across a space of more than 3,000 years, the scene is a touching one; so too are Akhenaton's frequent references to the wife he clearly treasured. He often referred to her as "Mistress of his Happiness, at hearing whose voice the King rejoices." He frequently swore by his family with the oath, "As my heart is happy in the Queen and her children."

Other artwork depicts Nefertiti taking an active role in the religion of Aton, offering sacrifices and performing ceremonial acts. Queens had never before been allowed to take part in religious services to this extent, leading some historians to suggest that she, and not Akhenaton, was actually behind the switch to the "new" religion of Aton.

Nefertiti disappeared from the historical record after the fourteenth year of Akhenaton's reign. Some historians interpreted her disappearance to mean that she was banished from the palace, possibly over a religious disagreement. It is more likely, however, that she simply died a few years before her husband.

The worship of Aton itself was not new. It had begun as early as the time of Akhenaton's grandfather, Thutmose IV. What was new was Akhenaton's insistence that Aton should be worshiped exclusively, or rather almost exclusively. From the beginnings of Egypt, pharaohs had held the status of living gods. Akhenaton was no different in this regard.

Although he is considered the founder of monotheism, in fact he upheld the tradition of pharaoh-worship, presenting himself as a go-between: the people would worship Akhenaton, who in turn would speak to Aton on their behalf. His worshipful "Psalm to the Blessed Aton" is considered one of the greatest works of ancient Egyptian literature.

The Amarna Period

It soon became clear that Akhenaton intended to completely reshape Egyptian religion, and thus Egyptian life. He ordered the closing of temples devoted to the gods as well as the seizure of the temples' property. Throughout the land, agents of Akhenaton destroyed statues and removed the names of rival deities. He even had all monuments to his father defaced, so as to remove the name Amon (also rendered as Amen) from "Amenhotep."

As part of his radical revolution, Akhenaton moved the capital to what later became known as Amarna (ah-MAHR-nah), along the Nile River almost exactly halfway from Memphis to Thebes. For this reason, Akhenaton's reign is known as the Amarna Period. In his time, however, the city was called Akhetaton (ahk-TAH-tuhn), or "The Horizon of Aton." Rather than take his old court with him from Thebes, Akhenaton surrounded himself with an entirely new group of associates.

In keeping with Akhenaton's radical departure from past ways, sculpture during the Amarna Period underwent a remarkable change. Prior to that time, Egyptian artwork had been very stiff and unreal-looking, with the pharaoh depicted as a man twice as tall as ordinary men. Amarna sculptors went in the opposite direction. To judge from their portrayals of their king, Akhenaton was not a handsome man. His hips and thighs were wide, his calves and arms skinny, his neck abnormally long, and his stomach flabby. For a time, this grotesque style of representation became the norm.

That he permitted such an unflattering depiction of himself says something about Akhenaton's complex personality. Sculptors of his time also produced numerous portrayals of Akhenaton and Nefertiti enjoying an ordinary family life. For instance, one such sculpture shows them playing with their children. Never before had pharaohs been depicted in such a human light.

The revolution that failed

When it came the religion, however, Akhenaton was uncompromising. He seems to have been unwilling to allow the people to get used to the radical changes he offered. Instead, he demanded that they accept the new religion all at once. They grudgingly gave in to the new system, simply because he was pharaoh. Once he died at the age of about thirty-five, though, they went back to worshiping a variety of gods—Aton among them.

Akhenaton had no sons. Of his six daughters, four died during his lifetime. One married a very young prince named Tutankhamen (toot-ahn-KAH-mehn; "King Tut"), who moved the capital back to Thebes and returned to the worship of Amon-Ra. Akhenaton had meanwhile been branded a *heretic*. Many of his statues were defaced. The Egyptians even tore down a number of the buildings he had constructed. Eventually Akhenaton and the three pharaohs who followed him would be erased from the list of Egyptian kings.

Hero or villain?

One effect of Akhenaton's revolution was that Tutankhamen, who died at the age of eighteen, was forgotten. The location of his tomb, an all-important part of an Egyptian king's *legacy,* was lost as well. Grave-robbers never found it, as they did the graves of virtually all the pharaohs. When the *Egyptologist* Howard Carter found it in 1922, the tomb contained a wealth in *archaeological* treasures. Tutankhamen became much more famous in death than in life.

Likewise, Amarna became an important archaeological site. When Tutankhamen's court hastily moved away, they left behind a vast array of records detailing, for instance, Egypt's relations with other countries of the time. Called the "Amarna

Letters," these records, written on some 380 clay tablets, were found accidentally in 1887.

Akhenaton, though he was removed from the memory of a nation shocked by his act of dishonor to the gods, has lived on in the minds of modern people. Some scholars believe that he simply used the new religion as a way to gain control over the politically powerful priests of Amon-Ra. Others have regarded him as a heroic figure who tried and failed to bring a new truth to a people unwilling to accept it. In the twentieth century, he has been the subject of numerous fictional books, a play by the mystery writer Agatha Christie, and an opera by composer Philip Glass.

Certainly what Akhenaton proposed was the wave of the future. The idea of monotheism took hold in the religion of the Israelites, who were probably living in Egypt at the time, and in turn influenced Christianity and *Islam*. Today Egypt is a *Muslim* country, where one of the most important beliefs, declared before prayers five times a day, is "There is no god but God."

For More Information

Books

Dijkstra, Henk. *History of the Ancient & Medieval World,* Volume 2: *Egypt and Mesopotamia.* New York: Marshall Cavendish, 1996.

Drury, Allen. *A God against the Gods* (fiction). Garden City, NY: Doubleday, 1976.

Encyclopedia of World Biography, 2nd ed. Detroit: Gale, 1998.

Silverberg, Robert. *Akhnaten, The Rebel Pharaoh.* Philadelphia: Chilton Books, 1964.

Stackton, David. *On a Balcony* (fiction). New York: London House & Maxwell, 1959.

Unstead, R. J. *An Egyptian Town.* Illustrated by Bill Stallion, et al. London: Kingfisher Books, 1986.

Web Sites

"Akhenaton." http://www.horus.ics.org.eg/html/akhenaton.html (accessed on June 26, 1999).

"Akhenaton." http://www.inetsonic.com/kate/tut/akhenaton.html (accessed on June 26, 1999).

"Akhenaton: Ancient Revolutionary." http://mars.acnet.wnec.edu/~ grempel/courses/wc1/lectures/03akhena ton.html (accessed on June 26, 1999).

"Eighteenth Dynasty." *Egyptian Ministry of Tourism.* http://interoz.com/ egypt/hdyn18d.htm (accessed on June 29, 1999).

"Neferneferuaten." *Ancient Sites.* http://www.ancientsites.com/~Hakima_ Ramesses/ (accessed on June 26, 1999).

"Nefertiti." http://www.horus.ics.org.eg/html/nefertiti2.html (accessed on June 26, 1999).

"Nefertiti: Royal Queen of Egypt." *Duke University.* http://www.duke.edu/ ~mcd3/ (accessed on June 28, 1999).

Alexander the Great

Born 356 B.C.
Died 323 B.C.

Greek king and conqueror

Though many ancient conquerors later had the title "Great" attached to their names, none was more deserving of it than Alexander III, king of Macedon. Coming from a mountainous kingdom to the north of Greece, he subdued the Greek city-states to the south. Then, at age twenty-two, he went on to take almost the entire known world. Eleven years later, having established a legend that would last throughout time, he was dead.

Even though the Romans would rule more land, no one man has ever subdued so much territory in so short a period. Yet Alexander did more than win battles. Trained in the classic traditions of Greece, he brought an enlightened form of leadership to the regions he conquered. His empire might have been a truly magnificent one if his life had been longer. As it was, he ensured that the influence of Greece reached far beyond its borders, leaving an indelible mark.

The Macedonians

Macedon (MAS-uh-dahn) was a rough, warlike country to the north of Greece. Although the Macedonians (mas-uh-

DOHN-ee-unz) considered themselves part of the Greek tradition, the Greeks tended to look down on them as rude and unschooled. But Greece's own day of glory had passed, and by the 300s B.C., the focus of power was shifting northward.

Philip II (382–336 B.C.; r. 359–336 B.C.), Alexander's father, proved himself the most extraordinary Macedonian leader up to his time. Had it not been for his even more remarkable son, he would be remembered as the greatest of all Macedonian leaders. Philip invented a new weapon called the pike, a spear some 16 feet (4.9 meters) long—a good 9 or 10 feet (2.7 or 3 meters) longer than the spears of Greek hoplites (HAHP-lytz), or foot soldiers. Armed with pikes, his army conquered most of southeastern Europe in the years between 354 and 339 B.C.

Alexander's mother was named Olympias, and she brought her son up on stories of gods and heroes. She believed that on his father's side, Alexander descended from Heracles (HAIR-uh-kleez; better known as Hercules). She herself claimed descent from Achilles (uh-KILL-eez), hero of the Trojan War and central figure of Homer's *Iliad*. The *Iliad* became Alexander's favorite book.

The education of Alexander

Added to the influence of his mother and father was that of Aristotle (see entry), who tutored Alexander in his teen years. It is intriguing that one of the ancient world's wisest men taught its greatest military leader. No doubt Alexander gained a wide exposure to the world under Aristotle's instruction.

He was not, however, a thinker but a doer. A natural athlete, Alexander proved his combination of mental and physical agility when at the age of twelve he tamed a wild horse no one else could ride. Impressed, Philip told the boy that anyone who could accomplish such a feat deserved to rule the world. Alexander named the horse Bucephalus (byoo-SEF-uh-lus), and the two would be companions almost for life. When Bucephalus died during Alexander's campaign in India, he would name a city for his beloved horse.

By the time he was sixteen, Alexander had the job of managing the kingdom's daily business while Philip was away at war. When Philip marched into Greece in 339 B.C., seventeen-year-old Alexander led a force that attacked Thebes (THEEBZ).

King of Macedon

The Greek city-states had never been truly united. Their disunity had worsened after the Peloponnesian War, which ended in 404 B.C. Philip saw himself as a fellow Greek bringing all of Greece together, but the Greeks regarded him as an outsider. After his victory at the Battle at Charonea (kare-uh-NEE-uh) in 338 B.C., however, the Greeks fell into line.

Back in Macedon, Philip took a new wife, who was determined that her own son would become his successor. This put the king into conflict with Olympias and Alexander. At one point the two men drew swords at each other. Alexander and his mother withdrew from the court for a year, but eventually father and son reconciled, in part because they realized that others in Macedon were willing to replace them both. Before they could fully patch up their differences, however, Philip was assassinated in 336 B.C.

Under the Macedonian system, a king's son could not simply expect to take the throne: he had to win the support of the nobles and deal with any potential enemies. Alexander was able to do this, killing as few opponents as possible. It was a policy he would pursue as a military leader, leaving as much good will as he could behind him while he pushed forward.

Achilles and the Gordian Knot

Alexander's immediate concerns in 335 B.C. were several tribes to the north of Macedonas well as some rebellious Greek city-states. The tribes were relatively easy to deal with. Alexander then made a lightning-quick movement into Greece, capturing Thebes and killing some 6,000 of its defenders. It was a brutal battle, but it could have been worse. Rather than slaughter the remaining 30,000 Thebans, he made them slaves and destroyed the city.

After that, he faced no serious opposition from the city-states. He embarked on a mission that had been Philip's dream: conquest of the vast Persian Empire to the east. The latter had once threatened Greece. Now Greece, led by Macedon, would take control of the Persians' declining empire.

The main body of Alexander's army, some 40,000 infantry (soldiers on foot) and 5,000 cavalry (soldiers on horseback), moved into Asia Minor. Meanwhile, their commander crossed the Hellespont with a smaller contingent so that he could go on a personal pilgrimage to the site of Troy. Alexander saw himself almost as a reincarnation of Achilles. When he arrived on Asian soil, he drove his spear into the ground as a symbol of conquest. Later he placed a wreath at a grave traditionally believed to be Achilles's.

Eventually Alexander and his army passed through the ancient Phrygian capital of Gordian. In that city was a chariot tied with a rope so intricately knotted that no one could untie it. According to legend, the fabled King Midas had tied the Gordian Knot, and whoever could untie it would go on to rule the world. Alexander simply cut the knot.

Conquering the world

Alexander's first military engagement in Asia Minor was not with a Persian commander but with a Greek mercenary named Memnon (MEM-nahn), who had been hired by the Persians. Memnon's forces were waiting for him at the River Granicus (gruh-NIKE-uhs). Alexander surprised him by charging straight at the center of his army. The seemingly reckless charge, which was characteristic of his style in battle, nearly cost Alexander his life. But he won the battle—and his troops' respect.

By April of 333 B.C., having dealt with various Persian and local forces in Asia Minor, Alexander had moved down into Cilicia (suh-LISH-uh), the area where Asia Minor meets Asia. The Persian emperor Darius III came to meet him with a force of 140,000. At one point, because Alexander's armies were moving so fast, Darius cut Alexander off from his supply lines. Darius chose to wait it out, letting Alexander's forces come to him; Alexander, taking this as a sign of weakness, charged on the Persians. Again Alexander nearly got himself killed, but the Battle of Issus (Is-sus; "Is" rhymes with "hiss") was a hands-down victory for the Greeks. Darius fled, leaving Alexander in control of the entire western portion of the Persians' empire.

Instead of raping and pillaging, as any number of other commanders would have allowed their troops to do, Alexander ordered his armies to make a disciplined movement through conquered territories. After the heavy tax burden the Persians had placed on their empire, Greek rule was a relief. People in some lands welcomed him as a liberator. As he had done in Macedon, Alexander left as few enemies behind him as possible so that he could more easily move forward.

In 332 and 331 B.C., Alexander's forces secured their hold over southwest Asia, conducting a seven-month siege on the Phoenician city of Tyre. By 331 B.C., he was in Egypt, where he founded the city of Alexandria, destined to become a center of Greek learning for centuries to come. In October of that year, he met a Persian force of some 250,000 troops (five times the size of Alexander's army) at the Assyrian city of Gaugamela (gaw-guh-MEEL-uh). It was an overwhelming victory for the Greeks. Although Darius escaped once again, he would later be assassinated by one of his own people.

No more worlds to conquer

Alexander now controlled the vast lands of the Persian Empire, but he did not want to stop there. He asked his men, who had been away from their homes for close to four years, if they would go on with him; it was a mark of his ability as a leader that they agreed to do so. Over the next six years, from 330 to 324 B.C., they subdued what is now Afghanistan and Pakistan and ventured into India. Alexander secured his position in Afghanistan by marrying the Princess Roxana, but he was aware that some of his troops were growing weary. He sent the oldest of them home.

He wanted to keep going east as far as he could, simply to see what was there and, if possible, add it to his empire. But in July of 326 B.C., just after they crossed the Beas River (BEE-ahs) in India, his troops refused to go on. There might have been a rebellion if he had tried to force the issue, but he did not. He sent one group back by sea to explore the coastline as they went and sent another group back by a northerly route. He took a third group through southern Iran, on a journey through the desert in which the entire army very nearly lost its way.

In the spring of 323 B.C., they reached Babylon. Alexander began plotting the conquest of Arabia. But he was unraveling both physically and emotionally, and he had taken to heavy drinking. He caught a fever and was soon unable to move or speak. During the last days of his life, Alexander—the man of action—was forced to lie on his bed while all his commanders filed by in solemn tribute to the great man who had led them where no conqueror had ever gone. On June 13, 323 B.C., he died before ever reaching his thirty-third birthday.

Alexander's empire

Alexander was no ordinary conqueror. His empire seemed to promise a newer, brighter age in which the nations of the world could join together as equals. Though some of his commanders did not agree with him on this issue, Alexander made little distinction between racial and ethnic groups. Instead, he promoted men on the basis of their ability.

From the beginning, Alexander's armies had recruited local troops, but with the full conquest of Persia, they stepped up this policy. It was his goal to leave Persia in the control of Persians trained in the Greek language and Greek culture. He left behind some seventy new towns named Alexandria. This began the spread of Hellenistic culture throughout western Asia.

But Alexander's empire did not hold. The generals who succeeded him lacked his vision. They spent the remainder of their careers fighting over the spoils of his conquests. Seleucus (suh-LOO-suhs; c. 356–281 B.C.) gained control over Persia, Mesopotamia, and Syria, where an empire under his name would rule for many years. Ptolemy (TAHL-uh-mee; c. 365–c. 283 B.C.) established a dynasty of even longer standing in Egypt. His descendants ruled until 30 B.C., when the last of his line, Cleopatra (see entry)—also the last Egyptian pharoah— was defeated by a new and even bigger empire, Rome.

Seleucus I controlled Persia, Mesopotamia, and Syria.
Photograph. The Library of Congress.

For More Information

Books

Gunther, John. *Alexander the Great.* Illustrated by Isa Barnett. New York: Random House, 1953.

Harris, Nathaniel. *Alexander the Great and the Greeks*. Illustrated by Gerry Wood. New York: Bookwright Press, 1986.

Krensky, Stephen. *Conqueror and Hero: The Search for Alexander*. Drawings by Alexander Farquharson. Boston, MA: Little, Brown, 1981.

Langley, Andrew. *Alexander the Great: The Greatest Ruler of the Ancient World*. Illustrated by Alan Marks. New York: Oxford University Press, 1997.

Lasker, Joe. *The Great Alexander the Great*. Illustrated by the author. New York: Puffin Books, 1990.

Macdonald, Fiona. *The World in the Time of Alexander the Great*. Parsippany, NJ: Dillon Press, 1997.

Web Sites

"Alexander III of Macedon (356–323 B.C.)." http://www.1stmuse.com/frames/project.html (accessed on July 11, 1999).

Alexander the Great. (http://www.geocities.com/Athens/1358/).

"Alexander the Great, King of Macedon." http://www.geocities.com/Athens/Aegean/7545/Alexander.html (accessed on July 11, 1999).

Aristotle

Born 384 B.C.
Died 322 B.C.

Greek philosopher

One of the most famous paintings of the Italian Renaissance is *The School of Athens* by Raphael (1483–1520), which shows a white-haired Plato (see entry) standing beside his pupil Aristotle. Plato points upward, as though indicating the world of ideas, which he considered the fundamental reality of existence. Aristotle, on other hand, stretches out his arm to take in the world around him. Thus Raphael brilliantly summarized the difference between the two greatest Greek philosophers.

Aristotle's interest in the world of experience took him beyond philosophy and into areas as diverse as biology and literary criticism. In the realm of pure philosophy, he identified the four types of cause (cause, as in the expression, "cause and effect": the cause is the reason why a certain effect or result happens) and established a framework for logic still in use today. As a scientist, he studied nature and from his observations made some remarkable conclusions. His comments on drama continued to affect the thinking of writers and film-makers at the dawn of the twenty-first century.

The man who chooses knowledge for its own sake will above all choose what is most truly knowledge.

Metaphysics

NYPL Picture Collection. Reproduced by permission.

The Macedonian philosopher

Born in the town of Stagira (stuh-JIE-ruh), Aristotle (AIR-uhs-taht-uhl) was not, strictly speaking, a Greek but a Macedonian. The Macedonians (mas-uh-DOHN-ee-uhnz), who lived to the north of Greece, shared in the Hellenic culture, but they were a rougher, tougher nation than the Greeks.

Perhaps this helped influence the later differences between Aristotle and his teacher Plato (PLAY-toh), who was raised in the much more refined world of Athens. In American terms, it was as though Aristotle came from New York or Boston and Plato came from Nebraska or Wyoming. To an Athenian, it might have made sense to believe that the world of ideas is more real than the physical world; but to a Macedonian, the physical was too ever-present to ignore its existence.

Aristotle came from an upper middle-class family. His father, Nichomacus (nik-oh-MAHK-uhs) was court physician to King Amyntas II (ah-MIN-tuhs; ruled c. 393–c. 370 B.C.) Perhaps his father's profession influenced his later interest in science; at age seventeen, however, Aristotle came under the sway of another man who would have a much greater effect on his future.

The brilliant rebel

Aristotle entered Plato's Academy in the same year that his teacher had what was no doubt a frustrating and even humiliating experience: he failed in his attempt to groom Dionysius the Younger as a philosopher-king. By then Plato was sixty years old and probably eager to know that his influence would last beyond his time. Certainly the brilliant young man from Macedon quickly caught his attention.

At one point, Plato read before the Academy a lengthy argument he had written on the nature of the soul. Diogenes Laertius (die-AH-jehn-eez lay-UHR-shuhs), a Greek writer of the A.D. 200s whose *Lives of the Eminent Philosophers* is one of the few sources of information about the thinkers of ancient times, wrote that Aristotle "was the only person who sat it out, while all the rest rose up and went away."

Aristotle spent twenty years at the Academy, during which time he wrote the Athenian Constitution (c. 350 B.C.) When Plato died in 347 B.C., the devoted pupil built an altar to his teacher, whom he loved and respected above all men. Yet he was destined to rebel against virtually everything the older man had taught him.

Wanderer and teacher

It was Aristotle's destiny to come in contact with a number of other remarkable thinkers. One of these was Hermeias (huhr-MAY-uhs), a fellow student at the Academy who had risen from slavery to become dictator of two cities in Asia Minor. In 347 B.C., Aristotle went to work in the court of Hermeias, presumably as an advisor and wise man. Three years later, at age forty, he married Hermeias's daughter Pythias (PITH-ee-uhs).

Two tragic events followed. First, Hermeias was assassinated by the Persians, who feared he was secretly allied with the new king of Macedon, Amyntas's son Philip II (382–336 B.C.; r. 359–336 B.C.). Aristotle and Pythias fled to the isle of Lesbos (LEZ-bohs), where he conducted studies in the island's natural history. Pythias died giving birth to a daughter.

In the midst of this second tragedy, Aristotle received an intriguing offer from King Philip. The king asked him to return to the Macedonian court in order to tutor his high-spirited son Alexander, then a boy of thirteen years. This Alexander, of course, would be known as Alexander the Great (see entry; 356–323 B.C.; ruled 336–323 B.C.), the greatest conqueror of all time.

Aristotle tutored Alexander for four years. Then Philip gave him another job, overseeing the restoration of Stagira, which had been destroyed in a war. Aristotle also wrote a new code of laws for the city. In 334 B.C., he returned to Athens.

The Lyceum

Possibly with funds from Alexander, who by then was king and had embarked on his journey of conquest, Aristotle purchased a school that had been dedicated to the god of shepherds, Apollo Lyceus. This became the Lyceum (lie-SEE-uhm). Just as the name of Plato's school, the Academy, has entered the English language, *lyceum* is a word for an auditorium, usually on a college campus.

The Lyceum, whose students typically came from the middle class, and the Academy, where most of the student body were aristocrats, became rival schools. In line with its middle-class style, the Lyceum featured afternoon courses for a popular audience of nonstudents, in addition to its regular morning courses. Thus it was also the first "extension campus," where nonstudents could expand their learning.

Aristotle put his students to work in all manner of scientific pursuits, from studying animals' organs, to listing the champions at the Pythian Games, to classifying the constitutions of various Greek cities. This tendency to classify was clearly dear to Aristotle's heart, as a look at Aristotelian (air-is-toh-TEEL-yun) thought will show.

The Aristotelian universe

Plato would have said that a red object is red because it participates in the form, or perfect idea, of "Red." Aristotle, on the other hand, would have called that nonsense. A red object is red, he would have insisted, because after repeated experience with red objects, humans eventually identified a color called "red." If this seems like mere common sense, it is a mark of how much Aristotle has affected the Western, and particularly American, approach to knowledge.

In order to explain how things existed, Aristotle identified four causes—material, efficient, formal, and final. A house, for instance, is made up of various items such as wood and glass, which are its *material cause,* or what it consists of. But these have to be put together by construction workers, who as the shapers of the house are its *efficient cause.* Yet they must have a blueprint to go by, a design or *formal cause.* Even if all these causes are present, there must also be a reason why the house was built—e.g., for people to live in it—and this is the "why," or the *final cause.*

People in modern times are accustomed to talking about "actualizing" their "potential." This idea is also a legacy of Aristotle, who maintained that the physical world is not fixed, as Parmenides had claimed; rather, it is constantly changing, and every living object contains the potential for change. Thus an acorn holds the potentiality for an oak. All beings are part of an ascending order of potentialities, he believed, the highest of which is God.

In contrast to Plato's emphasis on the universal—that is, on the forms, which exist in some heavenly realm and are the mystical essence of things on earth—Aristotle was concerned with particular and individual things. He believed that the goal of the individual person was not, as Plato claimed, to rise above the physical, but simply to be happy.

Aristotle's writings

Up to about 334 B.C., it appears that Aristotle followed the habit of ancient philosophers, focusing on classroom lectures rather than on written work. Then, in the last twelve years of his life, he began writing furiously, perhaps so that his lectures would not die with him.

He published a few books in his lifetime, works drawn from his popular lectures. These, unfortunately, did not survive. According to Diogenes Laertius, he wrote some 400 other works, many of them no doubt very short, of which about forty have survived.

The many interests of Aristotle

These books, which are classified according to discipline, reflect the wide range of Aristotle's interests. There was *Logic*, whose title refers to a system of reasoning. Aristotle developed the logical formula called the syllogism. He is generally considered the "father of logic" because he provided a system for it. There were the many volumes of science, ranging from *Physics* to *On the Soul*, a psychological study.

Aristotle was particularly successful in the area of biology, in which he produced several works. The first to attempt a scientific classification of animal life-forms, he dissected hundreds of animals to learn how they worked. He was about 2,000 years ahead of other scientists in realizing that the dolphin, though it swims like a fish, is actually a mammal.

The classification system in Aristotle's library gave a name to the branch of philosophy that deals with the fundamental nature of being: *Metaphysics*. Actually it was a name for the book in which he discussed that subject and simply meant "after *Physics*." He also wrote considerably on subjects such as *Ethics*, the area of philosophy concerned with morality;

Sophocles

The annual festival honoring the god Dionysus (die-oh-NIE-suhs) in Athens featured a contest in which playwrights presented a series of three tragedies and a short comedy. It is a hallmark of his success that Sophocles (SAHF-uh-kleez; c. 495–406 B.C.) won first prize more than twenty times.

Later Aristotle would write about tragedy, using the work of Sophocles as a model. As Aristotle explained it, a tragedy focuses on a great misfortune that befalls the hero. The tragedy usually ends with the hero choosing to go down fighting rather than merely submitting to fate. It is also a tragedy—in another sense of the word—that very few of Sophocles's plays survived. Of the 123 plays he is said to have written, 90 survive in fragments, but only 7 in their entirety.

One of these, however, has been proclaimed by Aristotle and by many other critics as the greatest play of all time: *Oedipus Rex* (*Oedipus the King*). At his birth, it was prophesied that Oedipus (ED-I-puhs) would kill his father and marry his mother. Because of the prophecy, his parents gave him up to die. He survived, however, and became a great hero, only to return to his hometown . . . where he met and killed an older man and then fell in love with and married a beautiful older woman. *Oedipus Rex* is the story of how Oedipus responds to the horrible news that he has fulfilled the ancient prophecy.

Politics, a book in which he advanced the now-accepted notion that human beings are happiest when they live in some kind of organized society; *Rhetoric* (RET-uh-rik), which dealt with speech and writing; and *Poetics.*

Poetics, though only a small part of it survives, was one of Aristotle's most important works. In it, he introduced the idea of *catharsis* (kuh-THAHR-sis), or the experience of emotional release that comes from watching a character on stage undergo difficult circumstances. Drama, he maintained, was therefore good for the soul. He particularly recommended the works of Sophocles [see sidebar].

The end of Aristotle

In 323 B.C., Aristotle received word of Alexander's death in Babylon. He feared that there might be an anti-Macedonian

Aristotle's tragedies were modeled after the work of Sophocles. *Archive Photos. Reproduced by permission.*

Sophocles introduced a number of important techniques such as scenery. Before his time, the stage in Greek plays had been bare. He also introduced a third actor on the stage: up to then, there had only been two actors, along with a *chorus* of twelve people who provided a sort of voice-over narration.

As an Athenian aristocrat, Sophocles was also active in political affairs. He served as treasurer of the Athenian Empire in 442 B.C. and later as a general under Pericles (see entry). In 413 B.C., after the defeat at Syracuse during the Peloponnesian War, he was appointed to a council of ten statesmen who provided advice on making an economic recovery from the defeat.

reaction in Athens. Remembering how the Athenians had killed his teacher's teacher, the great Socrates, he announced that he would not let the city "sin twice against philosophy." Therefore he left.

Aristotle moved to the city of Chalcis (KAL-suhs) on a nearby island. It had been the home of his mother, and he died there a year later, in 322 B.C. Some time after the death of his wife, Pythias, he had taken up with Herpyllis (HUHR-puh-lis), who like Praxiteles's (see entry) girlfriend Phryne was a high-class call girl; but when he died, he requested that he be buried beside his first love, Pythias.

His influence

For centuries, stories of Aristotle and Alexander have intrigued writers. During the Middle Ages, a whole literary tradition would develop around fanciful tales concerning the interaction of these two extraordinary figures. Plato, like Confucius (see entry), had tried and failed to cultivate a philosopher-king in Dionysius the Younger, yet ironically it was Aristotle who actually had an opportunity to influence a future world-conqueror. Certainly, Alexander was a typical conqueror in many respects, spilling blood and destroying cities, but in many regards he was far more enlightened than all but a handful of ancient rulers. Much of what he left behind was positive. His enlightened reign can in some measure be attributed to Aristotle.

Not that Aristotle needed Alexander to establish his legacy—he built enough of a legacy on his own. Most of his writings would not be published until centuries after his lifetime. During the Dark Ages in western Europe, much of his work would be preserved in the Byzantine Empire and by the Arab world. In the 1200s, Aristotle's ideas reappeared in western Europe, where St. Thomas Aquinas (uh-KWINE-uhs; 1255–74) developed an Aristotelian defense of the Catholic faith.

The rediscovery of Aristotle helped lead to the rebirth of learning known as the Renaissance. In fact, the hold of Aristotle became so powerful, some 2,000 years after his death, that he came to seem a symbol of old, established ways of thinking. But that was only a mark of his success: Aristotle, were he alive today, would be on the cutting edge.

For More Information

Books

Furan, Rodney. *Twelve Great Philosophers*. Mankato, MN: Oddo Publishing, 1968.

Illustrated Introduction to Philosophy. New York: DK Publishing, Inc., 1998.

Nardo, Don. *Greek and Roman Theatre*. San Diego, CA: Lucent Books, 1995.

Parker, Steve. *Aristotle and Scientific Thought*. New York: Chelsea House, 1995.

Ross, James Stewart. *Greek Drama*. New York: Thomson Learning, 1996.

Web Sites

"Björn's Guide to Philosophy—Aristotle." http://www.knuten.liu.se/~bjoch509/philosophers/ari.html (accessed on July 8, 1999).

"Great Books Index—Sophocles." http://www.mirror.org/books/gb.sophocles.html (accessed on July 9, 1999).

"Greek Philosophy: Aristotle." http://www.wsu.edu:8080/~dee/GREECE/ARIST.HTM (accessed on July 9, 1999).

"Sophocles" (ca. 495–406 B.C.) http://www.mala.bc.ca/~mcneil/tsoph.htm (accessed on July 9, 1999).

Wilson, Prof. Fred L. "Science and Human Values—Aristotle." *Rochester Institute of Technology.* www.rit.edu/~flwstv/aristotle.html (accessed on July 9, 1999).

Asoka

Born c. 302 B.C.
Died c. 232 B.C.

Indian emperor

In 1921, novelist and social critic H. G. Wells wrote: "Amidst the tens of thousands of names of monarchs that crowd the columns of history . . . the name of Asoka shines, and shines almost alone, a star." It was not because of Asoka's conquests that Wells wrote these words, though in fact he ruled over India's Mauryan Empire at its height. Rather, it was because of Asoka's kindness as a leader and his sincere godliness as a follower of Buddha (see entry).

At one time Asoka had been a typical ancient ruler: cruel, proud, and merciless. All of that changed, however, at the end of a bloody conquest in the eighth year of his reign. He recognized the evil in all people's hearts, particularly his own, and resolved to spend the rest of his life doing good. Thereafter he devoted himself to making life better for his subjects. He commanded that his principles of morality be carved onto rocks where his words can still be viewed today.

Chandragupta and the Mauryan Empire

In 326 B.C., armies under Alexander the Great (see entry) invaded India. They soon left, but the impressive conquests of Alexander inspired a dream in a young Indian monarch named Chandragupta Maurya (kahn-drah-GOOP-tah MOHR-yah; r. 324–301 B.C.) Chandragupta ruled over the kingdom of Magadha (MAH-guh-duh) in eastern India, a place where the Buddha had spent much of his career in the 500s B.C. His capital was Pataliputra (pah-tuh-lee-POO-trah), northwest of modern-day Calcutta, from which his armies swept over most of India.

The Mauryan Empire was a splendid and well-organized realm. Pataliputra was said to be the greatest city of that time. Like most ancient emperors, however, Chandragupta ruled with a fist of iron, maintaining a network of spies and punishing even a hint of rebellion. Yet in an eerie foreshadowing of his grandson's career, Chandragupta stepped down from the throne in 301 B.C. to become a Jain (JYN). The founder of Buddhism himself had once studied Jainism, which required an ascetic lifestyle that left the Buddha little more than skin and bones; as for Chandragupta, he died of starvation.

Chandragupta was succeeded by his son Bindusara (bin-doo-SAHR-ah), whose wife may have been named Subhadrangi (soob-hah-DRAHNG-ee). She bore her husband a son she named Asoka (ah-SHOH-kah), meaning "I am without sorrow" in the Sanskrit language.

"Black Asoka"

It was said that Asoka, like another famous priest-king, Akhenaton (see entry), was unattractive in appearance. Another story holds that Bindusara did not care for Asoka, yet he apparently trusted his son enough to give him the job of suppressing a revolt in the city of Taxila. After that, Asoka became prince over the city of Ujjain (oo-JINE) in west-central India. Until a few years before, Ujjain had been the capital of the ancient Avanti kingdom. Centuries later Ujjain would become capital of the Gupta Empire under Candra Gupta II [see sidebar].

Bindusara died in about 272 B.C. It appears that Asoka did not assume the throne until some time afterward. It is clear that there was a power struggle, though the story that Asoka murdered 99 of his brothers—presumably sons of Bindusara through various concubines—is probably a legend. A number

Kalidasa

Asoka's time represented one golden age in Indian history; another was the Gupta Empire (c. A.D. 320–c. A.D. 540), whose greatest ruler was Candra Gupta II (ruled c. A.D. 380–c. A.D. 415). The latter encouraged learning and the arts, and, under his reign, a variety of disciplines from literature to medicine flourished.

Among the prominent figures of the Gupta golden age was the playwright Kalidasa (kah-lee-DAH-suh; c. A.D. 340–c. A.D. 400). Though his name is hardly as well known in the West as that of Sophocles, he is viewed as the "Shakespeare of India." Yet he apparently wrote only three plays and four long poems. The most famous of his works are the *Meghaduta* (meg-hah-DOOT-ah), a poem translated as *The Cloud Messenger,* and the play *Sakuntala* (sah-koon-TAH-lah), or *The Lost Ring.*

The Cloud Messenger was much admired by the German poet Goethe (GUHR-tuh; 1749–1832), often considered the greatest of German writers. In the poem, a god separated from his wife sends a message to her on a rain cloud, which travels across India and settles for a time over Ujjain, the Gupta capital. The style of writing in the work reflects Kalidasa's rejection of traditional Indian poetic styles, which by that time had become stale.

As for *The Lost Ring,* it is taken from the *Mahabharata* and concerns two lovers who might be compared with Shakespeare's two main characters in *Romeo and Juliet.* However, Kalidasa's hero and heroine do not end their story tragically but are reunited after overcoming the curse that separates them. The play was originally translated in 1789 by Sir William Jones, a British judge in Calcutta who not only brought Kalidasa to the attention of the West but aided in the discovery of the link between European and Indian languages.

of such stories exist, all intended to convey the quite believable idea that Asoka was a ruthless leader. There are so many such tales, in fact, that they are collectively identified under the tradition of "Black Asoka," referring to the idea that before he became a Buddhist, Asoka was an evil man.

It appears that Asoka maintained a prison with an extensive network of torture chambers for dealing with his enemies. Iit is clear that he fought a number of wars, and spilled plenty of blood, in the course of securing his empire. Then, in 262 B.C., the bloodshed became too much for him.

The occasion for this abrupt about-face was his victory over the Kalinga (kah-LING-ah) people of southeastern India. In the course of the campaign, his troops captured more than 150,000 people and killed many times more, either directly or as a result of the general havoc created by the war. "Just after the taking of Kalinga," according to one of the many inscriptions he left behind, "His Sacred Majesty began to follow Righteousness, to love Righteousness, to give instruction in Righteousness."

A change of heart

His statement regarding his conversion comes from one of the 35 inscriptions that Asoka put in various places around India beginning in 260 B.C. Some of these edicts, or statements, were carved into rocks in high places; others on man-made pillars. Hence they are referred to either as rock edicts or pillar edicts.

Though he never identified the "righteousness" by name, it appears reasonably certain that Asoka adopted Buddhism. However, the inscriptions speak of morality in broad terms and make no mention of certain key Buddhist concepts. It is possible, therefore, that what Asoka embraced was a mixture of Buddhism and a "universal religion," or a belief that all people who worship with sincerity worship the same god.

Whatever the faith, Asoka set out to conquer the world with it, as he had once conquered with the sword. He sent missionaries to bring his message to far-flung places, including Egypt and Greece. Though Buddhism never took hold in those countries, it did spread to the island of Ceylon (seh-LAHN), where it replaced Hinduism as the dominant religion.

A good and just king

It is clear, however, that Asoka was not interested merely in "saving souls" (to use terminology drawn from Western religion), but also in making his people's lives better. According to one of his inscriptions, "There is no better work than promoting the welfare of the whole world. Whatever may be my great deeds, I have done them to discharge my debt to all beings."

In 257 B.C., he appointed officials to a position whose name is translated as "inspectors of morality." Such a term, however, suggests the image of religious thought-police telling people how to govern their lives; Asoka's "morality inspectors," by contrast, were charged with distributing gifts to the poor and making sure that people treated each other with kindness.

Not even Asoka himself could go all the way with his new faith of love and tolerance. Some of his inscriptions indicate that he reserved the right to punish those who did not respond to kindness. On the whole, however, he was thoroughly sincere. He devoted much of his time to traveling around the country, ensuring that his people were living well. He even oversaw the planting of trees to provide travelers with a shady place to rest.

A mission that failed

The sad fact, nonetheless, is that Asoka's mission failed. Though he had obviously moved past all greed, pettiness, and striving for power, not everyone had. It appears that during the 230s B.C., officials in his court—perhaps taking advantage of the fact that Asoka was consumed with humanitarian concerns—managed to gain influence over his grandson Samprati (sahm-PRAH-tee), whom Asoka had picked as his successor. It appears that Samprati forced his grandfather into virtual exile within the palace and that in his latter days Asoka lived on a meager ration of food.

And yet, as Wells wrote more than 2,100 years after Asoka's death, "the name of Asoka shines, and shines almost alone, a star." History is full of kings, as Wells observed, and the pages of time are piled high with the record of their killings and their conquests, but there have been precious few like Asoka. His name certainly deserves to be known throughout the world.

For More Information

Books

Chakrabarti, Atulananda. *Asoka for the Young.* Calcutta: Good Books Company, 1953.

Davar, Ashok. *The Wheel of King Asoka*. Illustrated by the author. Chicago: Follett Publishing Company, 1977.

Lengyel, Emil. *Asoka the Great: India's Royal Missionary.* New York: Franklin Watts, 1971.

Schulberg, Lucille and the editors of Time-Life Books. *Historic India.* New York: Time-Life Books, 1968, pp. 72-89.

Web Sites

"The Biographical Scripture of King Asoka." http://www.slip.net/ ~numata/AsokaTransIntro.html (accessed on July 7, 1999).

King Ashoka: His Edicts and His Times. http://www.cs.colostate.edu/ ~malaiya/ashoka.html (accessed on July 7, 1999).

"The Mauryans, 321–185 BC." http://www.wsu.edu:8080/~dee/ ANCINDIA/MAURYA.HTM (accessed on July 7, 1999).

"Rise of Religions and the Emergence of the State." *Discover India.* http://www.indiagov.org/culture/history/history2.htm (accessed on July 7, 1999).

Marcus Aurelius

Born A.D. 121
Died A.D. 180

Roman emperor and philosopher

[As a child I learned] to bear pain and be content with little, to work with my own hands, to mind my own business, to be slow to listen to slander.

Roman history is full of cruel emperors [see sidebar], but the list of distinguished ones is regrettably short. If any emperor belongs on the distinguished list, it is Marcus Aurelius, who ruled the empire at the height of its power but had to deal with a number of troubles on all sides. Nor was he only an emperor. As a philosopher, Marcus developed a Stoic view of life that advised patience and strength of character. These were qualities that would help him during the rocky years of his leadership.

His father died when he was two, and Marcus Aurelius was raised by his grandfather, a consul of Rome. His grandfather gave him a strong moral education, as Marcus later recalled in his great philosophical work, *The Meditations*. Among the things he learned from his grandfather, he said, were generosity, respect for the gods, "not only refraining from wrongdoing but even from thoughts of it," and a simple way of life.

In his youth, Rome was ruled by Hadrian (HAY-dree-uhn; ruled A.D. 117–138), second of the "good" emperors, of which Marcus would be the fourth and last. Hadrian took an interest in his education and helped see to it that Marcus received the best learning available. At the age of twelve, he embarked on a course of education that required three tutors, one of them a Greek expert on Homer.

One of his tutors exposed him to the philosophy of Stoicism (STOH-i-siz-um), which had originated in Greece. The Stoics were chiefly concerned with ethics, or morality, and placed an emphasis on dignity, bravery, and self-control. Today the word *stoic* in English refers to someone who withstands pain or misfortune without complaining. Marcus, who is described as having been serious even as a child, took to the Stoic philosophy instantly, wearing rough clothes and sometimes sleeping on the ground. A full range of training in sports, from boxing to riding to running, added to his physical discipline.

Later his tutors would include two highly distinguished men. Hadrian's role in securing their services showed how much he admired the young Marcus. Herodes Atticus (huh-ROH-deez AT-i-kuhs; c. A.D. 101–177) certainly did not need the job; he was an incredibly wealthy man. He agreed to tutor Marcus in Greek simply because Hadrian asked him to. Fronto (FRAHN-toh; c. A.D. 100–166), a consul and lawyer, took over Marcus's education in Latin. Both men were highly respected orators (OHR-uh-turz), or speakers.

Marcus becomes emperor

Grooming Marcus to one day lead Rome, Hadrian had arranged the young man's marriage to the daughter of his designated successor, Commodus (KAHM-uh-duhs). This arrangement fell through when Commodus died. Hadrian chose a new consul to replace him: Antoninus Pius (an-toh-NINE-uhs PIE-uhs; ruled A.D. 138–161). Hadrian directed Antoninus to adopt both Marcus and Lucius Verus (VEER-uhs; A.D. 130–169) as sons.

When he became emperor, Antoninus made Marcus consul, one of the chief leaders of Rome. Marcus was only eighteen at the time, below the minimum age. This appointment illustrated the trust Antoninus placed in the young man. Five years later, Marcus married Antoninus's daughter Faustina (faw-STINE-uh). When he was twenty-five years old, just after the birth of their first child, a daughter, Marcus was given even greater political power. He served as tribune, a position with

Nero

Very few men can compete with Marcus Aurelius for the title of "best" Roman emperor; the other end of the spectrum, however, is much more crowded. Surprisingly, some of the really terrible emperors came along when the empire was at its height. Later, in its decline, assassins ensured that unpopular rulers did not remain in power long enough to establish a reputation. The insane Caligula (kuh-LIG-yoo-luh; ruled A.D. 37–41) is a strong candidate for the title of "worst" emperor. Nero (A.D. 37–68; ruled A.D. 54–68) lasted much longer and established a much more impressive record, both for cruelty and incompetence.

Half frustrated artist, half overgrown child, Nero was all monster. He could hardly have turned out otherwise, given his upbringing. His father, Gnaeus Domitius Ahenobarbus (G'NAY-us doh-MISH-us uh-heen-uh-BAHR-bus), was every bit as terrible as his name. He is said to have killed a child for not drinking enough wine. At Nero's birth, he told the boy's mother, Agrippina (ag-ri-PIE-nuh), that their son would come to no good (an understatement).

Agrippina was no better than her husband, perhaps worse. She maneuvered to marry the absentminded emperor Claudius (ruled A.D. 41–54), her third husband. Later, Agrippina made advances toward her son. By then, having poisoned Claudius so that Nero could become emperor, she was fighting to keep Nero from killing her.

One of the few positive influences in Nero's life was the philosopher Seneca (SEHN-eh-kuh; c. 3 B.C.–c. A.D.65), who became his advisor. But the atmosphere around Nero affected Seneca as well. After Nero made an elaborate but botched attempt to kill Agrippina (by sinking a boat he gave her for her birthday in A.D. 59), Seneca arranged to finish off the job properly. Later, Nero forced Seneca to commit suicide.

Up until that time, as strange as it may sound, Nero had done a fairly responsible job of ruling. He even distributed funds to the poor. Although he had a habit of sneaking out at night to join

authority to bring bills before the senate, until the death of Antoninus in A.D. 161.

As soon as the senate proclaimed him emperor, Marcus asked that they allow Lucius Verus to become his co-ruler with the title "Augustus." This became a model for the sharing of power by later emperors, which in the future would create problems; in Marcus's case, however, it was a mark of his generosity.

gangs that robbed people in back alleys, few Romans knew about their emperor's late-night activities. Having removed all the restraining forces around him, however, Nero was free do do as he pleased.

Nero was fascinated with the arts. He fancied himself a singer and an actor. As a child he performed music publicly, something Roman nobles considered extremely undignified for one of their own. He had an insatiable appetite for approval. As emperor he could get all the approval he demanded. Thus he would later go to the Olympic Games and come home with more than 1,800 first prizes as an athlete, a singer, a harpist, and an actor.

Nero divorced his wife Octavia for Poppaea (pah-PEE-uh), whom he later killed—when she was pregnant with their child—because she complained about his lavish spending habits. His demand for the finer things in life led him to pass a law that every Roman citizen had to place him first in their will, an act which led to Boadicea's (see entry) revolt in Britain. The revolt of the Celts was an example of Nero's horrendous record in foreign policy, but what brought down his reign was his behavior in Rome.

The infamous fire of A.D. 64 started his downhill slide. Nero did not start the blaze or fiddle while the city burned, as popular legend has it, but he did benefit from the fire by purchasing a prime piece of burned property at a discount. This led Romans to speculate that he had started the fire for his own profit. Anxious to take attention off himself, Nero blamed the Christians, beginning a wave of persecutions that claimed thousands, most likely including the apostles Paul (see entry) and Peter.

His expensive tour of Greece in A.D. 68 bankrupted the imperial treasury. Nero's enemies began closing in. His own Praetorian Guard was prepared to kill him, but Nero escaped to do the job himself. He waited until the Praetorians were about to take him; then he plunged the knife into his chest. His last words were, "Death! And so great an artist!

That generosity extended to others as well. Marcus and Lucius gave the Praetorian Guard a gift equal to several years' pay. They also established a fund to support the children of the poor. At the same time, they spent little on themselves, maintaining a dignified but simple life at the court. All these measures won the Romans' hearty approval. Marcus would remain a popular emperor throughout his reign.

Famine, plague, and invasion

Marcus faced a series of difficulties almost from the beginning. In A.D. 161, the Tiber (TIE-bur) River flooded, causing a famine in Rome. Far away to the east, the Parthians invaded the Roman vassal kingdom of Armenia. At home, Marcus distributed grain to ease the famine. A Roman force soon dealt with the problems in Asia. One general, Avidius Cassius (uh-VID-ee-uhs KASH-uhs), went much further, invading Mesopotamia and establishing Roman control over it in A.D. 166.

Avidius would later cause trouble. In the meantime, the troops returning from Persia brought with them a plague that swept through Rome. Thousands upon thousands of people died. Not even Marcus's physician Galen (see entry), who fled the city to avoid dying himself, could help. Marcus, however, stayed on in Rome, risking his life in the process. He distributed funds for burials. As chief priest of Rome, he led public offerings to seek the gods' help in ending the disaster.

As if this were not enough, German tribes threatened the Italian border in A.D. 166. In 168 Marcus set about dealing with them. Meanwhile more soldiers were dying from the plague, and Lucius was among the casualties. Marcus had to build up his military by recruiting mercenaries and by offering slaves their freedom in exchange for a term of military service.

The costs of this military buildup were great, and tax revenue had dropped due to the plague. This led Marcus to take an extraordinary action for a Roman emperor. Over a period of two months, he auctioned off countless treasures from the palace, raising enough money to pay the public expenses without having to raise his peoples' taxes.

Revolt in the East

By A.D. 170, the Germans had moved into Italy while other tribes invaded Greece. The Romans lost more than 20,000 men, but Marcus defeated the Germans in A.D. 174. He was not able to secure his victory, however, because in A.D. 175, he learned that Avidius Cassius—now acting as governor of Syria—had been declared emperor by his troops.

This was a particularly serious crisis, because Cassius controlled Egypt, which supplied most of the empire's grain. But at least once in his career, things worked in Marcus's favor.

Before Marcus had a chance to march eastward, Cassius was murdered by one of his soldiers. The soldier sent the dead general's head to Marcus, but the emperor refused to look at it.

Although the threat from Cassius was over, Marcus decided to tour the eastern provinces in A.D. 175 in order to reestablish his control. In accordance with his Stoic philosophy, which required an individual to be much harder on himself than on others, he did not harshly punish those who had taken part in the revolt.

Final years

While he was in the east, Marcus also had an opportunity to discuss the Jewish religion with a well-known rabbi, Judah (c. A.D. 135–c. 220). This event is recorded in the Talmud. It is hard to imagine any other Roman emperor taking part in such an exchange. Marcus also took an interest in Christianity, or at least in Christians. At one point he wrote a letter to the senate urging moderation toward Christians—this at a time when they were regularly subjected to persecution in Rome.

Faustina died while they were in the east, and Marcus returned home to face more troubles with the Germans in A.D. 177. To further ease the financial burdens on his citizens, he ordered in A.D. 178 that all debts for the preceding forty-six years be canceled. He also ordered that the debt records be burned in the Forum at the center of Rome.

Between A.D. 178 and 180, Marcus managed to drive the Germans back, but again he missed the opportunity to consolidate Roman power in the north. This time it was because he was dying. He had ensured that his son Commodus (ruled A.D. 180–192) would succeed him. Just before he died on March 17, 180, he urged Commodus to finish the war he had started.

But Commodus was not his father. He negotiated a peace settlement with the Germans, not because he loved peace, but because this was the easiest solution. Therefore he left the German problem unsettled, and it would plague Rome for the remainder of its history.

With the end of Marcus's reign, Rome's golden age died out. The same problems Marcus had faced would continue to reappear. It would be a long time before Rome had

The ruins of the Roman Forum. *Popperfoto/Archive Photos. Reproduced by permission.*

another capable ruler. It would never again have one as kind-hearted and generous as Marcus.

For More Information

Books

Farquharson, A. S. L. *Marcus Aurelius: His Life and His World.* New York: Oxford University Press, 1951.

Powers, Elizabeth. *Nero.* New York: Chelsea House, 1988.

Warmington, B. H. *Nero: Reality and Legend.* New York: Norton, 1969.

Motion Pictures

The Fall of the Roman Empire. Facets Multimedia, Inc., 1964.

Quo Vadis? MGM Home Entertainment, 1951.

The Story of Mankind. Warner/Elektra/Atlantic Corporation, 1957.

Web Sites

"The Emperor Nero: 54-68." http://www.northpark.edu/acad/history/ WebChron/Mediterranean/Nero.html (accessed on July 11, 1999).

"Marcus Aurelius." http://www.kirjasto.sci.fi/aurelius.htm (accessed on July 11, 1999).

Quinn's Nero Page. http://www.ga.k12.pa.us/academics/MS/8th/romanhis/ Forum/QuinnC/in dex.htm (accessed on July 11, 1999).

"Web Resources for Marcus Aurelius." http://acs.rhodes.edu/~riley/aurelius _links.html (accessed on July 11, 1999).

Boadicea

c. A.D. 26
c. A.D. 62

Celtic queen

She was one of the few women of ancient times to lead troops into battle. She gave the mighty Roman Empire some of its fiercest resistance ever. She was Boadicea, queen of a Celtic tribe called the Iceni, who waged a bitter war against the Romans in Britain between A.D. 60 and 62.

The British Isles, consisting primarily of Britain and Ireland, have been inhabited for thousands of years. The first known settlers were those who built great structures, such as Stonehenge, throughout the islands. The identities of these peoples are unknown.

In about 500 B.C., the isles were invaded by the Celts (KEHLTZ), an Indo-European people referred to by the Romans as Gauls (GAWLZ). In fact the Romans typically called them "barbarians," though in fact they did not truly deserve the name. The Celts in Britain came to known as Britons.

Then in 55 B.C., the first Romans arrived: an army led by Julius Caesar (see entry). Caesar did not conquer Britain, however; that happened in A.D. 43, when the Emperor Claudius announced that his legions would "bring the barbarian peoples across the Ocean under the sway of the Roman People."

This the Romans did, killing and destroying as they placed the land under their control. It was a situation not unlike that of the Indians and the white settlers in America many years later. Just as the Native Americans had resistance leaders such as Chief Crazy Horse, the native people of Britain had a leader too—only she was a woman.

Trying to please the Romans

Her name was Boudicca (boo-DIK-uh). Ironically, she is better known by the Roman version of her name: Boadicea (boh-uh-duh-SEE-uh). Her husband, Prasutagus (preh-SHOOT-uh-guhs), ruled over a tribe called the Iceni (both I and i pronounced as "eye": I-SEE-ni).

Prasutagus tried to get along with the Romans. He did not offer any resistance to their invasion. Thus he must have been disappointed when, in A.D. 47, the Romans demanded that all Britons—including the peaceful Iceni—surrender their weapons. This should have told Prasutagus all he needed to know about the Romans, but apparently it did not.

Nero, Emperor of Rome, engraving. *Corbis Bettmann/ Michael Nicholson. Reproduced by permission.*

He died with no male heirs, only his and Boadicea's two daughters. In his will, he divided his property between the daughters and Emperor Nero, thinking that by so doing, he would please the Romans and thereby keep them from taking more. In fact his actions had exactly the opposite result.

Roman law dictated that in a will that left property to the emperor, the emperor had to receive the best share of the property. The Romans interpreted Prasutagus's will as favoring his daughters over Nero. Therefore they sent in soldiers to seize all of Prasutagus's property, which they did in the most savage fashion possible. Boadicea was publicly whipped, her daughters were raped, and many of their tribe were sold into slavery.

Deborah and Jael

Boadicea was not the first woman to prove that women could be every bit as fierce in battle as men. More than a thousand years before her lived the Israelite prophetess Deborah and a young woman named Jael (JAY-ehl). Deborah was a judge, one of the people who led Israel between the time of Moses (see entry) and that of the prophet Samuel, around the 1100s B.C. Her and Jael's story appears in chapters four and five of the Book of Judges in the Bible.

It was a frightening time to be alive in Israel, when the nation was threatened both by its own self-serving people and by outside enemies such as the Canaanites (KAY-nuhn-ightz). The author of Judges recorded that "the Israelites once again did evil in the eyes of the Lord"; therefore God allowed their lands to be invaded by a Canaanite general named Sisera [si-SARE-ah], whose forces had "nine hundred iron chariots."

At that time Deborah was judge. She was the only judge referred to as a "prophetess," which meant that she could hear the voice of God and let the people of Israel know what he wanted them to do. In the attack against Canaan, she had the role of commander-in-chief. She did not engage in the actual fighting but goaded the military commander, Barak (BARE-ak), to lead the Israelite forces into battle. Barak was timid and begged Deborah to go with him. Deborah replied that she would, "but because of the way you are going about this, the honor will not be yours, for the Lord will hand Sisera over to a woman" (4:9).

Deborah was not talking about herself, but about Jael, who came from a

The Britons revolt

As with her name, it is ironic that the record of Boadicea's career has primarily been preserved by Roman historians, both Tacitus (TAS-I-tuhs; c. A.D. 56–120) and Dio Cassius (DEE-oh KASH-uhs; c. A.D. 150–235). But Tacitus, one of the great historians of all time, was wise enough to view his own society critically. In his writings about Boadicea, he did not try to hide either the brutality of the Romans or his admiration for the rebels.

In A.D. 60 or 61, Boadicea raised a force of some 120,000 soldiers to attack a settlement of Roman army veterans at Camulodunum (kam-yuh-loh-DOO-nuhm; modern-day nation called the Kenites. Formerly allied with the Israelites, the Kenites had moved their tents into Canaanite territory, signifying a change of loyalties.

The ensuing battle was an overwhelming victory for Israel. Sisera fled on foot and wound up at Jael's tent. She told him (4:18), "Come, my lord, come right in. Don't be afraid." It was forbidden for a man to enter a woman's tent unless he were her husband or father; therefore it seemed that Sisera had found the ideal hiding place.

As it turned out, however, Jael had other plans. After he received some milk from her, Sisera told her to stand watch at the tent flap in case someone came by; then he fell asleep. While he was sleeping, she "picked up a tent peg and a hammer and went quietly to him. . .

. . . She drove the peg through his temple into the ground, and he died" (v. 21). It was an act that required not only great nerve, but great physical strength. If she had not struck the first blow firmly, Sisera would have woken up and overpowered her.

Chapter 5 of Judges is the "Song of Deborah," in which the prophetess celebrated the victory and paid special tribute, in verses 24 through 27, to Jael. After that time, the Bible says, there was peace for forty years. The region occupied by the Canaanites had long been promised to the people of Israel as "a land flowing with milk and honey." It is interesting, then, that the two women who saved Israel in Judges 4 were named Jael, which means "mountain goat," and Deborah, which means "bee"—milk and honey.

Colchester). Her troops consisted of many tribes, united in their hatred of Roman rule, and they sacked and burned Roman villages along the way. Tacitus wrote that the seas turned "a blood-red color" and the waters swelled with "shapes like human corpses." They destroyed Camulodunum completely, then turned their eyes toward the town of Londinium (luhn-DIN-ee-uhm).

The Romans had not sent a large force to Camulodunum because they did not believe the Britons could really pose a threat against battle-hardened veterans. In the case of Londinium, a settlement of some 30,000 people, the Roman governor decided it was not worth saving. Therefore he took his troops and left. Everyone who could escape the town did, but many women, children, and old people remained.

The attack by the Britons was horrible, and Boadicea left no one alive. Certainly the Britons proved themselves equal to the Romans for viciousness. After they destroyed another town, they prepared to meet the Romans for a battle that would decide the war.

Destruction of the Britons

The battle did decide the war, but not in the Britons' favor. Certain they would win, they had brought with them their wives and families, who would sit on ox-carts behind the army and watch them slaughter the Romans. The Romans had just 1,200 men against the Britons' 100,000. Though they were good fighters, the Britons were not a disciplined military force, as the Romans were. That lack of discipline would be their undoing.

First the Romans came at them with javelins, or spears, which cut down large numbers of men since the Britons had no armor. They drove the Britons back, but the rebels had nowhere to go: behind them were their families in oxcarts, and they found themselves pinned. By the end of the day, the Romans had massacred some 80,000 Britons, including women and children, not to mention their animals. Only about 400 Romans were killed.

Most likely Boadicea survived the battle, only to poison herself before the Romans could subject her to a much crueler death. Nothing is known regarding the fate of her daughters. Most of the Iceni were forcibly removed from Britain, and many were sold into slavery. The Romans took steps to ensure that the Celts who remained would never again mount a revolt such as the one led by Boadicea. The Britons paid dearly for their rebellion.

The first great British woman

As early as the time of Tacitus and Dio, Boadicea had already emerged as a legendary figure. Tacitus reported that before the last battle, Boadicea "drove round the tribes in a chariot with her daughters in front of her. 'We British are used to woman commanders in war,' she cried. 'I am not fighting for my kingdom and wealth now. I am fighting as an ordinary person for my lost freedom, my bruised body, and my outraged daughters.'"

The speech probably reveals more about Tacitus than it does Boadicea, since it is hard to imagine how any record of such a speech would have survived the battle. Probably he was so impressed by the idea of Boadicea that he invented the speech for her. Similarly, Dio was most likely presenting a romantic image when he described her thus: "She was very tall, the glance of her eye most fierce; her voice harsh. A great mass of the reddest hair fell down to her hips. . . . Her appearance was terrifying."

Through such highly charged image, the legend of Boadicea circulated centuries after her death. She is still celebrated as the first important figure in British history, long before there was an England. Today there is a statue commemorating her victory in London, a town she had once destroyed when it was a Roman settlement called Londinium.

For More Information

Books

Andrews, Ian. *Boudicca's Revolt*. Drawings by Graham Humphreys and Trevor Stubley. London: Cambridge University Press, 1972.

León, Vicki. *Outrageous Women of Ancient Times*. New York: John Wiley & Sons, 1998, pp. 71-78.

Matthews, John. *Boadicea: Warrior Queen of the Celts*. Plated by James Field. New York: Sterling Publishing Company, 1988.

McDonough, Yona. *Eve and Her Sisters: Women of the Old Testament*. Paintings by Malcah Zeldis. New York: Greenwillow Books, 1994.

Meltzer, Milton. *Ten Queens: Portraits of Power*. Illustrated by Bethanne Anderson. New York: Dutton Children's Books, 1998.

Sutcliff, Rosemary. *Song for a Dark Queen* (fiction). New York: Crowell, 1979.

Trease, Geoffrey. *Seven Sovereign Queens*. New York: Vanguard Press, 1968.

Web Sites

Boadicea. http://members.tripod.com/~ancient_history/boad.html (accessed on June 28, 1999).

"Boudicca, the Queen of the Iceni." *Athena Publications*. http://www.athenapub.com/boudicca.htm (accessed on June 28, 1999).

"Celts in Battle—Celts through Roman Eyes." *Encyclopedia of the Celts.* http://www.ealaghol.demon.co.uk/celtenc/celt_c3.htm (accessed on June 28, 1999).

"Deborah." http://www.geocities.com/Athens/Rhodes/1319/bibwomen/ deborah2.html (accessed on June 28, 1999).

"Deborah." http://info-center.ccit.arizona.edu/~ws/ws200/fall97/grp4/ part4.htm (accessed on June 28, 1999).

Buddha

Born c. 563 B.C.
Died c. 483 B.C.

Indian holy man, teacher, and founder of Buddhism

The Buddha, or "Enlightened One," has often been compared with Jesus Christ (see entry). Both were said to have been born under extraordinary circumstances. Both embarked, at about the age of thirty, on their life's work. In the course of that work, both would criticize the beliefs of an older religion and would establish the foundations of what became a new faith. Both would see the fulfillment of their work over a period of a few days in their mid-thirties.

On the other hand, the two could not have been more different. Whereas Jesus came from a humble background, the Buddha, whose given name was Gautama Siddartha, was born a prince. Their activities in their early thirties were different as well: Jesus was a teacher, Buddha a seeker of wisdom. And their acts of fulfillment differed sharply. After his ministry, Jesus was killed and, according to Christians, rose again; Buddha, in the view of Buddhists, achieved enlightenment, then began his ministry, which continued for some forty-five years.

All things must decay. Be diligent in striving for salvation.

The Buddha's last words

Miraculous birth

In the 500s B.C., a family by the name of Gautama (GOW-tuh-muh), from the Sakyas (SAHK-yahs) clan, ruled a kingdom in northern India, in what is now Nepal. To the king and queen was born a son named Siddartha (sid-AHR-tah). As many legends surround his birth as do that of Jesus nearly six centuries later.

As the New Testament relates how an angel appeared to Mary to tell her she would bear God's son, so Buddhist legend holds that Siddartha was not conceived by normal means. In the Buddhist story, his mother was visited in a dream by a white elephant, which touched her side with a fragrant blossom from the lotus tree. Soon afterward, she became pregnant. In both cases, the unusual conception showed believers that the one being born would rise above the established patterns of the world. Christ, in his virgin birth, broke the cycle of sin and death, just as the Buddha would break the cycle of death and rebirth known as reincarnation.

It was also said that Siddartha's mother experienced no pain in giving birth to him but that he simply came out of her side. At that moment, Buddhists believe, light flooded the world and many miracles occurred. The newborn baby told his mother, "This is my last rebirth—henceforth there is no more birth for me." He then began to walk, and lotus blossoms sprouted where his feet had trod.

His birth may have been painless, but the mother soon died. In the meantime, Siddartha's father, Suddhodana (sood-hoh-DAH-nuh), called in fortune-tellers to discover what was in store for this unusual child. The seers said that if he chose to become a ruler, Siddartha would be a world conqueror; if, on the other hand, he turned away from worldly pursuits to seek wisdom, he would bring spiritual salvation to all mankind. The father decided that his boy would become a king.

Questions about the world

Then, as now, the dominant faith in India was Hinduism, which taught that existence is an endless cycle of reincarnation. Though Hindus believe that people have some influence over the state of their future lives, to a large extent this is determined for them. Hand in hand with this idea went the notion of the caste system, a set of rankings for people. Those at the top of the social order, Hindus believed, were born that way because they had progressed further spiritually than those on the lower ranks.

Siddartha's family were members of a high caste. His father determined that Siddartha would never find out about the sufferings of the poor. He even prevented his son from knowing about sickness and death by never allowing anyone old or sick into the palace.

In order to maintain this illusion, Siddartha was kept a virtual prisoner, but in time he grew more and more curious about the world outside the palace walls. Finally he escaped and went on a series of sightseeing expeditions, in which he encountered what Buddhists call the Four Passing Sights.

He saw in turn an old man, a sick man, and a dead man, sights that made him ask why suffering existed. The fourth sight—that of a wandering Hindu holy man—led him to a decision. Siddartha had been married since the age of six-teen to a princess named Yasodhara (yah-sohd-HAHR-ah). They had a young son, but at the age of twenty-nine, Siddartha decided that he would give up his happy home life to seek enlightenment, or spiritual wisdom.

The quest for enlightenment

Over the next six years, Siddartha would renounce many more pleasures. First, he studied meditation for a year under two Hindu holy men. When he did not find what he was seeking, he joined the sect known as the Jains (JYNZ). The latter were ascetics (uh-SET-ikz), meaning they renounced all earthly pleasures, even such basic ones as food and shelter, in their search for spiritual truth.

After five years of study with the Jains, Siddartha's body had shrunk to mere skin and bone, but he had not reached the enlightenment he sought. Finally he left the Jains, and five ascetics left with him. One night, as his body and mind were recovering from all the stress of the years, he went to meditate under a fig tree near the town of Gaya (guh-YAH) in northeastern India.

Over the course of a single night beneath the tree, dur-ing which time he was tormented by demons, Siddartha came

Kanishka

Kanishka (kuh-NISH-kuh; C. A.D. 78–103) became the greatest ruler of the Kushan (koo-SHAHN) dynasty that ruled most of northern India for a short but very crucial period. The Kushans provided an important link between East and West. Thanks to Kanishka, the Kushans aided immeasurably in the spread of Buddhism from India to China.

The roots of the Kushans go back to the unification of China and the building of the Great Wall by Emperor Shi Huang Ti. This displaced two great nations, the Hsiung-Nu (shung NOO) or Huns, who ultimately went west; and the Yüeh-Chih (you-WAY CHEE).

The latter, after a defeat by the Hsiung-Nu, wound up in what is now Afghanistan in about 120 B.C.. The Yüeh-Chih consisted of five tribes, and one of these, known as the Kushans, became the most powerful. They invaded India. Under their third ruler, Kanishka, they controlled a vast territory that stretched from the southern end of modern-day Russia to the Ganges River valley in southeastern India. Between the arrival of the Aryan invaders in 1500 B.C. and India's conquest by Muslims more than 2,500 years later, no conqueror controlled more territory on the Indian subcontinent.

The Kushans stood at the crossroads of the world. They controlled the Old Silk Road, established in about 100 B.C., a vital trade route between China, India, western Asia, and ultimately Europe. Theirs was a multinational empire, with a variety of Eastern and Western belief systems. Thus they appear to have been strongly influenced both by Greece and Rome and by the cultures of the East.

to understand the meaning of existence. As he did, he was enlightened; hence his new name, Buddha.

He sat under the tree for many days and nights, during which time he came to a deeper understanding of what he had discovered. Then he preached his first sermon to the five ascetics, in a deer park—something like a forest preserve—near the town of Benares (bu-NAHR-uhs) in southeastern India.

The sermon contained what Buddhists know as the Four Noble Truths: that life is painful; that desire is the cause of pain; that only through a state of inner peace, or nirvana (nuhr-VAHN-uh), can one overcome desire; and that the key to nirvana is what he called the Eightfold Path. The Eightfold

Kanishka, Kushan King of India, praying to a statue of Buddha. *Illustration. Corbis-Bettmann. Reproduced by permission.*

Kanishka embraced a type of Buddhism called Mahayana (mah-ha-YAH-nuh; "Great Wheel"), which held that others could become buddhas by following the teachings of the Buddha. With Kanishka's blessings, a group of Buddhist monks came together to formalize the doctrines of Mahayana. Through his control of the Silk Road, the faith spread north and east, to China, and from there to most of eastern Asia.

The spread of Buddhism was perhaps Kanishka's greatest contribution to world civilization. His empire also helped transmit Greek ideas about art to India, where sculpture began to take on a distinctly Hellenistic cast. In addition, he built a 638-foot (194.5-meter) stupa in his capital, Peshawar (peh-SHOW-uhr), now in Pakistan on the Afghan border. The tower was one of the few structures built before modern times that exceeds the Great Pyramid of Egypt in height.

Path is a series of steps, such as facing the realities of life, that one must take in succession on the road to enlightenment.

His ministry

After his experience of enlightenment, the Buddha traveled a great deal, mostly in the area of Magadha (MAH-guh-duh). Magadha would become, two centuries later, the center of a great Buddhist empire whose greatest ruler was Asoka (see entry).

Buddhism was not a religion in the sense that Christianity is. Unlike Jesus, Buddha did not declare himself the son of God; many Buddhists do not believe in God as such. But all faiths have to have some system of organization. Buddha spent much of his remaining forty-five years providing that system. Thus he also had a function not unlike that of the Apostle Paul (see entry) in Christianity.

He set up monasteries (MAHN-uh-stair-eez), places where monks, nuns, and others could get away from the world's turmoil to seek spiritual wisdom. He also preached more sermons, including one at the time of his death. His last words to his disciples were a command to keep striving for salvation.

The spread of Buddhism

Buddha spoke about many things, but one thing he had no use for was the caste system. Thus Buddhism exerted a great appeal for people regarded as lower castes under Hinduism. Buddhists believe that their faith fulfills all the longings expressed in Hinduism, just as Christians believe that Jesus is the promised Messiah of Judaism. Jesus plays no role in Judaism, but he is treated as a great figure in the Islamic faith; similarly, Hindus believe that Buddha is the incarnation of the god Vishnu (VIZH-noo).

Many of Buddhism's holy sites are in India—not only the sites of the Buddha's enlightenment and his sermons, but also the eight temples, or stupas (STOO-pahz), to which the Buddha's ashes were divided after he was cremated. India would ultimately reject Buddhism, however; but thanks to Kanishka [see sidebar] and others, the faith would take hold farther north, in China and other countries.

For More Information

Books

Landaw, Jonathan. *Prince Siddartha: The Story of Buddha.* Illustrated by Janet Brooke. Boston, MA: Wisdom Publications, 1996.

Okada, Amina. *The Prince Who Became a Beggar.* Mankato, MN: Creative Education, 1997.

Rawding, F. W. *The Buddha.* Minneapolis, MN: Lerner Publications, 1979.

Roth, Susan L. *Buddha.* New York: Delacorte Press, 1994.

Rowe, W. W. *The Buddha's Question.* Ithaca, NY: Snow Lion Publications, 1994.

Schulberg, Lucille. *Historic India.* New York: Time-Life Books, 1968, pp. 57-71.

Motion Pictures

Little Buddha. Miramax Pictures Home Video, 1993.

Web Sites

Buddha at the Movies. http://buddhism.about.com/msub9.htmlpid =2818&cob=looksmart (accessed on July 5, 1999).

Buddhism 101. http://buddhism.about.com/msub8.htmlpid=2818&cob =looksmart (accessed on July 5, 1999).

The Historical Buddha. http://buddhism.about.com/msub2.htmlpid =2818&cob=looksmart (accessed on July 5, 1999).

Julius Caesar

Born 102 B.C.
Died 44 B.C.

Roman leader

The name of Julius Caesar is still quite literally a household word. After all, the seventh month of the year is named after him. He was without a doubt the most significant figure in the history of Rome. His career paved the way both for the end of the republic and the creation of the empire under his nephew Octavian [see sidebar].

A brilliant if not particularly moral leader, Caesar climbed to the top of Roman society partly through political maneuvering and bribery and partly through his own great skill. After forming the shaky First Triumvirate with Crassus and Pompey, he ultimately eliminated his opponents, along the way embarking on a well-known affair with Cleopatra (see entry). As dictator of Rome, he put through valuable reforms but earned the distrust even of his closest friends, who conspired in his assassination.

Marius and Sulla

The future dictator of Rome was born Gaius (GIE-yus) Julius Caesar on "Quintilis" (July) 13, 102 B.C., to an aristocratic but not wealthy family. Information about his early life is surprisingly scarce, though it is known that his father was a senator.

From a political standpoint, the most important event of young Caesar's life was his aunt Julia's marriage to the consul Marius (MAHR-ee-uhs; c. 157–86 B.C.). Marius helped Caesar's political advancement from an early age. Twenty-one-year-old Caesar further increased his standing by marrying Cornelia, daughter of the consul Cinna (SIN-uh)—an ally of Marius—in 83 B.C.. They later had a daughter, Julia.

At that time, Marius, as leader of the popular party, was locked in a struggle with Sulla (SUHL-uh; 137–78 B.C.), leader of the aristocratic party. The popular group, though aristocrats as well, favored a greater distribution of power. Because of his family association with Marius, Caesar allied himself with the popular faction.

Sulla established a dangerous example, one Caesar himself would later imitate, when in 88 B.C. he marched his troops into Rome. This ultimately meant the end of Marius's power. Sulla demanded that Caesar divorce Cornelia. Caesar refused and had to go into hiding, during which time he contracted malaria. His mother's family convinced Sulla to relent, and Caesar returned to Rome and entered the army.

The rise of Caesar

While serving in the Asia Minor in 80 B.C., Caesar earned a high military decoration for bravery in the battle to take Mitylene (mit-uh-LEE-nee) on Lesbos (LEZ-bohs). He went on to take part in a war against pirates from Cilicia (suh-LI-shuh), a region in southeastern Asia Minor. Following the death of Sulla, Caesar went back to Rome. In 77 B.C. he earned a name for himself as a prosecutor in an important legal case.

Already recognizing his ability as a speaker, Caesar traveled to the Greek isle of Rhodes (ROHDZ) for further training in rhetoric, but the Cilician pirates captured him and held him for ransom. After his release, he led a force to victory against the pirates. Then, without being commanded to do, Caesar led a successful attack against Mithradates of Pontus (mith-ruh-DAY-teez; ruled 120–63 B.C.; PAHN-tuhs). Soon after this, he gained his first elected office as military tribune.

Caesar Augustus

Born Gaius Octavius Caesar on September 23, 63 B.C., the man destined to become Caesar Augustus was known for the first thiry-six years of his life as Octavian (ahk-TAY-vee-uhn). His father died when he was four years old, and he was raised by his mother's uncle, Julius Caesar. The latter, having no legitimate sons, named him as his heir.

When Caesar was assassinated, nineteen-year-old Octavian administered his uncle's will. He quickly won the trust of the senate, unlike Caesar's junior associate Mark Antony. Octavian was put in command of an army to defend the city against Antony. He defeated him, but Antony escaped. Octavian decided that in order to prevent another civil war, it would be better to join forces.

Therefore Octavian, Antony, and Lepidus (LEP-i-dus) formed the Second Triumvirate and set about dealing with Caesar's killers. There was a bloodbath in Rome, in which several thousand leading citizens died; later at Philippi (FIL-uh-pie) in Macedon, the Triumvirate defeated Brutus and Cassius, who committed suicide.

But there was more unfinished business from Caesar's time. The son of Pompey, Sextus Pompeius (SEX-tus PAHM-pee-uhs; 75–35 B.C.), controlled the Mediterranean, and his naval forces were harassing Roman ships. To influence Sextus, Octavian married Sextus's relative Scribonia (SKRI-boh-nee-uh), by whom he had his only child, Julia. This helped relations, but when Octavian divorced Scribonia, Sextus resumed his piracy. Using ships borrowed from Antony's fleet and commanded by Marcus Agrippa (uh-GRIP-uh; c. 63–12 B.C.), Octavian destroyed Sextus.

Over the next seven years, Octavian edged Lepidus out of the Triumvirate and then dealt with Antony. The latter had married Octavian's sister Octavia, but it was clear that his true love was Cleopatra, once the lover of Caesar. In a brilliant move, Octavian persuaded the senate to declare war not on Antony (to do so would have constituted another civil war, something Octavian had pledged would never happen again) but only on Cleopatra and Egypt. The Battle of Actium on September 2, 31 B.C., destroyed Antony

In 69 B.C., Caesar was elected *quaestor*. Cornelia died in 67 B.C., but within a year, he had remarried. Again the marriage had a political angle: Pompeia (pahm-PEE-yuh), his new wife, was the granddaughter of Sulla. Of course Sulla had once been Caesar's enemy, but times had changed. Now Caesar wanted to establish closer ties with the ultra-wealthy Crassus (KRA-suhs;

and Cleopatra and left Octavian in sole power over the Roman state.

In the next few years, Octavian made one of the most cunning power plays in history, and he did it by appearing to give up power. For every office that he surrendered, the senate, grateful to him for restoring order to Rome, heaped more authority on him. He thus began to combine the functions of several offices without the titles of those offices. In doing so, he became far more powerful than his uncle Julius had ever been.

Titles were to come, however, and they were magnificent titles indeed. In 27 B.C., the senate gave him the name by which he would be known to history, Augustus, meaning "great." They lavished more titles on him, each conveying greater and greater authority and a status close to that of a god. Whereas Julius had offended decency when he renamed a month after himself, the senate itself declared that the month of Sextilius would thenceforth be called "Augustus," or August.

The senate's proclamation of him as emperor meant that Augustus now held all the leadership positions formerly occupied by a number of men; it did not, however, mean that he was an emperor in the traditional sense of the word, with a title he could pass down to his sons. Augustus was very careful about that, knowing as he did that the Romans had despised the idea of kings ever since they drove out Tarquinius Superbus half a millennium before. In a way, this position was unfortunate, because it always left open to question who would succeed the reigning emperor. Nero would be the last of Augustus's line to rule. In later years, men would succeed to the throne through treachery and assassination, often on the shoulders of the army.

Augustus, who died in A.D. 14, ruled over Rome in its greatest glory. He fostered the arts, aiding in the careers of such distinguished figures as Vergil (see entry) and overseeing the building of many magnificent structures. Whereas he had been ruthless in his rise to power, once he got to the top, he was a fair and just emperor.

---

c. 115–53 B.C.), a leading figure in the aristocratic party who had been friends with Sulla.

Parties and politics

To get ahead in Rome, a politician had to spend money on bribes and lavish entertainments for fellow politicians and the Roman citizens. As *aedile*, Caesar heavily outspent his colleague Bibulus (BIB-yoo-luhs; d. 48 B.C.), sponsoring the most magnificent set of gladiatorial games Rome had ever seen. Later, he obtained a position as governor in Spain, where he made back all the money he had spent—probably by means that were less than honorable.

Meanwhile, he had divorced Pompeia. It seems she had held a party for women in their home. Unbeknownst to her, a character named Pulcher (PUL-kur) had gotten into the house disguised as a woman. This created a scandal. Caesar informed his soon-to-be ex-wife, "I maintain that the members of my family should be free from suspicion as well as from accusation." That incident was recorded by Plutarch.

The historian Suetonius (soo-TOHN-ee-uhs) related a number of revealing details about Caesar, including his spending. According to Suetonius, at one point Caesar had a mansion built, then ordered it torn down because he did not care for it. As for his personal habits, "He was somewhat overnice in the care of his person, being not only carefully trimmed and shaved, but even having superfluous [extra] hair plucked out." His baldness "troubled him greatly. . . . Because of it he used to comb forward the scanty locks from the crown of his head, and of all the honors voted him by the senate and the people there was none which he received or made use of more gladly than the privilege of wearing a laurel wreath at all times."

Caesar in Gaul

Back from Spain in 59 B.C., Caesar was elected co-consul with Bibulus and managed to establish such a degree of control that the comedians of the day referred to "the consulship of Julius and Caesar, instead of Bibulus and Caesar." By then, however, it was clear that only three men in Rome really mattered: Caesar, Crassus, and Pompey (PAHM-pee; 106–48 B.C.).

Caesar had just returned from his defeat of Mithradates, and together the three formed the First Triumvirate (try-UM-vuhr-eht), or government of three. Pompey even married Caesar's daughter Julia. Despite their mutual claims of loyalty, however, the First Triumvirate was an uneasy alliance, since none of the three trusted one another. The inevitable conflict would be delayed for many years while Caesar went to Gaul (modern-day France).

Anxious to gain military glory in Gaul, Caesar went looking for a war, and he soon had one. When the Helvetii (hel-VEE-shee-ie), from what is now Switzerland, tried to cross Gaul without permission from Caesar, he drove them back. Other tribes then asked him to drive out the Suebi (SWAY-bee) from Germany, which he did; then he conducted the first Roman invasion of Britain in 55 and 54 B.C. to prevent the Celts on that island from aiding their cousins on the mainland. After this, he had to fight more tribes in Gaul. Caesar killed perhaps a million people but put all of Gaul firmly under Roman control.

Back in Rome, the alliance with Pompey had grown shaky. Julia died in 54 B.C., breaking that bond between the two men. In the following year, Crassus was killed in Asia. Pompey began marshalling forces against Caesar. Although Caesar managed to win a few more allies with some carefully placed bribes, it was clear that a showdown was near.

Julius Caesar, sword raised.
Library of Congress.

From the Rubicon to Egypt

That showdown came on January 10, 49 B.C.. Pompey had ordered Caesar back to Rome. Caesar, knowing he would be killed if he went back alone, brought his army with him. By crossing the River Rubicon (ROO-bi-kahn), a shallow stream that formed the southern boundary of Cisalpine Gaul (siz-AL-pine), he made his intentions clear. The expression "crossing the Rubicon" still means passing a point of no return.

Pompey moved his forces to Greece in order to regroup while Caesar defeated Pompey's legions in Spain. The two met in battle at Pharsalus (fahr-SALE-uhs) in Greece in 48 B.C. Though Caesar's armies won, Pompey managed to escape. He fled to Egypt, where Pharaoh Ptolemy XII (TAHL-uh-mee) had him killed. Caesar is said to have reacted in horror when he learned the fate of his former colleague.

Egypt, of course, is where Caesar met Cleopatra and began his celebrated affair with her. He aided her in a war against Ptolemy and declared her queen of Egypt. But he had other troubles elsewhere: Mithradates's teenaged son Pharnaces (FAR-nuh-seez), taking advantage of Caesar's distraction in Egypt, had attempted to regain his father's kingdom in Pontus. Caesar went to Asia Minor and destroyed Pharnaces's army in just five days. It was then that he made his famous report of his victory: "I came, I saw, I conquered." The saying is even shorter in Latin: *Veni, vidi, vici* (VAY-nee VEE-dee VEE-chee).

The dictator of Rome

In 47 B.C., Caesar was at the high point of his career. He returned to Rome, where he assumed the powers of a dictator and quickly pushed through a series of reforms. Most notable among these was his effort to reduce unemployment, a growing problem, by requiring that every landowner hire one free man for every two slaves working in his fields. He increased the membership in the senate from 300 to 900 and included Celtic chieftains from Gaul in Rome's legislative body.

Caesar managed to combine the authority of numerous political offices, giving himself more power than any Roman leader had ever enjoyed; yet he seemed to want more. Though it is common practice today for the portrait of a leader—usually a deceased one—to appear on coins, at that time only deities were depicted on Roman currency. Caesar decreed that his image would grace the back of coins. He declared that the month of his birth would no longer be called Quintilis (kwin-TIL-is) but "Julius," or July.

The calendar reform has endured, but to the Romans of that time, it seemed that Caesar was going too far. Instead of standing before the senate when he spoke to them, as rulers had always done before, he sat, more like a monarch than a citizen. His junior colleague Mark Antony even tried to convince him to wear a crown.

The Ides of March

Had Caesar accepted the crown, it would have been such an offense to the Romans' views on government that he would have been an instant target for assassination. As it was, assassination was not long in coming. Caesar planned to go to Persia to conduct a campaign against the Parthians, who had killed Crassus. Before he left, he planned to address the senate on the Ides, or fifteenth, of March, 44 B.C..

Unbeknownst to him, however, a group of some sixty influential Romans had joined forces to assassinate him. Although the group included his opponents, the majority were his former allies. The ringleaders, Brutus and Cassius, were supposedly his friends. As he walked into the senate, the assassins jumped at him with daggers, stabbing him twenty-three times. It would fall to his nephew Augustus to avenge the murder.

For More Information

Books

Gunther, John. *All About Julius Caesar.* London: W. H. Allen, 1967.

Nardo, Don. *Caesar's Conquest of Gaul.* San Diego, CA: Lucent Books, 1996.

Nardo, Don. *Julius Caesar.* San Diego, CA. Lucent Books, 1996.

Ochoa, George. *The Assassination of Julius Caesar.* Englewood Cliffs, NJ: Silver Burdett, 1991.

The Roman World. New York: Marshall Cavendish, 1989.

Shakespeare, William. *Julius Caesar for Young People* (drama). Edited and illustrated by Diane Davidson. Fair Oaks, CA: Swan Books, 1990.

Motion Pictures

Cleopatra. CBS/Fox Video, 1963.

Cleopatra (TV). American Broadcasting Company, 1999.

Julius Caesar. MGM Home Entertainment, 1953.

Julius Caesar. Commonwealth United Entertainment, 1970.

Web Sites

"Augustus and Tiberius." http://vroma.rhodes.edu/~bmcmanus/augustus.html (accessed on July 11, 1999).

"Caesar." http://www.cs.uh.edu/~clifton/caesar.html (accessed on July 11, 1999).

"Caesar Augustus." *Virgil.org.* http://www.virgil.org/augustus (accessed on July 11, 1999).

"Julius Caesar: Historical Background." http://vroma.rhodes.edu/~bmcmanus/caesar.html (accessed on July 11, 1999).

Cleopatra

Born 69 B.C.
Died 30 B.C.

Greek queen of Egypt

Cleopatra seemingly needs no introduction, since her name is a household word. Virtually everyone learns about the beautiful Egyptian queen who seduced two famous Romans. But the truth about Cleopatra is far more complicated. Cleopatra—or, more properly, Cleopatra VII—was not Egyptian but Greek. She was a descendant of one of Alexander the Great's (see entry) generals. More important, from the comments of ancient historians, not to mention a bust sculpted in her lifetime, it is clear she was no great beauty, as she has almost always been represented in movies.

Instead, what drew both Julius Caesar (see entry) and Mark Antony to her was her intelligence and wit. Certainly she knew how to use her gifts to her advantage, and she was no innocent victim. But from the perspective of modern history, it is easy to understand how a brilliant woman ruler, seeking to save her empire from a much stronger one, might have felt that she had no other choice but to do what Cleopatra did.

The Greeks in Egypt

Cleopatra belonged to a dynasty that descended from Ptolemy (TAHL-uh-mee; c. 366–c. 283 B.C.), one of the Macedonian generals who carved up the empire created by their leader, Alexander the Great. By the time of her birth in 69 B.C., all the other Greek dynasties had long since died out; only the ptolemies, a name they used as a title like "pharaoh," remained. They ruled from the Egyptian city of Alexandria, the most famous of the many cities so founded and named by Alexander.

The ptolemies' endurance is surprising, since the aspects of Egyptian culture that they adopted tended to separate them from the Egyptians rather than bring them closer to the people. Like the pharaohs, they claimed to be gods, but the pharaohs were powerful rulers and the ptolemies were not. Also like the pharaohs, they practiced intermarriage. (Cleopatra's first two husbands were her brothers.) Intermarriage only kept their bloodline more Greek and more cut off from the Egyptians.

Trying to bribe Rome

Cleopatra's father, Ptolemy XII (ruled 80-51 B.C.), was particularly unpopular. Hoping to protect Egypt from Roman invasion, he spent great sums of money bribing senators in Rome. Apparently, he made little effort to explain his actions to the people of Egypt, who saw only that he was robbing the treasury to give money to a foreign power. In 59 B.C., he seemed to have bought himself a little time when he convinced Pompey (pahm-PAY; 106–48 B.C.), one of Rome's principal leaders, to spare Egypt. In the following year, however, Rome seized the island of Cyprus (SIE-pruhs) from Egypt. The people revolted against Ptolemy, who fled to Rome.

Eleven years old at the time, Cleopatra had already shown herself to be a bright young girl. She must have received an outstanding education, because she had an astonishing command of languages. She became the only ptolemy to ever learn Egyptian (a telling detail). Undoubtedly it was also clear to her that Egypt could only survive as an independent country if Rome allowed it to.

Fathers, brothers, and lovers

In the absence of Ptolemy, Cleopatra's older sister Berenice (bare-uh-NIE-see) took the throne. Then, in 55 B.C., Ptolemy bribed more Romans and returned to power. Appar-

Antiochus the Great

Though he is far less famous than his descendant Cleopatra, Antiochus III (an-tee-AHK-uhs; 242–187 B.C.; ruled 223–187 B.C.), known as "the Great," came much closer than she did to achieving her dream of empire. Like her, he ruled over what remained of lands claimed by one of Alexander's generals. The Seleucid (seh-LOO-sid) Empires at one point included most of western Asia. By the time of Antiochus, its holdings had shrunk considerably.

Throughout his nearly forty-year reign, Antiochus waged nearly constant war with a variety of enemies—not only with foreign powers but with rebellious members of his own family. After a crushing defeat by forces under Ptolemy IV of Egypt in 217 B.C., he went on to a string of victories. In 213 B.C., he recovered Asia Minor from his cousin Achaeus (uh-KEE-uhs); regained control of Armenia in 212; and in quick succession reconquered all of Persia and Bactria (modern Afghanistan). By 205 B.C., his armies had reached the Hindu Kush Mountains on the Indian border. Before leaving the region, he looted a temple to help repay the cost of his wars. It was an act he would repeat frequently in the years that followed.

Back home, Antiochus won back Palestine. In 195 B.C., he scored a major victory over Egypt. Ptolemy V gave up

ently seeing a threat in Berenice, he had her executed. Now Cleopatra, age fourteen, was his oldest child.

But as a girl, of course, she was not likely to take the throne if there were a boy available—even though she was very much the intellectual superior of her brother. The father arranged for her and her oldest brother to marry. When Ptolemy XII died in 51 B.C., Cleopatra became joint ruler with the brother, Ptolemy XIII.

To put it lightly, Cleopatra did not exactly have a normal home life. She was eighteen and her brother/husband nine or ten years old. Although it appears that they did not have a sexual relationship, they did not share the loyalties of a brother and sister either. Eventually two hostile parties developed around them. By 48 B.C., Ptolemy's group forced Cleopatra out of Egypt. But 48 B.C. was also the year the Romans arrived.

lands to Antiochus and agreed to marry Antiochus's daughter Cleopatra—whose name would be passed down through the generations. Antiochus had won back the empire of his forefathers and was hailed as the greatest conqueror since Alexander.

However, he did not known how to quit when he was ahead. He joined forces with the Macedonian king Philip V (238–179 B.C.) against Rome. But Philip was defeated in 197 B.C., and the Romans warned Antiochus not to invade Greece. He got the same advice from someone who knew about Roman power: Hannibal (see entry), to whom Antiochus had given refuge. Antiochus went ahead with his plans, nevertheless, and Rome defeated him at Thermopylae (thuhr-MAHP-uh-lee) in 191 B.C. A year later, the Romans crippled Antiochus's forces at Magnesia. Antiochus was killed in 187 B.C. while trying to loot a temple.

The defeat of Antiochus brought an end to the Seleucid Empire as a powerful force. This defeat, however, was not really in the long-term interests of Rome. Because the Seleucids were Greek, their defeat spelled the end of European influence in the area. Rome would control much of the region for a time, but without the European influence of the Seleucids, western Asia later became one of the first parts of the Roman Empire to break away.

Winning and losing Caesar

As members of the First Triumvirate (try-UM-vuhr-eht), Pompey and Julius Caesar had come into conflict. Pompey expected to find allies in Egypt; instead he was assassinated by forces loyal to Ptolemy. Caesar, who arrived shortly thereafter, was horrified by what had happened. Meanwhile, Cleopatra managed to make her way back into Alexandria and, smuggled in a rolled-up rug, arrived at Caesar's quarters. This intrigued Caesar, who was fifty-four at the time; Cleopatra was twenty-one.

The reason was not her great beauty but rather her intelligence. The historian Plutarch (PLOO-tahrk), explaining her later appeal to Mark Antony, a young general under Caesar, wrote that "her beauty in itself was so striking that it stunned the onlooker, but . . . the persuasiveness of her talk, and the charac-

Mark Antony, bust.
Drawing by E. Krell.
Library of Congress.

ter that surrounded her conversation, was stimulating." She overwhelmed Antony, who was no great genius; with Caesar, on the other hand—a man often considered the greatest of the Romans—she found an equal.

Because of Cleopatra, Caesar became involved in Egyptian politics. He joined her in a war that left Ptolemy dead in 47 B.C. Then Cleopatra married another brother, who took the throne as Ptolemy XIV. Of course the relationship with this brother, twelve years old at the time, was not that of a husband and wife. In 46 B.C., Cleopatra went with Caesar to Rome and later bore a child whom she named Cesarion (seh-SARE-ee-uhn). She claimed the boy was Caesar's, though some historians dispute this.

The whole Egyptian royal house had moved to Rome, including not only Ptolemy but a sister, Arsinoë (ahr-SIN-oh-ee), who had tried to take the throne herself. Cleopatra later had Arsinoë murdered. In 44 B.C. she did away with Ptolemy in order to make way for Cesarion. But 44 was also the year of Caesar's assassination; with her lover gone, she fled Rome.

Wooing Mark Antony

Many Romans believed that Cleopatra had joined in the plot against Caesar or at least had not tried to stop it. This is highly unlikely—she had every reason to want Caesar to stay in power. But the force of public opinion was strong. Therefore, in 41 B.C., one of the members of the Second Triumvirate, Mark Antony (c. 82–30 B.C.), demanded that she meet him at Tarsus in Asia Minor for questioning. Cleopatra, however, had other plans.

She took her time arriving. When she did finally arrive, she came on a perfumed ship with purple sails. Dressed as Venus, goddess of love, she welcomed Antony as Bacchus

(BAK-uhs), god of wine. Certainly Antony, a much simpler man than Caesar, loved to have a good time, but he had come on official business and did his best to stay focused. Cleopatra played him like an instrument, persuading him to come to her quarters for a lavish feast. Soon they were lovers.

At the time, Mark Antony was joint ruler of the world's leading superpower, and his co-ruler Octavian (63 B.C.–A.D. 14), nephew of Caesar, was out to get him. When the triumvirate divided up the Roman world, Octavian had taken command over Italy and left Asia to Antony. Not only did he control the most important part, but Octavian could now claim that Antony did not have Italy's best interests at heart.

In a further maneuver, Octavian arranged for his beautiful sister Octavia to marry Antony in 40 B.C. Supposedly this would create a bond between the two rulers, but Octavian knew that Antony would end up leaving Octavia for Cleopatra—another fact he could use against him. In 40 B.C., Cleopatra bore twins by Antony just as he was trying to make his marriage to Octavia work. Octavia gave him a daughter in 39 B.C. But in 37 B.C., just as Octavian had predicted, Antony left her to join Cleopatra.

The lovers' last stand

The two met in Antioch (AN-tee-ahk), Syria, where Antony proceeded with an extremely ill-advised campaign against the Parthians. Apparently he wanted to prove himself by winning an empire in Asia; instead, as many as 30,000 Roman soldiers lost their lives. In 36 B.C., Cleopatra gave birth to a son by Antony. Perhaps during this time, the couple—they had apparently been married in a secret ceremony—made plans for a trans-Mediterranean empire. They would build this empire, combining Greece, Rome, and Egypt, once they had dealt with Octavian.

After a successful campaign against Armenia, they finally turned their attention to the more pressing matter of dealing with Octavian. By now, Cleopatra's ability to control Roman rulers had won her the admiration of the Egyptian people. The opposite was true of Antony in Rome, where citizens saw him as the weak-willed servant of a foreign seductress. Playing on these sentiments, Octavian in 32 B.C. produced a document—most certainly a forgery—that he claimed was Antony's will. It stated that in the event of Antony's death, he would leave his part of Rome's possessions in Cleopatra's hands. When the outraged Roman Senate heard this, it declared war against both Antony and Cleopatra.

The forces met in a naval battle near the town of Actium (AK-tee-uhm) in Greece on September 2, 31 B.C. Antony and Cleopatra's side never stood a chance. As the battle ended in disaster for them, they fled separately to Egypt. Octavian sent a message to Cleopatra that if she would give up Antony, he might make a deal with her. She refused. Antony, having heard a rumor that she had killed herself, took poison and died in her arms.

The Romans caught Cleopatra and put her in prison, but she managed to have asps, highly poisonous snakes, smuggled in. With these snakes, she killed herself. She died hoping that her children's lives would be saved, but in fact seventeen-year-old Cesarion was executed by Octavian, soon to be known as Augustus Caesar, founder of the Roman Empire. Cleopatra and Antony's son was adopted by Octavia but may have died of disease, along with one of the twins. The other twin, Cleopatra Selene (seh-LEEN), married Juba (YOO-buh), king of Numidia and Mauretania. She was later killed by the mad Roman emperor Caligula (kuh-LIG-yoo-luh).

For More Information

Books

Brooks, Polly Schoyer. *Cleopatra: Goddess of Egypt, Enemy of Rome.* New York: HarperCollins Publishers, 1995.

Encyclopedia of World Biography, second edition. Detroit: Gale, 1998.

Historic World Leaders. Detroit: Gale, 1994.

Hoobler, Dorothy and Thomas. *Cleopatra.* New York: Chelsea House, 1986.

Meltzer, Milton. *Ten Queens: Portraits of Power.* Illustrated by Bethanne Anderson. New York: Dutton Children's Books, 1998.

Noble, Iris. *Egypt's Queen Cleopatra.* New York: Messner, 1963.

Stanley, Diane and Peter Vennema. *Cleopatra.* Illustrated by Diane Stanley. New York: Morrow Junior Books, 1994.

Trease, Geoffrey. *Seven Sovereign Queens.* New York: Vanguard Press, 1968.

Web Sites

"Ancient Egypt in the Movies." http://res3.geocities.com/~amenhotep/ wwae/movie/main.html (accessed on July 2, 1999).

"The Cleopatra Costume on Stage and in Film." http://www.xsite.net/ ~videoc/Cleo/Cleopatra1.html (accessed on July 2, 1999).

"The Cleopatra Forum." http://pharos.bu.edu/Egypt/Alexandria/History/ cl_forum.html (accessed on July 2, 1999).

"Cleopatra Home Page." http://hargray.com/~jwoggon/cleohome.htm (accessed on June 26, 1999).

"Cleopatra VII." *Egyptian Ministry of Tourism.* http://interoz.com/egypt/ cleopatr.htm (accessed on June 26, 1999).

"Cleopatra VII." http://www.netsrq.com/~dbois/cleopatr.html (accessed on June 26, 1999).

"History of Alexandria: Cleopatra." http://pharos.bu.edu/Egypt/Alexandria/ History/cleo.html (accessed on July 2, 1999).

Confucius

Born 551 B.C.
Died 479 B.C.

Chinese philosopher

> [A man should say] I am not concerned that I have no place; I am concerned how I may fit myself for one. I am not concerned that I am not known; I seek to be worthy to be known.

One of the most influential individuals who ever lived was a minor Chinese scribe and teacher named K'ung Ch'iu. He came to be called K'ung Fu-tzu, or Master Kung. He is best known throughout the world by the Latinized version of his name, Confucius. Though he never professed to be a religious leader, a religion later developed around him. Aside from his contemporary Buddha (see entry), he remains perhaps the most admired figure in the Eastern world.

Confucius taught a philosophy of mutual respect and social harmony, a belief in shared obligations between ruler and ruled. He stressed the value of education. Out of his teachings emerged a new class of scholar whose influence in China would grow in coming centuries. Later monarchs would twist his ideas, but the essence of what Confucius taught would remain the foundation of Chinese society more than 2,000 years after his death.

An age of philosophers

Confucius lived at almost exactly the same time as the Buddha. Because his views related more to human society than to spiritual life, it is perhaps more important to note that his dates also more or less coincided with those of Pythagoras. Confucius was born around the time when Thales, father of Greek philosophy, died. Confucius would die just before the birth of the man who transformed Western thought, Socrates [SAHK-ruh-teez; see sidebar].

Though the Greeks and Chinese were unaware of one another's existence, it is interesting that philosophy, a discipline that seeks to reach a general understanding of values and of reality, blossomed in both societies at about the same time. In China, it was an age that would see the likes of Lao-tzu (low-TSOO), Mo-tzu (MOH-zoo), Confucius's follower Mencius (MIN-see-uhs), and the sinister Legalists.

Both in China and Greece, the flowering of philosophy did not seem to require a state of peace; in fact, it seemed to thrive on turmoil. Thus Confucius was born into a land caught up in the Spring and Autumn Period (722–481 B.C.), a time when, despite its pleasant-sounding name, China saw almost constant warfare between rival states. He was born in the town of Ch'u-fu (choo-FOO), located in what is now Shantung Province in northeastern China. In his time, however, it was the capital of one of those warring states.

A hunger for learning

As with many world-changing individuals, there are legends concerning Confucius's birth. For instance, one story tells of how dragons kept watch over his mother as she delivered him. Supposedly he descended from Huang Ti, one of China's legendary early emperors—not to be confused with Ch'in Shih Huang Ti (see entry).

Though his family possessed a noble title, the family had no money. His father, seventy years old at his birth, died before Confucius was three years old. His mother was able to give her boy little more than encouragement. He worked after school to help support her but did not think of quitting school: from the age of fifteen, he determined that he would be a great scholar.

Apparently Confucius married at the age of nineteen, then divorced four years later. In the meantime, he had become a teacher at age twenty-two. Perhaps as a result of his

Socrates

If there was ever anyone who represented "Western Culture"—or, more properly, Western Civilization—it was the Greek philosopher Socrates (c. 470–390 B.C.). He embodied the qualities that would later serve as a foundation for the Western mind: a restless curiosity, an unwillingness to accept easy answers, a striving for improvement. Other cultures value these qualities as well, but only in the West did they become central aspects of the society. Out of these longings came a desire for discovery and invention, which would later help the West in areas such as technology and science.

Like Confucius, Socrates (c. 470 B.C.–399 B.C.) was the father of a whole way of thinking, yet he wrote nothing himself. In the case of Socrates, however, he had a pupil who became as famous as he: Plato (see entry), who along with the historian Xenophon (ZEHN-uh-fahn; c. 431–c. 352 B.C.) is the major source of information on his life.

It was said of Confucius that his appearance had "49 remarkable peculiar-ities"; likewise Socrates was rather strange-looking, with a flat nose, bulging eyes, and a fat stomach. Again like Confucius, he came from humble circumstances: his father was a stonemason and his mother was a midwife. Later, with Confucius-like humility, Socrates would describe himself as a mere midwife for the ideas of others, helping them birth what was already within them.

Unlike Confucius, however, Socrates did not lead a quiet life. As a citizen of Athens, he served as a hoplite during the Peloponnesian War, where he gained a reputation for toughness. It was said that he walked barefoot over snow and ice while the Athenian army was fighting in northern Greece. Later he was a member of the assembly, Athens's chief governmental body, but he had no desire to take part in politics and soon became a full-time philosopher.

Socrates soon gathered around himself a group of devoted students, including Plato. He did not so much teach them a new philosophy as he encouraged

own childhood hardships, he believed in offering an education not on the basis of what a student could pay but on the basis of how much the student hungered for learning.

Confucius the teacher

Confucius believed, as he said, that "it is not easy to find a man who has learned for three years without coming to them to question everything—even, or especially, themselves. He adopted as his own a motto inscribed on the walls in the temple at Delphi: "Know thyself." Likewise there was the statement, attributed to Socrates, "The unexamined life is not worth living." He believed that knowledge, and particularly self-knowledge, was the key to excellence in all things, but he did not believe that he himself possessed any great knowledge. The one thing he knew, Socrates claimed, was that he knew nothing—and that, of course, made him the wisest of men.

Just as he questioned himself, Socrates questioned the society around him. This attitude finally got him into trouble. After the loss to Sparta in the Peloponnesian War, Athens took on something of a witch-hunt atmosphere. It was in this climate in 399 B.C. that Socrates was arrested and charged on two counts: not respecting the gods, and corrupting young minds. The only truth to the first charge was that Socrates had encouraged people to think for themselves. As for the second, it was true that several of his pupils, among them Alcibiades (al-seh-BY-eh-deez), had turned out to be dishonorable men. But there is no reason to blame Socrates for this, since he taught that reasonable argument and discussion—not violence and treachery—were the solutions to problems.

The leaders of Athens condemned Socrates to die by drinking a cup of poison called hemlock. Though Socrates could have saved himself, he chose not to. He used his trial as an opportunity to criticize his society one last time. "Athenians," he said, using a sarcastic tone, "I am not going to argue for my own sake . . . but for yours, that you may not sin against God by condemning me, who am his gift to you." He went on to compare Athens to a horse, and himself to a fly—specifically, a gadfly—who stirs the horse to life. Then he drank the poison. While he waited for it to take effect, he talked with his pupils, Plato among them. After that, he died.

be good." This idea is similar to Socrates's identification of virtue with learning. The two men's methods of teaching shared similarities as well. As with the Socratic dialogue, the Confucian method of teaching was based on asking questions rather than on pounding a point home.

Neither Confucius nor Socrates was merely a teacher to their students; they were like fathers and friends to them as well. Of the 3,000-odd young men who studied under Confucius during his career, the ones most eager to learn lived with the master and ate and drank with him. They also joked with him; it appears he had a great sense of humor. He loved to hear his students tell a story about a man who had described him (Confucius was apparently rather odd-looking) as having the downcast appearance of a stray dog.

Confucius and Socrates both favored the spoken word over the written word. Each left no writings of his own. The famous *Analects* (AN-uh-lektz), and other Confucian Classics, were actually compiled by students. Also like Socrates—or at least, the Socrates of Plato's *Republic*—Confucius believed that an education in music was essential to cultivating a well-developed mind.

Principles of a good society

A significant difference between Confucius and Socrates, however, lay in their attitudes toward their personal contribution to society. Whereas Socrates saw himself as an outsider in the society of Athens, Confucius had an interest in influencing the political life of Chou Dynasty China. He shared with the Socrates of the *Republic,* as opposed to the real Socrates, an interest in establishing the best possible political state—a realm in which men of learning would lead.

Looking around him at the problems of his times, he saw princes who thought only of their own interests and not of the people as a whole. Therefore he sought to influence the princes through a new corps of civil servants with a strong training in morals. Because morality and education went hand in hand, he believed, it was necessary to focus on learning. But learning had another purpose as well: in a world of crafty, self-serving princes, it was best for the scholar to know as much as he could.

Socrates would later say that he knew nothing, but that he helped others formulate ideas of their own. Confucius was similarly humble, as befit his image of the proper scholar. He claimed that he had thought of nothing new, but rather had recombined old ideas. Though this was far from the case, it is true that the Confucian social philosophy was based around a new interpretation of two old concepts in Chinese thought: *li* (LEE), or one's proper place in society; and *jen* (ZHEN), which might be described as inner virtue or conscience.

It is very hard to find English equivalents for either term, since both are deeply rooted in the Chinese culture. In any case, someone who developed a proper awareness of both *jen* and *li* became mature. He became what Confucius described as a "gentleman," or *chun-tzu* (joon-ZOO). Confucius's ultimate goal, through cultivating scholars, was to raise up a generation of rulers possessing both *jen* and *li*. Only when all people, from the top down, appreciated their place within the fabric of social life, could there truly be peace and happiness in the world.

Mao Zedong (Mao Tse-tung), with Lin Biao (clapping hands). Respect for the teachings of Confucius permeated Zedong's rule in the twentieth century.

Confucius in government

For a long time, Confucius had wanted to put his principles to work in the real world, as a minister of government. That opportunity escaped him, however, primarily through his own doing: He received several job offers from princes he did not respect and refused them all. Then, in about 500 B.C., he received a series of official appointments from Duke Ting in the state of Lü.

There would come to be legends about the success of Confucius in government. For example, when he became Lü's Minister of Crime, it was said, crime all but ceased. Whether or not this was the case, it is clear that he had plenty of enemies who set about to sabotage him. Within a very short time, he became so disgusted with Ting's unwillingness to carry out his reforms that he left office of his own accord.

For many years thereafter, Confucius and his students wandered. Those were dark days; twice they were attacked by bandits. Then, in about 484 B.C., when Confucius was sixty-seven years old, he received an appointment from a new prince of Lü, Duke Gae (GIE). His last five years were happy ones.

The legacy of Confucius

Perhaps Confucius died thinking that his work had been in vain. But he had attracted around himself a group of men, most notably Mencius (MIN-see-uhs; c. 370-290 B.C.), who preserved his ideas. More than three centuries after his death, under the reign of Han Wu Ti (see entry), Confucian scholars began to take a significant role in government.

Eventually the scholars would come to dominate the government and would maintain their hold almost to the establishment of Communism in 1949—2,428 years after the death of Confucius. By then, Confucianism had become stale and rigid. It was hard to recognize that it had once brought progress to China. Respect for Confucius continued to some degree, however, even in the darkest days of rule by Mao Zedong (1893–1976). Today the K'ung family—Confucius's descendants—still live in the town of Ch'u-fu and make up most of its population.

For More Information

Books

Hoobler, Thomas and Dorothy. *Confucianism.* New York: Facts on File, 1993.

Johnson, Spencer. *The Value of Honesty: The Story of Confucius.* Illustrated by Pileggi. La Jolla, CA: Value Communications, 1979.

Nardo, Don. *The Trial of Socrates.* San Diego, CA: Lucent Books, 1997.

Rowland-Entwistle, Theodore. *Confucius and Ancient China.* New York: Bookwright Press, 1987.

Silverberg, Robert. *Socrates.* New York: Putnam, 1965.

Turlington, Bayly. *Socrates, The Father of Western Philosophy.* New York: F. Watts, 1969.

Wilker, Josh. *Confucius: Philosopher and Teacher.* New York: Franklin Watts, 1998.

Web Sites

Chinese Philosophy Page. http://www-personal.monash.edu.au/~sab/ (accessed on July 8, 1999).

"Confucius, K'ung-fu-tzu." http://www.friesian.com/confuci.htm (accessed on July 8, 1999).

"Greek Philosophy: Socrates." http://www.wsu.edu:8080/~dee/GREECE/SOCRATES.HTM (accessed on July 8, 1999).

Kong Zi—Confucius. http://sac.uky.edu/~mdtuck0/Resources/Confucius. html (accessed on July 8, 1999).

The Last Days of Socrates. http://socrates.edu/index.htm (accessed on July 8, 1999).

"The Master Confucius." http://www.csun.edu/~hbchm009/confucius. html (accessed on July 8, 1999).

"Stories about Confucius." http://www.sh.com/culture/legend/confu.htm (accessed on July 8, 1999).

Constantine

Born A.D. **285**
Died A.D. **337**

Roman emperor

Last of the truly powerful Roman emperors, Constantine I, or Constantine the Great, may also be considered the first figure of medieval times. By accepting Christianity and making it the state religion of Rome, he broke all ties with the empire's ancient past. He opened the way for the rise of the popes who would dominate Europe during the Middle Ages. During his rule, it became abundantly clear that one man could never hope to rule the whole empire. Constantine therefore established a capital, named after himself, for its eastern half.

A hostage in Rome

By the time Constantine (KAHN-stun-teen) was born, at Naissus (nay-IE-sus) in what is now Serbia, many Romans already perceived that the empire was on a downward spiral: thirty-five years before Constantine's birth, a commentator had written, "You must know that the world has grown old . . . . The rainfall and the sun's warmth are both diminishing; the metals are nearly exhausted; the husbandman [farmer] is failing in the fields."

It had always been difficult for one man to rule the vast Roman Empire, but by the late A.D. 200s it had become all but impossible. Therefore the emperor Diocletian (die-oh-KLEE-shuhn; ruled A.D. 284-305) introduced a number of reforms, among them a complex system whereby various men shared the titles of Caesar and Augustus, which had once been held by a single ruler.

Later, as emperor, Constantine would establish a number of reforms himself, but he would differ in one significant way from Diocletian, who was particularly severe in his persecution of Christians. Constantine's later conversion probably resulted from the influence of his mother, Helena (HEL-uh-nuh), who became St. Helena (c. A.D. 248–c. A.D. 328). His father, Constantius (kahn-STAN-chee-us; ruled A.D. 305–306), did not share his wife's beliefs and divorced her when Diocletian's co-ruler Maximian (mak-SIM-ee-un) declared him Caesar.

Part of Diocletian's delicate system of power-sharing required that the designated Caesar bring someone to Rome as a hostage, thus ensuring he would not revolt against his two fellow rulers. Eight-year-old Constantine was that hostage. Over the coming years, he would find himself caught between a number of others who each claimed authority over Rome.

Competing emperors

As a youth, Constantine proved himself an able military commander in victories over the Parthians, but as the intrigue in Rome heated up, he began to fear for his life. In A.D. 306, he got away from Rome to be by his father's side on a campaign in Britain. Shortly thereafter, Constantius died, but not before naming Constantine his successor as emperor.

The years that followed would be characterized by an incredibly complex battle for power. The details of this jockeying are so intricate that a person would literally have to draw a diagram of all the figures involved in order to understand the battle. At one point Rome had no less than six emperors, three in the East and three—among them Constantine—in the West.

By marrying Maximian's daughter Fausta (FOW-stuh), Constantine allied himself with his fellow Western emperors, Maximian and the latter's son Maxentius (mak-SEN-shee-uhs). But this, too, was no simple matter. At one point Constantine helped his father-in-law against his brother-in-law. Then Max-

Attila

In its latter days, Rome was overwhelmed by a variety of "barbarian" tribes, some of whom hardly deserved that title. None, however, created as much terror in Roman hearts as the Huns, especially their leader, Attila (c. A.D. 400–453).

They came originally from China, where they were known as the Hsiung-Nu (SHAHNG-noo). The building of the Great Wall had forced them out, and the Huns had migrated to central Asia. Unlike most nomads, however, who lived by herding, the Huns lived by conquering other nations. By A.D. 434, the Huns had arrived in what is now eastern Austria. Attila had emerged as their leader.

No reliable portrait of him exists, but he was said to be incredibly frightening in appearance (though this description came from people who already had reason to fear him). It is rumored that he was extremely short, perhaps even a midget. Certainly the Huns, as an Asiatic people, were shorter than Europeans, and their Eastern features must have appeared frightening to the Romans and others. Their hardy lifestyle, too, meant that they were sturdy people. Years of rough living in the windswept plains of Asia gave the Huns a leathery, weatherbeaten look.

The Huns were masters of warfare, which they conducted almost entirely on horseback. Their victories over the Romans would change the face of warfare, ending the dominance of foot soldiers in favor of cavalry(soldiers on horseback), a style of

imian turned on Constantine and joined forces with his son against him. Constantine had Maximian executed in A.D. 309 and then focused his attention on Maxentius. They fought several battles in northern Italy, but the decisive battle occurred on October 28, A.D. 312.

The location was outside Rome, on the Milvian Bridge (MIL-vee-uhn), which spanned the Tiber River (TIE-bur). Constantine later claimed that on the afternoon before the battle, he saw a flaming cross in the sky superimposed over the Greek words meaning "In this sign [you shall] conquer." He then directed his troops to decorate their shields with the Greek letters *chi-rho* (KIE-ROH; X-P), a symbol of Christ. Constantine's forces won the battle, making him undisputed ruler of the Western Empire.

fighting that would prevail until the invention of firearms a thousand years later. Attila himself was certainly a fearsome military leader, but he was no savage. He often spared the lives of people he admired, and in particular he admired those with spiritual wisdom.

After harassing the Eastern Empire for a time, Attila in A.D. 448 took advantage of Rome's troubles with the Vandals in Africa to move farther west. He demanded that the emperor of the West, Valentinian III (val-un-TIN-ee-uhn), give him his sister Honoria (hoh-NOHR-ee-uh) as a bride. When the Romans declined, he used this as an excuse to rampage through Gaul.

The Romans defeated him at Châlons-sur-Marne (shah-LAWN syoor-MAHRN), about 100 miles (161 kilometers) east of Paris, in A.D. 451. By the following year, however, he had recovered enough to march on Rome. Pope Leo I went to negotiate with him. Perhaps because of Attila's respect for spiritual leaders, the Hun chieftain agreed to withdraw. This great victory for the pope helped establish the political authority of the Church.

A year later, Attila's years of hard living caught up with him. He had just taken a new bride and was about to celebrate his wedding night when he began bleeding heavily from his nose. He died that night, and with him died the threat of the Huns. With no leader like Attila, they faded into the growing population of tribes in Europe.

Christianity and Constantinople

Constantine never completely gave up the pagan traditions of Rome. For example, on his return to the city, he accepted the title of chief priest of Rome, held by many emperors. He did, however, declare an end to the persecution of Christians. He legalized Christian worship, which under Diocletian had been punishable by death, in A.D. 313. In the following year he strengthened his control by arranging the marriage of his sister Constantia (kahn-STAN-shuh) to Licinius (lie-SIN-ee-uhs; ruled A.D. 308–324), the emperor in the East.

Constantine disbanded the Praetorian (pray-TOHR-ee-uhn) Guard, an institution established by Augustus. In the past, these personal bodyguards of the emperor had used their power to choose emperors themselves. He put more gold and silver coins into circulation to strengthen the economy and reorganized the military.

By A.D. 323, Constantine was strong enough to go after Licinius, leading the troops personally while his son Crispus (KRIS-pus) commanded the navy. Having gained victory over Licinius in Greece, he had him executed and declared Licinius a usurper, meaning that all the laws he had passed were null and void. For reasons that are not clear, he then accused Fausta, Crispus, and Constantia of treason. He had them executed along with Licinius's son and others.

Now sole ruler of the Roman Empire, Constantine decided it was time to establish a second capital. For this he chose the Greek city of Byzantium (bi-ZAN-tee-um). Not only did it occupy a commanding position overlooking the Bosporus but it made administration of the Eastern Empire much more practical in an age before telephones and airplanes. By the time the Western Roman Empire collapsed in A.D. 476, the Eastern Roman Empire had become the Byzantine Empire (BIZ-un-teen), which preserved Greco-Roman culture for more than a thousand years. Today Byzantium is the Turkish city of Istanbul (EE-stahn-bool). Until 1453 it was known by the name Constantine gave it: Constantinople (kahn-stan-ti-NOHP-ul).

The age of Constantine

In the last dozen years of his reign, Constantine placed his stamp all over Western civilization. Adapting the basilica (buh-SIL-ih-kuh), a type of public building common in Rome, he made its open floor plan a model for churches up to the present day. Today worshipers in many churches repeat a version of the Nicene Creed (NYE-seen). A council of Christian bishops adopted the creed in a conference sponsored by Constantine in A.D. 325.

At that time, the Christian world was divided over the issue of Christ's relationship to God. Arius (AHR-ee-uhs; c. A.D. 250–337), a Greek Christian heavily influenced by the ideas of Plato (see entry), had advanced the idea that God was separate from all of his creation and that Christ was one of those creations. This, of course, meant that Christ was not really God. Arianism threatened to shake the foundations of Christianity. Wanting to end the controversy, Constantine in 325 called the Council of Nicaea (nye-SEE-uh), a city in Asia Minor. There 220 bishops adopted the Nicene Creed, a statement of faith that in effect declared Arianism as heresy (HAIR-uh-see)—a doctrine at odds with the Christian faith.

During his latter years, Constantine dealt with threats both at home and abroad. He campaigned against Shapur in Persia from A.D. 335 to 337, but he had worse problems back in Rome. There he tried to pass leadership on to his three living sons along with two of his nephews. He hoped he would ensure a bloodless succession that way, but after his death there would be more struggles for power.

Constantine died on the Feast of Pentecost, May 22, A.D. 337, in the city of Nicomedia (nik-uh-MEED-ee-uh) in Asia Minor. He was baptized just before his death, and laid to rest in the Church of the Holy Apostles, which he had built in Constantinople.

Among the monuments he left in Rome was the Arch of Constantine, which celebrated his victory at the Milvian Bridge. It was decorated partly with statues and relief sculpture taken from monuments to Marcus Aurelius (see entry) and other emperors from Rome's golden age. Artists of Constantine's time, however, also contributed their work. Their representation of the human figure differed sharply from that of earlier sculptors. The men they depicted in the battle scenes were crudely outlined. The design of the scenes suggested that artists were losing their sense of spatial relationships. It was a frightening sign that Roman civilization was declining—that the world, in the words of an earlier writer, was growing old.

Vatican City, Vatican. The interior of St. Peter's.
AP/Wide World Photos. Reproduced by permission.

For More Information

Books

Paton Walsh, Jill. *The Emperor's Winding Sheet.* London: Macmillan, 1974.

Vardy, Steven Béla. *Attila.* New York: Chelsea House, 1991.

Walworth, Nancy Zinsser. *Constantine.* New York: Chelsea House, 1989.

Web Sites

"Attila the Hun." http://art1.candor.com/barbarian/attila.htm (accessed on July 11, 1999).

"Attila the Hun (aka 'Scourge of God')(406–453)." http://www.mala.bc.ca/~mcneil.attila.htm (accessed on July 11, 1999).

"*Catholic Encyclopedia:* Constantine the Great." http://www.knight.org/advent/cathen/04295c.htm (accessed on July 11, 1999).

"Constantine I." http://history.hanover.edu/ancient/constant.html (accessed on July 11, 1999).

"Constantine Converts to Christianity." http://www.northpark.edu/acad/history/WebChron/EastEurope/ConstantineConverts.html (accessed on July 11, 1999).

"History 303: Later Roman Emperors, 306–395 A.D." http://homeport.tcs.tulane.edu/~August/H303/chronologies/Later_Roman_Emperors.htm (accessed on July 11, 1999).

David

Died c. 960 B.C.

King of Israel

Sometimes he is referred to as King David, or as King David of Israel, but in fact he can be identified simply by the name of David. He was the most important figure of ancient Israel, and thus in the Jewish religion, after Abraham and Moses (see entry). Through stories and songs, more is known about him than about any other ancient monarch.

The best-known story concerning David involves his defeat of the giant Goliath as a boy, but this is far from the greatest of his achievements. The Bible presents him as a warrior and a great king, who ruled Israel at the height of its glory. He was also a poet and songwriter, credited with writing much of the Book of Psalms. But perhaps the most important thing about David, from the viewpoint of both Judaism and Christianity, was that despite his many errors and sins, he was judged a righteous man.

An unlikely king

David grew up in an era when Israel was led first by the judges and later by the prophet Samuel. For years, however,

> [God] testified concerning him: 'I have found David son of Jesse a man after my own heart.'
>
> *Acts 13:22*

83

the people had wanted a king so that they could be like other nations. According to the eighth chapter of 1 Samuel in the Bible, God did not want them to be ruled by a king; however, the Israelites insisted. Finally God chose a tall, handsome young man named Saul and told Samuel to anoint him—that is, to pour oil over his head as a symbol that God had chosen him to lead.

Such political issues probably meant little to David, a boy growing up in the little town of Bethlehem. As the seventh and youngest son of Jesse from the tribe of Judah (JOO-duh), it was his job to tend his father's sheep while his older brothers went about more important business. Even as a young shepherd boy, however, he displayed remarkable abilities. According to the Bible, he had killed lions and bears defending his father's flocks.

At first Saul was a great success as a king, but on several occasions, the Bible reports, he disobeyed orders from God delivered through Samuel. Therefore God sent Samuel to anoint a son of Jesse. Jesse was thrilled, of course. He assumed God's choice would be one of his older sons—not David, a mere boy. But God had other plans and chose David, described in 1 Samuel 16:12 as having "ruddy [reddish] cheeks, with fine eyes and an attractive appearance."

The giant-killer

It would be decades before David actually took the throne. Saul was still king, and David went to work at the palace as a harp player whose music soothed the king's troubled nerves. Soon, however, he was given a more serious role.

For years, the Israelites had fought with the Philistines (FIL-i-steenz), a neighboring people. In Saul's time, the Philistines had a new weapon: the giant Goliath, a fierce-looking warrior who stood some nine feet tall. He challenged the Israelites to send a man who would fight him one on one. No one dared take up the challenge, but finally David—armed only with his slingshot and his faith in God—stepped forward. When David killed Goliath with a single shot, it terrified the Philistines, and they fled.

David was now a great hero. He received the hand of Saul's daughter Michal (MEE-kal) in marriage. He also became

best friend of Saul's son Jonathan. As a general, he won battle after battle with God's help. But he had one problem. The favor God had shown to David made Saul jealous, and Saul decided to kill him.

Years of exile

David would spend many years in exile. During the first part of this time, he remained in Israel, an outlaw building up his own private army. Saul pursued him. Several times David had an opportunity to kill Saul but refused to do so. In those years of hiding, he composed many of the songs to God contained in the biblical Book of Psalms (SAWLMS).

Later he went into Philistine country. With his army—referred to as the "mighty men of David"—he served as a mercenary, or hired soldier. He never helped the Philistines in any attacks on Israel, however. When it came time for the two nations to go into battle, the Philistines forced him to stay out of the fight.

David fires his slingshot, knocking the mighty Goliath down with a single stone. This victory caused the Philistines to flee, and David was deemed a hero by the Israelites. *Archive Photos. Reproduced by permission.*

Fearful about the upcoming battle, Saul consulted witches, who raised the ghost of Samuel. The ghost of the prophet, recently dead, told Saul he would die in the battle. This passage, in 1 Samuel 28, has been a difficult one for biblical scholars. The Bible clearly forbids witchcraft and seances, yet the words of the spirit—whether it was really Samuel's ghost or some other being—were true: Saul did die in the battle, by his own hand, along with Jonathan. Instead of rejoicing, David mourned for his father-in-law and his beloved friend.

Taking the "City of David"

After a period of civil war during which the kingdom was divided between the tribe of Judah and the other Israelite tribes, who called themselves Israel, David emerged as king. In order to hold the kingdom together, it was vital to gain control of the city of Jerusalem, held by a rival people known as the Jebusites (JEB-yoo-sightz). In a daring assault, David and his mighty men took the city, which thereafter would be known as the "City of David."

Celebrating his victory, David arranged for the sacred Ark of the Covenant to be brought into the city. Not only was he a king and a conqueror, as well as a man of God, but he was a poet and a songwriter. On the occasion of bringing in the ark, "David and the whole house of Israel were celebrating with all their might before the Lord" (2 Samuel 6:5). His wife Michal told him he looked like a fool. According to the Bible, God was angry with her for this and made her unable to have children.

A great and flawed king

David's early career had been characterized by conflict with his father-in-law—a conflict for which he was not to blame. His forty-year reign would see a number of problems with his wives and children; and in these situations, however, he was often quite guilty. Never was this more true than in the case of Bathsheba (bath-SHEE-buh), a beautiful woman he saw from his rooftop at a time when, the Bible indicates, he should have been out leading his troops in battle. He got her pregnant and all but murdered her husband by sending him into a dangerous battle situation.

David paid dearly for this sin, the most striking of several misdeeds recorded in the books of 2 Samuel and 1 Chronicles.

Ruth

The life of Ruth was as quiet as that of David was exciting. The Book of Ruth, which other than Esther is the only biblical book named after a woman, consists of just four chapters. Set during the time of the judges, the book tells how Ruth, from the land of Moab (MOH-ab)—whose people the Israelites despised—came to live in Israel.

The book's two principal figures are Ruth and her mother-in-law, Naomi. Naomi had come with her two sons to Moab, where the boys married two girls, Ruth and Orpah (OHR-puh). The sons later died, leaving no children; therefore Ruth and Orpah did not have any obligation to remain with Naomi, particularly when Naomi decided to return to Israel.

Naomi told them they had no obligation to her. At first both daughters-in-law protested, but Naomi insisted that they stay behind. Orpah did, but in one of the Bible's most moving statements, Ruth declared, "Where you go I will go, and where you stay I will stay. Your people will be my people and your God my God" (1:16).

So Ruth went with Naomi back to Israel, where a wealthy relative of Naomi's named Boaz (BOH-az) took an interest in Ruth. Ultimately Ruth and Boaz were married, and they had a son named Obed (OH-bed). Obed in turn fathered a son named Jesse, whose son was David. Therefore Ruth, a brave and faithful woman, became the great-grandmother of King David—and out of her line would come Jesus as well.

The prophet Nathan informed David that because of his sin with Bathsheba, whom he had meanwhile married, his children would suffer. Although he repented, his and Bathsheba's son died.

More troubles followed for David, and many revolved around his children. Worst was a rebellion led by his son Absalom (AB-suh-luhm), who very nearly took over the kingdom. David managed to put down the revolt, but his general Joab (JOH-ab)—against David's orders—killed Absalom.

Solomon

But despite his many wrongs, David was still beloved

of God, who had often promised to bless him. Thus a second son by Bathsheba, Solomon, would grow up to become a great king. In his old age, David gave Solomon a number of warnings concerning what he could expect as king, knowledge that David had gained the hard way. He also instructed Solomon regarding the friends he should protect and the enemies he should kill—including Joab.

Solomon would be known for his wisdom and for the riches of his kingdom, and he would build the temple in Jerusalem. The building of the temple was an extremely important job that had been denied to David. As David had his Psalms, Solomon had his Proverbs, a book of wisdom mostly attributed to him. He also is credited as author of the Song of Solomon, a tender and sensuous love poem, and of Ecclesiastes (eh-klee-zee-AS-teez), a philosophical book that questions the very meaning of life.

Living on through his descendants

After Solomon, the kingdom would divide along the lines that it had before David took the throne, with separate rulers over Israel and Judah. Eventually the people of Israel would go into captivity, first under the Assyrians, then the Babylonians, and finally the Persians. They would return home, but Israel would pass through the hands of various empires until Rome gained control.

Christians believe that during the Roman occupation of Israel, God's promises to David were fulfilled through Jesus, born into the tribe of Judah in the city of Bethlehem. It is also interesting to note that when Israel became an independent nation again in 1948, its leader would be named David—David Ben-Gurion (GYOOR-ee-uhn; 1886–1973).

For More Information

Books

Alex, Marlee. *Ruth: A Woman Whose Loyalty Was Stronger Than Her Grief.* Grand Rapids, MI: W. B. Eerdmans Publishing Company, 1987.

Asimov, Isaac. *The Story of Ruth.* Garden City, NY: Doubleday, 1972.

Cohen, Barbara. *David.* New York: Clarion Books, 1995.

De Regniers, Beatrice Schenk. *David and Goliath*. Illustrated by Richard M. Powers. New York: Viking Press, 1965.

Eisler, Colin T., ed. *David's Songs: His Psalms and Their Story*. Illustrations by Jerry Pinkney. New York: Dial Books, 1992.

Patterson, Lillie. *David, the Story of a King*. Illustrations by Charles Cox. Nashville, TN: Abingdon Press, 1985.

Rosenblum, Morris. *Heroes of Israel*. New York: Fleet Press Corp., 1972.

Smith, F. LaGard, ed. *The Narrated Bible*. Eugene, OR: Harvest House, 1984.

Storr, Catherine, reteller. *Ruth's Story*. Pictures by Geoff Taylor. Milwaukee, WI: Raintree Children's Books, 1986.

Hannibal

Born 247 B.C.
Died 183 B.C.

Carthaginian general

> I swear that so soon as age will permit . . . I will use fire and steel to arrest the destiny of Rome.

Many leaders of ancient times, from Boadicea to Spartacus to Zenobia, made a name for themselves by opposing the power of Rome. But none came as close to defeating the Romans, and none burned their name as deeply into human history, as a youthful general from Carthage named Hannibal.

The people of Carthage had long been enemies of Rome. Hannibal despised Rome with a particularly strong passion. On the battlefield, however, he was all cool calculation. His legendary crossing of the Alps during the Second Punic War, followed by an equally brilliant fifteen-year campaign on the Italian Peninsula, proved him one of the most brilliant military minds of all time.

A history of ill will

Carthage (KAHR-thehj) occupied a commanding position on the coast of what is now Tunisia in North Africa. Its people were neither African nor European, however, but Phoenician. The Phoenicians had established the city as a trading colony in about 800 B.C. From the Phoenicians came the name for the wars Rome fought with Carthage: *Punic* (PYOO-nik), an adjectival form of the Romans' word for "Phoenician."

In time Carthage emerged as a great city, the rival of any in Phoenicia. With its strong navy, it also took a position of military leadership in the western Mediterranean, fighting wars with the Etruscans and others. An ancestor of Hannibal's, Hamilcar (hah-MIL-kahr), died in one such assault on Sicily in 480 B.C.

Eventually the Carthaginians (kahr-thuh-JIN-ee-uhnz) did establish colonies on Sicily as well as in Spain. They also controlled the western end of the Mediterranean, preventing sea passage by other nations [see sidebar].

Hannibal's oath

Given the rising power of Carthage, and Rome's own growing ambitions for territory, there was bound to be a showdown. It came with the First Punic War (264–241 B.C.), in which Hannibal's father, Hamilcar Barca (BAHR-kuh; c. 270–c. 229 B.C.), served as a naval commander.

With the end of the First Punic War, Rome controlled not only Sicily but two large islands to the west, Corsica (KOHR-si-kuh) and Sardinia (sahr-DIN-ee-uh). Hannibal was six years old at that time; three years later, on a visit to a temple in Carthage with his father, the boy swore his eternal hatred for Rome.

The Second Punic War begins

Hamilcar was assassinated in 228 B.C. Hannibal was only nineteen years old but had prepared to lead an army. Soon the new commander of the Carthaginian forces, his brother-in-law Hasdrubal (HAZ-droo-bahl), called on him to do just that. Hannibal crossed the Mediterranean to Spain, Hasdrubal's base of operations, but in 221 B.C., Hasdrubal was also assassinated.

Hasdrubal's killers were local tribesmen, possibly Celts. The real threat, as Hannibal well knew, came from Rome. Now in charge of the troops in Spain, Hannibal faced a conflict with Rome over the colony of Saguntum (suh-GUN-tum). The colony was well within Carthaginian territory. After the Romans laid claim to it, Hannibal attacked the city and destroyed the Roman resistance.

Pytheas

The Greek explorer Pytheas (PITH-ee-uhs; c. 380 B.C.–300 B.C.) lived long before the Punic Wars, at a time when Carthage was still firmly in control of the western Mediterranean. Therefore when he set out on a journey from the Greek colony of Massilia (muh-SIL-ee-uh), which is now the city of Marseilles (mahr-SAY) in southern France, he had to be careful to avoid trespassing on Phoenician territory.

His goal was Britain, source of tin for much of Europe. The Greek colonists wanted to find a route to the island, but no one knew exactly where it was. Pytheas set off on his journey some time about 310 B.C. Careful to avoid the western tip of Europe at Gibraltar (ji-BRAWL-tuhr), an important spot heavily guarded by the Carthaginians, he probably traveled overland across France.

Eventually he got to Britain and found the tin mines in what is now Cornwall on the southwestern tip of the island. He also explored much of Britain. He provided the first written observations of the Celtic tribes who inhabited it. But Pytheas kept on going, to a place in the far north he called Thule (TOO-lee).

The place he described was probably Norway, but the name Thule eventually came to be used for any place in the frozen north. (Today it is the name for a tiny settlement above the Arctic Circle in Greenland.) On his journeys, Pytheas heard of places even farther north, places where the sea was ice and where the sun never set in summertime. Later, when he returned to his sunny Mediterranean home and told about such things, people assumed he was making up tall tales and laughed at his stories.

Crossing the Alps

Hannibal had long been preparing for war with Rome. Now he apparently decided that if the Romans really wanted a war, he would bring it to them. Therefore in 218 B.C. he started out on his famed journey: northward from Spain; across what is now southern France; and ultimately over the Alps, the high range that separates the modern nation of Switzerland from Italy. With him he took an army that consisted primarily of mercenaries hired from various parts of Europe and north Africa—as well as thirty-seven elephants.

The elephants were not only frightening creatures in battle, but they gave Hannibal's army a distinctive appearance that added greatly to the legends surrounding him. Unfortunately, all but one of them died in the agonizing journey over the mountains, which Hannibal's army accomplished in an almost unbelievable two weeks. Once he entered Italy, he and his forces met the Romans for the first of many battles.

Hannibal (center) crossing the Alps on horseback, surrounded by his army, during the Second Punic War. *Archive Photos. Reproduced by permission.*

A series of brilliant maneuvers

Military history can sometimes be rather dry, with accounts of which army went where, and which general attacked another generals' flank (that is, the side of a military formation). Reading about Hannibal's Italian campaign, though, is like watching a boxer dazzle and gradually destroy an opponent. Of course any fight is most interesting if the two sides are equally matched, as was the case in the Second Punic War.

The amazing thing about Hannibal, however, is that he managed to claim the upper hand again and again when it was the Romans who had (to use another sports metaphor) the "home team advantage." One of his earliest victories was against forces led by the consuls Scipio (SKIP-ee-oh; d. 211 B.C.) and Sempronius (sehm-PROH-nee-uhs). Scipio had already tried to catch Hannibal in Spain and missed him there. He then tried to stop the Carthaginians on the way into Italy and ended up running for his life.

As they faced Hannibal, now inside their borders, Scipio had enough experience to urge caution, but Sempronius was certain he could defeat the enemy. That was exactly what Hannibal wanted him to think. The defeat of the Roman forces in 218 B.C.—thanks to an ambush staged by Hannibal's younger brother Mago—was such a humiliation that Sempronius gave up all hope of being taken seriously as a leader again.

Bringing Italy to its knees

In 217 B.C., two new consuls faced the prospect of a Carthaginian movement down the Italian Peninsula. Again, Hannibal outflanked them, driving through a hole in the Apennines (AP-uh-nynz), a mountain range that runs through central Italy. His pursuers did not know where to find him. At one point his army stood on high ground and listened to the Roman soldiers going by in the mists below. It was not a painless victory, however. Hannibal lost the sight in his right eye; many of his men were killed; and his last elephant died.

The first consul who proved remotely effective against Hannibal was Fabius (FAY-bee-uhs), declared dictator in 217 B.C. The Carthaginians and their mercenaries had long been living off the land, but Fabius ordered the people of Italy to start burning their crops and homes so that there would be nothing left for the invaders. This helped to create an atmosphere of hatred toward the enemy, and it hurt the Carthaginians—but not enough, in the eyes of the Roman Senate, who removed Fabius from power.

Hannibal dealt Rome one of the most severe blows in its history at Cannae (KAH-nee), where His forces killed some 50,000 Romans in 216 B.C. For comparison, the United States lost about that number in the entire Vietnam War, from the early 1960s to 1975. Hannibal sold into slavery the Romans he did not kill. This had the effect not only of humiliating the Romans but of removing valuable citizens from the land and raising more money for his army.

The defeat of Hannibal

It must have seemed as though Hannibal could go on terrorizing Rome until it fell to its knees, but in 210 B.C. the Romans finally brought in a general with enough skill to take on Hannibal: Scipio the Younger (c. 236–c. 183 B.C.) His father, one of the first two generals to face Hannibal, had been killed in battle the year before; therefore Scipio was like a mirror image of Hannibal—he was a man with a burning grudge.

First Scipio attacked Spain, cutting off Hannibal's supply lines. Then he returned to Italy, where he met and destroyed a force commanded by Hannibal's brother Hasdrubal (not to be confused with the earlier brother-in-law.) He cut off Hasdrubal's head and sent it to Hannibal.

From then on, Hannibal found himself in an unusual spot for him: on the defensive. By 203 B.C., Scipio (who later gained the name Scipio Africanus for his campaigns on the African coast) was launching attacks close to Carthage. This forced Hannibal to return home, and Scipio's forces struck the final blow in the Battle of Zama in 202 B.C.

Hannibal's end

For a time, Hannibal remained in the Carthaginian government, but by 195 B.C. he had to flee. For the last twelve years of his life, he was on the run. For a time he found refuge with Antiochus III, but when Antiochus suffered a defeat at the hands of the Romans, Hannibal knew his time was almost up.

He would die in Asia Minor, where he committed suicide rather than let the Romans catch him. Forty years after his death, Rome—no doubt still smarting from its defeat by Hannibal—wiped Carthage off the face of the Earth in the Third Punic War.

In spite of his inability to defeat Rome, Hannibal would be admired, throughout the world of people who hated the Romans' cruelty, for his valiant attempt. In time he would be recognized not only as a military genius but as an early practitioner of guerilla warfare.

For More Information

Books

Connolly, Peter. *Hannibal and the Enemies of Rome.* Illustrated by the author. Morristown, NJ: Silver Burdett Company, 1978.

Frye, John and Harriet. *North to Thule: An Imagined Narrative of the Famous "Lost" Sea Voyage of Pytheas of Massilia in the Fourth Century B.C.* Illustrations by Harriet Frye. Chapel Hill, NC: Algonquin Books, 1985.

Green, Robert. *Hannibal.* New York: Franklin Watts, 1996.

Hirsh, Marilyn. *Hannibal and His 37 Elephants.* Illustrated by the author. New York: Holiday House, 1977.

Nardo, Don. *The Battle of Zama.* San Diego, CA: Lucent Books, 1996.

Rosen, Mike. *The Journeys of Hannibal.* Illustrated by Tony Smith. New York: Bookwright Press, 1990.

Web Sites

"Brief History" (Pytheas). http://www.nostos.com/education/brief.htm (accessed on July 6, 1999).

"Colonial Punic Wars and Hannibal." http://www.phoenicia.org/punicwar.html (accessed on July 6, 1999).

"Focus on Tunisia—History." http://www.focusmm.com.au/~focus/tunisia/tn_hist.htm (accessed on July 6, 1999).

"Hannibal." http://clever.net/enc/hannibal.html (accessed on July 6, 1999).

"Hannibal 247–183 BC." *Epilepsy International.com.* http://epilepsy-international.com/english/history/hisfolk43.html (accessed on July 6, 1999).

"Thule Culture." http://www.digitalbanff.com/thulium/thule.html (accessed on July 6, 1999).

Hatshepsut

Born c. 1510 B.C.
Died 1458 B.C.

Egyptian pharaoh

Hatshepsut was not the only woman ruler of ancient times; however, as queen of Egypt during the Eighteenth Dynasty, she was the only woman to rule a world power at the height of its greatness. Hers was not an eventful reign, certainly not when compared with that of Zenobia of Palmyra [see sidebar] or Egypt's own Cleopatra (see entry). But Zenobia's realm was a tiny city-state in a world dominated by Rome; and Cleopatra ruled a nation well past its prime. In Hatshepsut's case, it was as though a woman had ruled the Persian or Roman empires before those empires declined.

The peaceful character of her reign was not simply because she was a woman, as some historians have supposed. Hatshepsut had usurped, or seized, the throne. She was never fully comfortable with her grip on power and would not have risked a military defeat. Instead she devoted herself to building monuments, one of which records a historic visit to another country. Her construction of obelisks (ceremonial columns) and other structures suggests a desire to provide legitimacy for her rule. Perhaps she guessed—and she would have been right—that her successor would attempt to remove from history the fact that a woman had once ruled Egypt.

Those who shall see my monument in future years [will say] . . . 'How like her this is, how worthy of her father.'

Inscription on obelisk erected by Hatshepsut

Library of Congress.

97

Zenobia of Palmyra

Some 150 miles (241.4 kilometers) northeast of Damascus, capital of Syria, was the ancient city-state of Palmyra (pal-MIE-ruh). Built on an oasis at the northern edge of the Syrian Desert, it lay on an important caravan route between Asia Minor, Mesopotamia, and Palestine.

The city had long been in contact with the cultures of Europe. Corinthian columns—a remnant of the Hellenistic era—lined its main avenue. But by the time a young girl named Bat Zabbai (BAHT ZAH-bie) was born, in about A.D. 231, the empire of Alexander was long gone. In its place was Rome, which valued Palmyra as an important military post. As the 200s wore on, however, the power of Rome had begun to fade.

Little is known about the early life of the young woman, better known by the name the Romans called her: Zenobia (zeh-NOH-bee-uh). When she came of age, she married the prince Odenathus (ahd-i-NAY-thuhs), whom the Romans acknowledged as king over Palmyra. He had helped Rome defend its eastern frontier. For this aid the empire gave him an esteemed title, normally set aside only for emperors: "Corrector of all the East."

In A.D. 267, however, Odenathus was murdered, along with his heir, a son by another wife. Some suspected Zenobia of the murder. In any case, her son Vaballath (vah-BAH-lahth) became the recognized heir, and Zenobia became his regent. These events occurred during a time when Rome had a series of rulers in quick succession. As each new ruler assumed the throne, he reviewed the agreements made by his predecessor. In

"King's daughter, king's sister"

Hatshepsut (hah-CHEHP-suht) was the elder of two daughters born to the Pharaoh Thutmose I (TUHT-mohz) and his wife Ahmose (AH-mohz) during the Eighteenth Dynasty (1539–1295 B.C.) Her younger sister died in childhood, however—a frequent occurrence in ancient times, even among royalty—making Hatshepsut an only child.

Hatshepsut's name, variously rendered as Hashepsowe, Hatasu, Hatshopsitu, Maatkare, meant "foremost of the royal ladies." When she was still a young girl, her parents married her to her half-brother Thutmose II, son of Thutmose I by a different wife. Marriage between relatives was common in

A.D. 268, a new Roman emperor refused to recognize the arrangement, but in 270, the emperor Aurelian named Vaballath the legitimate heir once again.

By then Zenobia had taken advantage of the confusion in Rome and had begun building a Palmyran empire that she intended to rule jointly with her son. Not only did she take over most of Syria but she annexed Egypt as well. However, her demand that the mint in the Syrian city of Antioch make coins with the image of herself and her son rather than that of the Roman emperor was too much for Aurelian.

In 271, Rome restored Egypt to the empire. Aurelian personally came east to deal with Zenobia. There ensued an extraordinary battle of wits and wills between the two, along with a series of bloody conflicts between their armies. In the end, however, the sheer power of Rome won. Zenobia was paraded through the streets of Rome, a captured princess weighted down with impossibly heavy gold and jewels.

There is a legend that Zenobia was not executed but married a Roman senator and lived out her days in comfort. Whether or not this is so, it is certain that she was an extraordinary woman. Though she claimed relation to Cleopatra, whose ancestry was Greek, most likely she was an Arab. She spoke five languages. Those who had seen her attested to her great beauty. However, a Roman historian wrote, "Such was her continence, it is said, that she would not know her own husband save for the purpose of conception."

Egypt. In the case of Thutmose II, it strengthened his claim on the throne since he, unlike Hatshepsut, did not have two royal parents.

When Thutmose II took the throne, Hatshepsut had no reason to believe she would ever rule. Soon after becoming his queen, she had ordered the construction of a tomb for herself. This was an important act for a monarch in Egypt, where people believed that after death, they returned to live on Earth. She never finished construction on the tomb, but an inscription listing her titles says a great deal about an Egyptian queen's place in the shadow of men: "king's daughter, king's sister, wife of the god, great wife of the king."

Regent for the king

In the eighth year of his reign, Thutmose died. Some historians later suggested that Hatshepsut had him poisoned in hopes of becoming pharaoh herself. It is unlikely that she did, but if so, she was in for a disappointment. Egypt was not about to crown a woman, and if Hatshepsut had a son, the child would have become king. But she had no son, so a boy born to Thutmose by one of his concubines became Thutmose III.

Thutmose III was only ten years old, but just as Thutmose II had done, he married the daughter of the king and queen—that is, Hatshepsut's daughter—to strengthen his claim on the throne. The girl died a few years later. Meanwhile, in about 1480 B.C., Hatshepsut had begun to rule Egypt as regent for its young king.

For a long time, her role was little more than that of a guardian for the underage Thutmose. Soon after she became regent, she sent an expedition southward, to Upper Egypt, in order to acquire granite for a pair of obelisks. These would be covered in gold and placed in the Temple of Karnak, an important ceremonial center. Leading the expedition was her chief advisor, Senenmut (seh-NEHN-moot).

Ruling as "king of Egypt"

In the second year of Thutmose's reign, however, Hatshepsut claimed that the god Amon had spoken to her personally and told her to take the throne. She therefore proclaimed herself "king" of Egypt. Thereafter she would often be depicted as a man, complete with a ceremonial beard. Powerful officials, most notably Senenmut, helped her secure her position, though she maintained the fiction that she ruled jointly with Thutmose III.

In the sixth year of her reign as pharaoh, probably about 1472 B.C., she sent five boats south along the Red Sea to the land of Punt. Though Hatshepsut claimed hers was the first expedition, Egypt had actually been trading with this country, which historians have located anywhere from modern-day Eritrea to Somalia, for as many as seven centuries. A relief sculpture in her tomb records the voyage and depicts the people of Punt as physically similar to the Egyptians themselves: slender, delicate of features, with long hair. The queen of Punt, however, was apparently an odd-looking woman in comparison—short and fat, with long arms and a prominent behind.

Carving her name in stone

Egyptian pharaohs normally enjoyed a special celebration upon reaching the thirtieth year of their reign. Hatshepsut celebrated hers a little early, after just sixteen years. It was thirty years since the death of Thutmose III, however. Her haste to commemorate her rule suggests that she was aware of her uneasy grasp on power.

For much the same reason, she never waged a war, though undoubtedly she was tough enough to see one through. Had she not possessed nerves of steel, she could never have seized the throne as she did. However, she could not afford to risk a defeat. Instead, she devoted herself to recording the fact that she had ruled. Thus she sent another expedition to Upper Egypt, as well as quite a few to the Sinai (SIE-nie) Peninsula, to acquire rock for monuments.

Her inscriptions on these monuments portray her as a queen chosen by the gods for the special mission of resurrecting Egypt from the damage left by the Hyksos (HIK-sohs) when they invaded about two centuries before: "I raised up what was dismembered," one inscription reads, "even from the time when the Asiatics were . . . overthrowing what had been created. They ruled in ignorance of Ra [the sun-god] and acted not by divine command, until my august [great] person." This exaggerated the situation considerably, no doubt in an attempt to further justify herself as ruler. She also used the inscriptions to identify herself with her father Thutmose I, a powerful pharaoh.

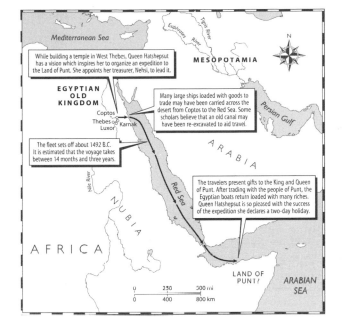

Map of Egypt and Arabia showing route of ancient Egyptian expedition sent by Queen Hatshepsut to the Land of Punt, c. 1492 BC.
Illustration by XNR Productions. Gale Research.

The disappearance of Hatshepsut

Some scholars have suggested that Hatshepsut and Senenmut were lovers; whatever the case, the bond between them was strong. In the nineteenth year of her reign, he disappeared from the official record. Perhaps he fell from favor, either with Hatshepsut or with other powerful figures. Three years later, the name of Hatshepsut too disappeared from the list of pharaohs. Presumably she died, though it is possible she was removed from power by the new king, Thutmose III, who was no doubt angry at her for keeping him from the throne for so long.

As would happen with Akhenaton (see entry) a century later, there would be an attempt to remove all evidence that Hatshepsut had ever ruled. Thutmose, who went on to wage near-constant war and assert Egypt's imperial position among the nations of the Middle East, had her statues destroyed and her name removed from a number of monuments. The later king lists would include a fictional pharaoh, "Amensis," in her place. Despite all these efforts to erase her memory, however, the name of Hatshepsut has endured, and along with it the knowledge that a woman once ruled the most powerful nation on Earth.

For More Information

Books

Carter, Dorothy Sharp. *His Majesty, Queen Hatshepsut.* Illustrated by Michele Chessare. New York: J. B. Lippincott, 1987.

A Dictionary of Biography, Past and Present. Detroit: Gale, 1974.

Encyclopedia of World Biography, 2nd ed. Detroit: Gale, 1998.

Green, Roger Lancelyn. *Tales of Ancient Egypt, Selected and Retold by Roger Lancelyn Green.* Illustrated by Elaine Raphael. New York: H. Z. Walck, 1968.

Meltzer, Milton. *Ten Queens: Portraits of Power.* Illustrated by Bethanne Anderson. New York: Dutton Children's Books, 1998.

Web Sites

"Hatshepsut." http://www.mala.bc.ca/~MCNEIL/hatshep.htm accessed on (June 27, 1999).

"Hatshepsut: The Female Pharaoh." http://www.soonernet.com/hatshepsut /article.htm (accessed on June 27, 1999).

"The Woman Who Was King." http://eyelid.ukonline.co.uk/ancient/k-q1.htm (June 27, 1999).

"Zenobia, Palmyra's Martial Queen." http://www.corrieweb.com/historica5.htm (accessed on June 29, 1999).

"Zenobia, Queen of Palmyra (b. 231?–d. after 271 AD)." http://www.mala.bc.ca/~MCNEIL/zenobia.htm (accessed on June 29, 1999).

Herodotus

Born c. 484 B.C.
Died c. 424 B.C.

Greek historian

> I, Herodotus of Halicarnassus, am here setting forth my history, that time may not draw the color from what man has brought into being.
>
> The History, *opening words*

He is known as "the father of history," but his reputation rests on a single book: *The History,* a chronicle of the world up to the conclusion of the Greeks' war with Persia. In setting down his history, Herodotus drew on all manner of geographical, social, and political details from the known lands of the world and produced a work that has seldom been paralleled for sheer readability. His reputation only grows with the passage of time.

The inspiration of Homer

It is ironic that only a smattering of facts are known regarding the man who would chronicle his own world with an artist's attention to detail. The family of Herodotus (hur-AHD-uh-tus) was wealthy and lived in Halicarnassus (hal-ih-kahr-NAS-us) in Asia Minor.

Halicarnassus was home to one of the ancient world's Seven Wonders. More important, the city lay only about forty miles from the great cultural center at Miletus (muh-LEE-tuhs) in Ionia (ie-OHN-ee-uh). Miletus had given birth to a number of notable figures such as Thales, but the Ionian who had the most effect on Herodotus was Homer.

From his readings of the *Iliad* and the *Odyssey*, Herodotus came to appreciate the vast scope of human experience—not only the greatness of human ambitions but also the many forces that conspire to frustrate those ambitions. Looking around him at the Greece of his day, fresh from its victory over the Persians, he realized that the recent conflict with Persia was the Trojan War of his own day. He decided that he would write about the Persian Wars as Homer had written about Troy.

Pyramids along Nile River, Cairo. *Hulton-deutsch Collection/Corbis. Reproduced by permission.*

Research, writing, and travels

It was Herodotus's good fortune to come from Asia Minor, a land rich with a mixture of cultures. In the course of his career, he would travel throughout most of the known world. This heightened exposure—he later said that he interviewed people from thirty foreign nations in writing his *History*—gave great depth to his writing.

Tacitus

Tacitus (TAS-I-tus; c. A.D. 56–120) ranks perhaps as high among Roman historians as Herodotus does among Greeks; but his methods were not always as careful as those of Herodotus. He is admired more as a commentator on morals than as a recorder of historical facts.

His early life is a mystery. What little historians do know about him comes from his friend Pliny the Younger (PLI-nee). Tacitus's later involvement in public life makes it easier to know about his career from about the age of twenty. It also helps to illustrate the Roman system of civil service, which gave employment to many young men of noble families.

Tacitus most likely started out in his late teens at some minor post, at which he showed his abilities. Then, as was the custom, he served a term as an officer in the military. A young man could then choose either to stay in the army or to return home for a career in civil service. The choice of civil service usually involved an early marriage, since this helped career advancement. Thus in A.D. 77, Tacitus returned to Rome and married the daughter of Agricola (uh-GRIK-uh-luh; A.D. 40–93), a noted general.

In A.D. 82, when he was about twenty-six years old, Tacitus took a job as a *quaestor* (KWES-tur), a post concerned chiefly with financial administration. From there he probably went on to the position of *aedile* (EE-dile), a type of magistrate responsible for overseeing all manner of details involving life in Rome, from organizing public games to regulating traffic to checking weights and measures. Having succeeded at that job, he was elected to the highly prestigious position of *praetor* (PREE-tur)—something like a

Supposedly Herodotus took part in a revolt at Halicarnassus. For that involvement he was exiled to the isle of Samos (SAH-mohs) off the west coast of Asia Minor when he was thirty-two years old, in about 452 B.C. From there he went on to Athens, where he lived for some time during the Age of Pericles (see entry). In 443 B.C., when he was about forty-one, he traveled to Thurii (thoor-ee-EYE) in southern Italy, where Pericles had recently founded an Athenian colony.

Over the course of the next two decades, as he wrote the book that would make him famous, Herodotus traveled far and wide. His research took him to Phoenicia and into Egypt district attorney—in A.D. 88. A year later, in a move typical of a Roman civil servant on his way up the career ladder, he went for another tour of military duty somewhere in the provinces.

Around the time Tacitus returned to Rome, in A.D. 93, Agricola died. The empire had come under the control of the cruel, mentally imbalanced emperor Domitian (doh-MISH-un; ruled A.D. 81–96), who refused Tacitus permission to write a biography of his enemy, Agricola. The next three years were fearful ones, as Domitian conducted a reign of terror, killing many of Tacitus's friends. Meanwhile Tacitus laid low, writing his *Agricola* in secret. He published it in A.D. 96, the year Domitian was assassinated.

Tacitus published his next work, *Germania,* in A.D. 98. This work presented one of the few contemporary accounts of the Germans and the Britons. With their love of freedom over pleasure, these "barbarians" were the opposite of the Romans. They clearly impressed Tacitus, who longed for a return to the simple ways of early Rome. He would put that longing into his two other historical works, *Histories* (c. A.D. 109) and *Annals* (c. A.D. 116).

The last two books formed a history of the empire from the death of Augustus in A.D. 14 through the assassination of Domitian. As historical works they are unreliable because Tacitus allowed his own foregone conclusions—rather than the evidence—guide his narrative. They are nonetheless impressive for their portrayals of various characters and for their passionate criticism of the Romans' moral decline.

as far south as Elephantine (el-uh-fan-TINE), near modern-day Aswan. While there, he wrote extensively on the Pyramids. Although he came up with some bizarre ideas about how they were built, he also offered a detailed firsthand look at great structures already more than 2,000 years old at that time.

Later he traveled westward, to Cyrene (sie-REEN) in what is now Libya; then he ventured east, to inspect the ruins of Baby-lon. There he wrote extensively about what he saw and marveled at what had been. He traveled to Persia, home of the Greeks' recent foes, and around the Black Sea in what is now Russia and other former Soviet republics. As he went, he interviewed people, made notes, and collected material for his *History.*

The History

The History, which Herodotus apparently published in stages between 430 and 424 B.C., comprised a record of the world from its origins (or at least, what the Greeks understood of its origins, which was myth rather than history or science) to the present day. What made Herodotus "the father of history" was his method. He did not simply record lists of kings and names, as others before him had done. Nor did he, at least in reporting on relatively recent events, rely on myths or superstitions to guide his narrative. Instead, he conducted tireless research and sifted through what he learned to find the truth.

Curiously, he did relate a great number of outlandish stories he had heard in his travels. He explained these by writing, "I must tell what is said, but I am not bound to believe it, and this comment of mine holds [true] about my whole History." Though clearly trained in the Athenian traditions of logic and philosophical inquiry, he was also wise enough to understand that logic does not explain everything. In particular, he realized that while myths, rumors, and superstitions are not "true," they often contain some grain of truth about the human condition.

Humanity, in fact, was really the subject of The History. Though many later historians operated under the belief that history is simply a matter of kings and military leaders, Herodotus gave at least as much attention to "ordinary people." On the one hand, his book is a narrative of events leading up to the Persian Wars, from the destruction of Croesus by the Persians to the defeat of Xerxes (see entry) at Salamis; on the other hand, The History is much more than that.

Herodotus celebrated the diversity and varied splendor of humankind in the pages of his History. In his view, all men and women were subject to the forces controlling destiny. It was not his place to judge any group of people whose customs might differ from those of his own nation. This was a highly progressive viewpoint for someone in the 400s B.C.

"The father of history"

Herodotus died, probably in Thurii, at about the time his History appeared. People have been talking about him ever since. It was Cicero who gave him the title "father of history." Others acclaimed him also as the first true geographer, anthropologist (a scientist who studies human cultures), and collector of folklore.

There were plenty who looked down on Herodotus as well. Greeks in his own time complained that he was too tolerant of other peoples' religions. He fell out of favor in the West because he seemed too admiring of the East and its differing ways of life. Up through the early twentieth century, scholars tended to smirk at Herodotus, often laughing him off as a teller of tall tales.

But as the writing of history itself has matured, so has historians' appreciation of Herodotus. This growing appreciation of his work is signified by the many references to him in the 1996 motion picture *The English Patient*. The film, which won the Academy Award for Best Picture, exposed a whole new generation, twenty-four centuries after his death, to his compelling account of Kandaules and Gyges.

Herodotus was not the "father of history" simply because he was the first known historian. He established the method historians use today: gathering facts, weighing those facts for truth and falsehood, finding an overall picture among the many details, and then writing this information as a narrative, or story. Only a handful of historians since his time have done their job as well as Herodotus.

For More Information

Books

De Selincourt, Aubrey. *The World of Herodotus*. San Francisco, CA: North Point Press, 1982.

Gaines, Ann. *Herodotus and the Explorers of the Classical Age*. New York: Chelsea House Publishers, 1994.

Herodotus. *The History*. Translated by David Greene. Chicago, IL: University of Chicago Press, 1987.

Hill, Frank Ernest. *Famous Historians*. New York: Dodd, Mead, 1966.

Mellor, Ronald. *Tacitus: The Classical Heritage*. New York: Garland Publishers, 1995.

Web Sites

"Herodotus." *Perseus Encyclopedia*. http://www.perseus.tufts.edu/cgibin/text?lookup=encyclopedia+Herodotus (accessed on July 10, 1999).

"Reading from Herodotus." http://www.fcs.net/maclark/Herodotus.htm (accessed on July 10, 1999).

"Works by Tacitus." *The Internet Classics Archive.* http://classics.mit.edu/Browse/browse-Tacitus.html (accessed on July 10, 1999).

Imhotep

Born 2600s B.C.

Egyptian architect, engineer, government administrator, physician, philosopher, mathematician, priest, and scribe

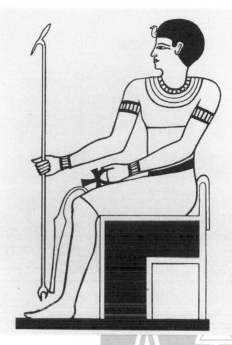

The Step Pyramid of Egypt's King Zoser was the first large-scale building in history. The equivalent of a twenty-story skyscraper in height, it had a base of almost 150,000 square feet (13,935 square meters)—nearly the size of three football fields—and an extensive network of surrounding structures, most of which have long since disappeared. It was particularly impressive because the people who built it were a Stone Age civilization apparently without knowledge of the wheel.

As remarkable as the Step Pyramid was, however, it was no more so than the man who designed it, an official named Imhotep. A truly extraordinary individual, Imhotep appears to have been not only an architect, an engineer, and a vizier or chief minister in the Egyptian government, but also a doctor, a mathematician, and a philosopher. No wonder, then, that he was later worshiped as a god. In the end, the glory of the Step Pyramid's designer exceeded that of the king for whom he designed it. The image of Imhotep remains as an example of wide-ranging genius seldom equaled in any age.

Shadowy origins

For a number of reasons, not the least of which was the fact that he lived so long ago, most details from the early life of Imhotep (im-HOH-tehp) are shrouded in mystery. He was probably born and raised in a suburb of Memphis, the Egyptian capital at the time, which lay on the Delta of the River Nile in northern Egypt.

It appears that Imhotep's father was named Kanofer (probably pronounced "KAH-noh-fehr"), and his mother Khreduonkh (probably "KRAY-doo-awnk"). Kanofer was reportedly an architect, and an important one at that. It is safe to guess that he was a prosperous civil servant and that the family lived well.

Certainly Imhotep's varied achievements would lead one to conclude that he received the best education available in Egypt at the time, which probably included training as a scribe. If so, he was in a distinct minority: very few people in ancient Egypt knew how to read and write. Images of Imhotep showed him dressed as a scribe, holding a papyrus (a scroll).

The first "person"

To appreciate just how long ago Imhotep lived, it is important to remember that Egyptian history only really began just half a millennium before his time, when the semi-mythical King Menes (MEHN-eez) united Upper and Lower Egypt. Five hundred years might seem like a long time, but in the grand sweep of history it is not much, especially considering that it was all that lay between Imhotep's time and prehistory.

Imhotep qualifies as the first true "person" in history. Certainly he was the first non-king or "ordinary" person, though he was far from common. Of course there were people before Imhotep, but none about whom historians know much. What few names survive from the prehistory of Near Eastern civilizations are either of legendary figures such as the biblical Adam and Eve, or of semi-legendary ones such as Menes. Though there was certainly a factual basis for the idea of Menes, the facts about him are so shadowy that he is almost like a figure out of mythology.

On the other hand, Zoser, or Djoser (ZHOH-suhr), the pharaoh for whom Imhotep designed the Step Pyramid,

Pythagoras

The Greek mathematician and philosopher Pythagoras (puh-THAG-uh-ruhs; c. 580–c. 500 B.C.) is one of the few figures in ancient times, or indeed in any age, who warrants comparison to the extraordinary Imhotep. Although he is best known for his famous geometrical theorem, his accomplishments ranged far beyond mathematics and involved areas as diverse as music, politics, and religion. Like Imhotep, he was a figure larger than life. Some historians suggest that he never really lived; in fact it appears highly likely that he did live some time during the 500s B.C. (Imhotep was only a bit less ancient to Pythagoras than Pythagoras is to modern people.)

Born on Samos (SAH-mohs), an Ionian (ie-OHN-ee-uhn) island off the coast of Asia Minor, Pythagoras later settled in Crotona (kruh-TOH-nuh) in southern Italy. There he gathered around him a school of followers, usually referred to as the Pythagoreans (puh-thag-uh-REE-uhnz), who had their own way of looking at life. It is possible that the Pythagoreans took control of Crotona, which may have led to Pythagoras's expulsion in about 509 B.C.

Certainly the Pythagoreans were interested in politics, along with most other subjects. Pythagoras and his followers envisioned a world of small communities. In each community people would share property. Women would have the same rights as men—an extremely radical idea, particularly in the Greek world. Everyone in this utopia would take an active interest in mathematics and music, concepts which in Pythagoras's mind were closely linked.

Pythagoras believed that the universe was highly ordered and could be explained mathematically. He was able to establish a complex relationship between the movements of the planets and the intervals between notes on the musical scale, an idea his followers termed "the music of the spheres." His ideas of precise relationships between different elements had a strong influence on Greek sculpture and architecture, both of which were heavily concerned with proportion.

Other Pythagorean ideas, particularly his belief in reincarnation, gained less acceptance in the world at large. This belief seems to be at odds with his scientific interests, but in Pythagoras's time, there was no clear division between religion and science.

Similarly, he treated numbers as though they were something mystical and possessed a real and highly concrete existence. This idea, not to mention Pythagoras's utopian politics, would heavily influence the philosopher Plato (see entry). It was a measure of Pythagoras's broad views, however, that he also had a great effect on Aristotle (see entry), a philosopher with ideas quite different from those of Plato.

was most certainly a historical figure who probably reigned from about 2630 to 2611 B.C. But more is actually known about Imhotep.

The Step Pyramid

Because Egyptians believed that, with proper preparation, they could go on living on Earth after their deaths, an essential part of an Egyptian pharaoh's reign was the building of a structure that would house his body in the afterlife. Prior to Imhotep's time, kings had been laid to rest in a type of burial mound called a mastaba (MAHS-tuh-buh). Built of mud bricks, a mastaba was rectangular in shape, with sloping sides. In comparison to later structures, it was far from impressive.

Zoser had appointed Imhotep vizier and given him the assignment of creating a suitably magnificent tomb. Imhotep's solution was to stack six mastabas on top of one another, each smaller than the one below; hence the steplike profile of Zoser's pyramid, which was built in the town of Saqqara (suh-KAR-uh) near Memphis. Unlike the mastabas of previous times, however, the pyramid was constructed not of bricks but of stone.

Around the pyramid was an elaborate walled complex that included a temple as well as buildings that looked like temples but were not. The buildings had false doors and could not be entered, a tactic intended to fool grave robbers. There was also a long court on which King Zoser, watched by crowds from all over Egypt, once ran a course to prove to his subjects that he was physically fit. This was perhaps the world's first recorded spectator sporting event.

Wide-ranging achievements

Imhotep may rightfully be called the father of the pyramid. After his time, pharaohs and their architects improved on his stepped design, developing smooth-sided structures that became larger and larger. Out of this movement would emerge the Great Pyramid of Cheops at Giza less than a century later.

As though it were not enough to be remembered as the creator of some of history's greatest structures, Imhotep established himself in a number of careers. As chief vizier, he oversaw the courts, the treasury, the military, and the nation's agriculture. He is also credited as the first true physician in history, one who sought causes for disease in science rather than in religion. Not that Imhotep was opposed to religion. Among the many vocations attributed to him was that of priest, not to mention philosopher and mathematician, areas considered close to religion in his time.

Casting a long shadow

Centuries after Imhotep's death, when Zoser had become a mere footnote to history, Imhotep would be worshiped, and those closest to him—including his parents and his wife, Ronpe-nofret (perhaps "RAWN-pay-NAW-fret")—were depicted as the close relatives of a god. Those who deified Imhotep believed that he was the offspring of the god Ptah (TAH) as well as his mortal father.

Sculpture of Imhotep.
Library of Congress.

The worship of Imhotep would later spread to Greece and Rome, where he was associated with the god of medicine, Asclepias (ah-SLEE-pee-uhs). The symbol of Asclepias was the caduceus (kuh-DOO-see-uhs), a staff with a serpent or serpents coiled around it. The caduceus remains the symbol of medicine to this day.

Because of the myths that later came to surround him, it is difficult to find reliable information about Imhotep. Many people who write about him in modern times are interested in proving points about him that cannot be supported by historical evidence. For instance, there are those who assert that Imhotep was ethnically the same as sub-Saharan Africans, when in fact there is no reason to believe he was racially different from other Egyptians, who were and are more closely related to the peoples of southwest Asia. Others have tried to make various claims about the "mystery religion" associated with him and its relation to Christianity.

Such controversy is a measure of the long shadow cast by Imhotep, but it hardly adds to the already great stature of the man himself. It is enough to recognize him as the model for an extremely rare type of genius, one with achievements in a wide array of areas. As such, Imhotep was first in a very short list that includes figures such as Greek mathematician and philosopher Pythagoras [see sidebar], Italian artist and scientist Leonardo Da Vinci (1452–1519), and American founding fathers Benjamin Franklin (1706–1790) and Thomas Jefferson (1743–1826).

For More Information

Books

Aldred, Cyril. *Egypt to the End of the Old Kingdom.* London: Thames & Hudson, 1984.

Asimov, Isaac. *Great Ideas of Science.* Illustrated by Lee Ames. Boston: Houghton Mifflin, 1969.

Brumbaugh, Robert S. *The Philosophers of Greece.* Albany, NY: State University of New York Press, 1981, pp. 30-42.

Durant, Will. *The Story of Civilization,* Volume I: *Our Oriental Heritage.* New York: Simon and Schuster, 1954, p. 147.

Hurry, Jamieson Boyd. *Imhotep, the Vizier and Physician of King Zoser, and Afterwards the Egyptian God of Medicine.* Chicago: Ares Publishers, 1978.

Shepherd, Walter. *Heroes of Science.* Illustrated by Gay Galsworthy. New York: Fleet Press, 1970.

Valens, Evans G. *The Number of Things: Pythagoras, Geometry, and Humming Strings.* New York: Dutton, 1964.

Web Sites

"The Ancient Egypt Site: Imhotep." http://www.geocities.com/~amenhotep/who/imhotep.html (accessed on June 30, 1999).

"McDonald's Proof of Pythagoras' Theorem." http://www.math.uio.no/~einara/McPyth.html (accessed on June 30, 1999).

"Pythagoras of Samos." http://www-groups.dcs.st-and.ac.uk/~history/Mathematicians/ Pythagoras.html (accessed on June 30, 1999).

"The Step Pyramid of Djoser (Zoser)." *Egyptian Ministry of Tourism.* http://interoz.com/egypt/Stepyram.htm (accessed on June 30, 1999).

Tirabassi, Michael. "Foundations of Greek Geometry." http://www.perseus.tufts.edu/GreekScience/Students/Mike/geometry.html (accessed on June 30, 1999).

"Vizier Imhotep." *Ancient Sites.* http://www.ancientsites.com/~Wbn-RaMPt_Horemheb/vizier/03imh.htm (accessed on June 30, 1999).

Jesus Christ

Born c. 6 B.C.
Died c. A.D. 30

Israelite rabbi, teacher, and founder of Christianity

Who was Jesus Christ? Christians say he was the son of God, yet also a man; that he felt all the temptations of a man, yet had all the powers of God. Non-Christians tend to view him as a very good man, though perhaps a misguided one. Jewish religious teachers of his day condemned him as a dangerous upstart. The Romans ruling over the region aided in the execution of a man who could clearly command the support of discontented masses.

In subsequent centuries, Christ has been presented as the savior promised in the Bible's Old Testament, as an advocate of political revolution, or in any number of roles, depending on the viewpoint of the person describing him. Virtually all would agree, however, that he was the most significant religious figure in the history of the Western world.

The hoped-for Messiah

All dates are rendered in relation to the year of Christ's birth, yet that year is not certain; it could have been anywhere from 6 B.C. to A.D. 4. Whatever the year, Christ was born about

The scroll of the prophet Isaiah was handed to him. Unrolling it, he found the place where it is written: 'The Spirit of the Lord is on me. . . . He has sent me to proclaim freedom for the prisoners and recovery of sight for the blind.' The eyes of everyone . . . were fastened on him, and he began by saying to them, 'Today this scripture is fulfilled in your hearing.'

Luke 4:16-21

Archive Photos. Reproduced by permission.

four centuries after the last event recorded in the Old Testament: the return of the Israelites from years of exile in foreign lands. During that period, they had increasingly begun to believe in the coming of a Messiah, a savior for all of Israel.

Some believed the Messiah would be born from tribe of King David (see entry) in the city of Bethlehem. The Bible reports that King Herod the Great (73–4 B.C.), who at the time of Jesus's birth ruled over the region of Judea (joo-DEE-uh), ordered the killing of all boys born in Bethlehem. Perhaps he feared the coming of a rival; certainly historians have recorded that Herod suffered mental instability in the later years of his life.

Miraculous birth

Christians believe that Jesus was born of a virgin and that his mother, Mary, conceived him through an act of the Holy Spirit not through sexual relations with her husband, the carpenter Joseph. The virgin birth clearly illustrated God's direct intervention in human history. The miraculous birth also established Jesus's freedom from the curse of sin and death that began with the temptation of Adam and Eve in the Garden of Eden.

The Bible records that the Roman Emperor Caesar Augustus commanded a census, or count of the population, in the year of Jesus's birth. Mary and Joseph therefore returned to the home of Joseph's family, in Bethlehem. The story of events that occurred there, including the birth in the manger and the visit by the Three Wise Men, is such a part of Western culture that it hardly needs to be repeated.

Sketchy details of early life

Virtually all the information available about Jesus comes from the first four books of the New Testament—the Gospels of Matthew, Mark, Luke, and John. Historians in Jesus's time were concerned with important figures, not carpenters' children. Except for a few later references by Josephus, there exists hardly any mention of Jesus in historical writings.

The Gospel writers, of course, were not historians but religious believers whose purpose was to spread Christ's message; therefore they provided little information about his early life. They did recount that his family escaped Herod's soldiers and went to Egypt. They told that by the time Jesus was twelve years old, the family had returned to the village of Nazareth (NAZ-uh-rehth). There Jesus sat and discussed the scriptures with the wise men of the temple, who were amazed at his wisdom and his learning.

That fascinating incident is the last recorded event of Jesus's life for almost eighteen years. What did Jesus do during that time? People have offered all sorts of fanciful theories, but it is most likely that he lived the life of an ordinary Jewish carpenter's son, working in his father's shop and attending services every Sabbath at the temple. Then, when he had reached the age of thirty, the Gospel account resumes.

Ministry begins

Jesus had a cousin, John, better known as John the Baptist, who went around the land preaching about the coming of the Messiah. When Jesus went to him to be baptized, or lowered into water as a symbol of death and rebirth, John recognized him as that Messiah. The Bible says that following the baptism of Jesus, the sky opened up and the Holy Spirit came down as a dove. Then a voice from Heaven said, "This is my Son, whom I love; with him I am well pleased" (Matthew 3:17).

Following this spiritual high point, however, came a great trial, as Jesus spent forty days and nights fasting in the desert, during which time he was tempted by the Devil. Jesus overcame the Devil's temptations, however, and went on to begin his ministry, which lasted only about three years.

He performed the first of many miracles at a wedding feast, where he turned water into wine. There would be many other miracles, including feeding 5,000 followers with a few loaves of bread and fishes, walking on water, healing the blind and sick, and even raising the dead. Though these miracles naturally made Jesus quite popular, that was not his purpose; rather, he performed them in order to show the power of faith. The power of faith is a central concept in the Bible. The Gospels are full of passages in which he either praised people with great faith or condemned those who lacked it.

Lowly friends, powerful enemies

Though he preached a number of sermons to large groups—most notably the Sermon on the Mount (Matthew 5:1–7:29)—Jesus's primary focus was on his twelve disciples, whom he chose early in his ministry. Just as Jesus seemed an unlikely Messiah, they seemed unlikely religious motivators. Several, including Peter and John, were fishermen; Matthew was a hated tax collector; and Judas Iscariot belonged to a group of anti-Roman political revolutionaries. Perhaps Judas hoped Christ would lead that revolution. If so, he was in for a disappointment. Jesus repeatedly said that his was a spiritual message rather than a political one.

Jesus taught a message of love, both for God and for one's fellow man. He lived out his message by befriending the lowest of the low. He spent time with prostitutes and other sinners, teaching that God's grace was for them as well. When people asked him to explain his teachings, he used little stories, or parables. Thus, when someone asked "Who is my neighbor?" he told the story of the Good Samaritan. This parable no doubt raised some eyebrows, since Jews hated Samaritans.

Just because Jesus taught about love did not mean he never lost his temper. He often spoke in sharp, harsh, language that did not seem calculated to win friends and influence people. No one inspired more wrath from Jesus, or responded to him in turn with more anger, than a group of religious teachers known as the Pharisees. Jesus himself, of course, was a Jew, known as a rabbi, or teacher. He did not attempt to remove the Old Testament, but to build on it. He angered the Pharisees by telling them that he was the promised Messiah. He seemed to be challenging their control over Israel, and they saw in him a threat.

Crucifixion and resurrection

In the third year of his ministry, Jesus came to Jerusalem to celebrate the Jewish feast of Passover. He entered the city like a conquering king, before cheering crowds; by the time the week was out, however, those same crowds would be calling for his blood.

The Pharisees had made an arrangement with Judas, who had agreed to turn Jesus over to them in exchange for thirty pieces of silver. On the night before he was to die, Jesus celebrated a last supper with his disciples. The meal became the model for a religious ritual celebrated by Christians to this day. The bread they ate and the wine they drank, he explained, were symbols of the sacrifice he was about to make of his body and blood, in order to wipe away the sins of humankind.

A few hours later, after painful moments of soul-searching in the Garden of Gethsemane (gehth-SEHM-uh-nee), Jesus was taken by the Pharisees, who would eventually bring him before the Roman governor, Pontius Pilate. Because Jesus had called himself King of the Jews, he was considered a threat both to the Pharisees and the Romans. Pilate was unwilling either to condemn him or to free him. In the end, he simply let the crowd decide. The crowd called for the Roman soldiers to crucify him.

Placed between two thieves and wearing a crown of thorns, Jesus hung on the cross for some six hours. Finally, he called out, "Father, into your hands I commit my spirit" and he died. A wealthy believer allowed Jesus to be buried in a tomb that he had prepared for himself.

A risen savior

There the story of Jesus's life ends, in the view of non-Christians. Christians, however, believe that by paying the debt of sin on the cross, Jesus ultimately overcame sin and death, and after being dead for three days, he returned to life. This event is celebrated each spring at Easter.

The New Testament went on to record that Jesus, after being resurrected, gave his disciples power to perform miracles as great or greater than his own. The disciples became apostles, and they went out into the world to preach about Jesus. The history of Christianity as a formal religion begins at this point—and with it the controversy surrounding Jesus's life, death, and resurrection.

Historians can never fully answer the question "Who was Jesus?" because that is a matter of religious faith rather than of scientific evidence. On a less profound level, however, it is clear enough that Jesus was one of the central figures of Western history, as his gospel eventually triumphed over even the mighty Roman Empire and became the faith of billions. Because the West went on to be a dominant force in the world for many centuries, Christianity too had an effect felt around the world.

For More Information

Books

Bloom, Daniel Halevi. *The Man from Galilee*. New York: Adama Books, 1987.

De Paola, Tomie. *Mary: The Mother of Jesus*. New York: Holiday House, 1995.

Dickens, Charles. *The Life of Our Lord; Written for His Children by Charles Dickens*. London: Collins, 1970.

Fitch, Florence Mary. *Young Jesus Asks Questions*. New York: Lothrop, Lee & Shepard, 1970.

Kissinger, Warren S. *The Life of Jesus: A History and Bibliography*. New York: Garland, 1985.

Makhlouf, Georgia. *The Rise of the Major Religions*. Translated and adapted by Walter O. Moeller, illustrations by Michaël Welply. Englewood Cliffs, NJ: Silver Burdett, 1988.

Smith, F. LaGard, ed. *The Narrated Bible*. Eugene, OR: Harvest House, 1984.

Wilson, A. N. *Jesus: A Life*. New York: Norton, 1992.

Motion Pictures

The Greatest Story Ever Told, MGM Home Entertainment, 1965.

Jesus of Nazareth, CBS/Fox Video, 1977.

The King of Kings, MGM Home Entertainment, 1961.

Moses

Born 1300s B.C.
Died 1200s B.C.

Israelite prophet, leader, and lawgiver

O f the many powerful figures in the Old Testament, none was more important to the nation of Israel, and to civilization itself, than Moses. Born at a time when the people of Israel were enslaved, he grew up in luxury. He could have continued in that easy life, as an adopted son of the Egyptian pharaoh, but instead he chose a much harder road.

It was a road that would ultimately lead to freedom for his people, but it would take a long time. Along the way, he grew as a servant and prophet of the Israelites' God, Yahweh. Through Moses would come the Ten Commandments, which became the basis for morality in the Western world. Moses would ultimately lead the Israelites to their Promised Land but would never set foot on it himself.

Slaves in Israel

The biblical Book of Genesis ends with Joseph and all the descendants of Jacob settling in Egypt. The Book of Exodus (EX-uh-duhs; "to go out from a place")—the only significant record of Moses's life—begins some four centuries later. By that

The Lord would speak to Moses face to face, as a man speaks with his friend.

Exodus 33:11

Moses and the Burning Bush, illustration. *Archive Photos. Reproduced by permission.*

Moses receiving the Ten Commandments, painting.
Archive Photos. Reproduced by permission.

time, the Israelites had fallen into disfavor with the Egyptians, who feared their growing numbers. Therefore, according to the Bible, the Egyptians made slaves of the Israelites. The pharaoh set out to kill all boys born to the people of Israel. Probably this pharaoh was Seti I (SEH-tee).

Among the Israelites from the tribe of Levi (LEE-vie) was a couple named Amram (AM-ram) and Jochebed (JACH-uh-bed), who apparently was Amram's aunt (Exodus 6:20). They had a son, who they kept hidden for three months. When she could no longer hide the boy, Jochebed put him in a basket made of reeds and let it float down the Nile River past the pharaoh's palace. There the pharaoh's daughter found it.

Rescued from the river

The princess instantly knew that the baby was an Israelite, but she decided to save him. The boy's sister Miriam, who was hiding nearby, asked her if she wanted a Hebrew woman to nurse him. The princess agreed to the idea, and even sent money to Jochebed, who raised him until he was old enough to go live in pharaoh's house.

The boy was named Moses, which comes either from a Hebrew word meaning "to draw out" (of the water) or from an Egyptian one meaning "is born." The story of his rescue from the water is a familiar one in the history of the Near East; a similar legend was told concerning Sargon of Akkad (see entry).

Escape from Egypt

One day when he was grown, Moses saw an Egyptian beating an Israelite, and he killed the Egyptian. Perhaps he thought he would be a hero to his people, but if so, he was mistaken. The next day, when he saw two Israelites fighting, and tried to break up the dispute, one of them said, "Who made you ruler and judge over us? Are you thinking of killing me as you killed the Egyptian?" (Exodus #2:14).

Moses realized that his crime was known. He had to flee Egypt just ahead of the pharaoh, who wanted to have him killed. He wound up in a desolate place called Midian (MID-ee-uhn), near the Sinai (SIE-nie) Desert. After he defended the daughters of a priest named Jethro against some local shepherds, Jethro invited him to stay with the family. Eventually Moses married Jethro's daughter Zipporah (ZEF-uh-ruh), and they had two sons.

Called to lead Israel

The Bible indicates that Moses lived in Midian for a period of some forty years. During this time, the old pharaoh died. The one who took his place was probably Ramses II. As the Bible records, "The Israelites groaned in their slavery, and their cry for help . . . went up to God" (Exodus #2:23). Apparently their labor was being used in a giant building project for Ramses.

One day Moses was tending his father-in-law's sheep when "the angel of the Lord appeared to him in flames of fire from within a bush" (Exodus #3:2). God then related the details of his covenant with Abraham, which included taking the Israelites to "a land flowing with milk and honey"—Canaan (KAY-nuhn). To accomplish this, the Israelites needed someone to lead them out of slavery, and God had chosen Moses.

Spartacus

Like Moses, Spartacus (SPAHR-tuh-kuhs; d. 71 B.C.) led a slave revolt. His had no religious overtones, however, yet he remained a powerful symbol for revolutionary political movements even in the twentieth century.

Spartacus was probably born in Thrace, in about 100 B.C. Apparently he had served in the Roman army. He then deserted and was caught; because of his desertion, he was sold into slavery. Eventually he was sent to the Italian city of Capua (KAP-yoo-uh), where there was a school for the training of gladiators (GLAD-ee-ay-tohrz).

Gladiators were warriors who fought to their deaths in a ring, watched by cheering spectators. It is not surprising, then, that some seventy slaves at the gladiatorial (glad-ee-uh-TOHR-ee-uhl) school revolted in 73 B.C. The escapees took refuge on Mount Vesuvius (veh-SOO-vee-uhs), site of a volcanic eruption some 150 years later. They defeated two legions of Roman soldiers and built up an army that numbered between 90,000 and 120,000 men. By then Spartacus had emerged as their leader. He simply wanted to lead an escape from Roman territory; other slaves, however, wanted revenge on Rome itself.

Moses was extremely reluctant, but God answered every one of his objections. He also performed the first of many miracles through Moses by turning a staff, a long stick used for herding sheep, into a snake, and then back into a staff.

Hardening pharaoh's heart

Back in Egypt, Moses met his brother, Aaron, and they went before the leaders of Israel to gain their allegiance. Then they went to the pharaoh and demanded that he release the Israelites for a three-day religious festival in the desert. Pharaoh was at first amused and then annoyed. He made Israelites' workload greater by refusing to provide them with straw for their bricks.

Exodus records that God "hardened Pharaoh's heart." Nothing Moses and Aaron did seemed to soften it. God sent a series of misfortunes, or plagues (PLAYGZ) against Egypt, each

The Roman economy was based on slavery, and the idea of a slave revolt threatened the very foundations of their system. The rebellion lasted two years, by which time Rome had brought in one of is most influential generals, Crassus (KRA-suhs; c. 115–53 B.C.), as well as one of its ablest, Pompey (PAHM-pee; 106–48 B.C.). In the end it was Crassus who secured the victory, fighting the rebels to the tip of Italy, where they had hoped to board boats for Sicily or Africa. Spartacus died fighting.

It was perhaps a better way to die: the slaves taken prisoner in that last battle of what came to be known as the Gladiatorial War (73–71 B.C.) were crucified. The bodies of some 6,000 men hung every 100 paces along the more than 90 miles (144.8 kilometers) of the Appian (AP-ee-uhn) Way from Capua to Rome.

The Gladiatorial War, by bringing together Pompey and Crassus, helped lead to the formation of the First Triumvirate with Julius Caesar (see entry) just a few years later. As for slavery in Rome, it did not so much end as it faded away. Once Rome stopped making overseas conquests in the A.D. 100s, it no longer had a source for slaves. As its economy declined, few people could afford to keep them. Feudalism eventually took the place of slavery.

worse than the one before; each time, the pharaoh's resistance simply increased.

Then came the tenth and worst plague, the killing of all the Egyptians' firstborn sons—just as the earlier pharaoh had tried to kill the Israelites' sons. On the night when this happened, the Israelites protected themselves from the angel of death by placing the blood of a lamb on the frames of their front doors; then they ate a solemn feast. This was called the Passover, still celebrated by Jews to commemorate the way that God passed over their houses and did not take their sons.

Exodus

The pharaoh was not so fortunate. When he lost his firstborn son, he finally gave in. Moses then led the Israelites and others, a group numbering as many as 2 million, out of Egypt. The Bible reports that when they came to the Red Sea,

God parted the waters and let them walk on dry land. When the pursuing army of the pharaoh (who had meanwhile changed his mind) tried to follow them, the sea swallowed them up.

Soon afterward, an even more significant event occurred at Mount Sinai. Leaving Aaron in charge of the people, Moses went up to the top of the mountain. There he received from God the Ten Commandments, which were carved into two stone tablets. He also received a long series of laws, chiefly concerning the ways that God should be worshiped.

Moses remained on the top of Mount Sinai for so long that the people of Israel became impatient and demanded that Aaron make them an idol that they could worship. This he did, making a calf out of gold—a direct violation of the Second Commandment. When Moses saw this, he became so furious that he broke the two stone tablets. God later replaced these, but he dealt severely with the Israelites, killing many of them.

Moses as leader

Despite God's violent response to the Israelites' sins, Exodus records far more examples of how he took care of Israel. He provided the people with water on many occasions, as well as bread from heaven called manna (MAN-uh). He also helped the Israelites prevail in the first of many battles with enemy peoples. Moses spent the entire period of the battle praying, until Israel had its victory.

The Bible is clear that God had a special relationship with Moses. He spoke to him directly on many occasions, and once Moses all but saw God. After the Golden Calf incident, God considered destroying everyone except Moses and only relented when Moses begged him not to.

The strains of leadership showed on Moses, however. At one point, Jethro suggested that he appoint others, answerable to him, who would take charge of the day-to-day responsibilities of leadership. Moses did this, but even so, the stress of his role had a deep-seated effect on him.

The wilderness

Despite their triumphal exodus from Egypt, it would be forty years before the Israelites finally claimed the Promised

Land. Soon after their exodus, they arrived in Canaan. Moses sent twelve spies to observe the military strength of the Canaanites. All but two spies came back and said that Canaan appeared too powerful to defeat. This lack of faith and courage enraged God, who told them he would not help them if they invaded the land. Against Moses's warnings, Israel invaded and suffered a terrible defeat.

Therefore Israel wandered for an entire generation—forty years—in what the Bible calls a wilderness, the Sinai Desert. Of course it would not take forty years to cross such a relatively small area, but this long period of homelessness was God's punishment for disobedience.

The Promised Land

Moses himself would never enter the Promised Land. This happened because of an incident in which God told him to speak to a rock so that it would produce water. Instead, Moses, no doubt weary from the people's ceaseless complaints, struck the rock. By this act, he showed not only a lack of faith—even if it was temporary—but also suggested that he had come to believe that he, and not God, was the source of miracles.

In the end, Moses passed his authority on to Joshua, who led Israel in conquering Canaan. He died within sight of the Promised Land. Although he never entered it, his name would pass down through the generations, and he would be remembered as Israel's greatest leader.

For More Information

Books

Bollinger, Max. *Freedom-Fighter: The Story of Moses*. Tring, England: Lion Publications, 1988.

Durant, Will. *The Story of Civilization,* Volume III: *Caesar and Christ.* New York: Simon and Schuster, 1944, pp. 137-38.

Hodges, Margaret. *Moses.* Illustrated by Mike Wimmer. San Diego, CA: Harcourt Brace, 1999.

Houghton, Eric. *They Marched with Spartacus.* New York: McGraw-Hill, 1963.

Kessler, Brad. *Moses the Lawgiver.* Illustrated by John Collier. New York: Rabbit Ears Books, 1996.

Nederveld, Patricia L. *Safe at Last: The Story of Moses and the Red Sea*. Grand Rapids, MI: CRC Publications, 1998.

Plutarch. *Lives of the Noble Romans*. Translated by John Dryden, edited by Edmund Fuller. New York: Dell Publishing, 1959, pp. 152-57.

Smith, F. LaGard, editor. *The Narrated Bible*. Eugene, OR: Harvest House, 1984.

Storr, Catherine, reteller. *Moses and the Plagues*. Pictures by Jim Russell. Milwaukee, WI: Raintree Children's Books, 1985.

Youd, Pauline. *Adopted for a Purpose: Bible Stories of Joseph, Moses, Samuel, and Esther*. Nashville, TN: Abingdon Press, 1986.

Motion Pictures

The Prince of Egypt, Dream Works SKG, 1998.

Spartacus, Universal Studios Home Video, 1960.

The Ten Commandments, Paramount Home Video, 1956.

Nebuchadnezzar II

Born c. 630 B.C.
Died 562 B.C.

Babylonian king

Nebuchadnezzar II remains the most famous of all Mesopotamian rulers. In large part, the enduring stature of this Babylonian king rests on the book of a people whom Nebuchadnezzar held captive for many years, the Israelites. He is known primarily through the biblical books of Daniel and Jeremiah. Legend also assigns Nebuchadnezzar a role in the building of one of the ancient world's Seven Wonders, the Hanging Gardens of Babylon.

Under his reign, Babylon reached the height of its magnificence. His armies conquered many lands. Babylonian influence would recede quickly after Nebuchadnezzar's death, but the name of the king himself would long outlast the city and the empire he built.

> Nebuchadnezzar, King of Babylon, glorious Prince, worshiper of Marduk . . . firm, not to be destroyed . . . King of Babylon am I.
>
> *from the Inscription of Nebuchadnezzar*

Nabopolassar and the Chaldeans

For centuries, Babylonia and Assyria warred for control of Mesopotamia and surrounding areas. Some time after the Assyrians sacked Babylon in 689 B.C., the Babylonians revolted. Although the Assyrians put down this revolt, it was clear that Babylon was on the rise. The leaders of this resurgence were a group called the Chaldeans (kal-DEE-uhns) from southern Babylonia. Their leader was Nabopolassar (nab-oh-poe-LASS-uhr; ruled 625-605 B.C.).

Nabopolassar formed an alliance with the Medes (MEEDZ) in northern Iran. Together they attacked the Assyrian capital at Nineveh (NIN-uh-vuh) in 612 B.C. The Assyrian court retreated to the west, where Egyptian forces protected them.

This led to a showdown between the Babylonians and Medes on the one side and the Egyptians and Assyrians on the other. The two forces met at Carchemish (KAR-kuh-mish) on what is now the border of Turkey and Syria, in 605 B.C. The leader of the Babylonian forces at Carchemish was Nabopolassar's twenty-five-year-old son, Nebuchadnezzar II (neb-you-kuh-D'NEZ-ur), who led his armies to victory. After this, Babylonia claimed most of the Assyrian Empire.

The new king

On August 15, 605 B.C., while he was near the city of Damascus in Syria, Nebuchadnezzar received word that his father had died. He rushed home, covering nearly 600 miles in just two weeks—an impressive speed in the age of horseback travel. On September 7, he was crowned King Nebuchadnezzar II in Babylon.

Aside from Babylonian inscriptions and a document called the *Chaldean Chronicles,* translated in the twentieth century, the primary sources of information on Nebuchadnezzar's life come from the Babylonian priest Berossus (buh-RAH-suhs; c. 290 B.C.), whose research and conclusions later reappeared in the work of Josephus (joh-SEE-fuhs; A.D. 37–95) and in the Old Testament. Berossus is the source of the story that Nebuchadnezzar married the Median princess Amyntis (ah-MIN-tis) in order to seal the alliance between the two nations.

The Bible paints a fascinating picture of a man who destroyed Israel, yet sought the wisdom of the Israelites' god, Yahweh; a man who worshiped the Babylonian god Marduk (MAHR-dook), whom Yahweh despised, but who eventually (according to the Book of Daniel) came to recognize the god of Israel as superior. Long before that time, however, Nebuchadnezzar became known as the conqueror of Judah (JOO-duh), the last holdout from the tribes of Israel, who had been overwhelmed earlier by the Assyrians.

Conquering rebellious peoples

Nebuchadnezzar's first foreign-policy task was to bring Judah under Babylonian rule. It was a truly international conflict: the Babylonians employed Greek mercenaries, while the Judean king, Jehoiakim (jeh-HOY-uh-kim; ruled c. 609–598 B.C.) formed an alliance with Necho II of Egypt (NEHK-oh; ruled 610–595 B.C.).

The prophet Jeremiah [see sidebar] warned Jehoiakim against the alliance with Egypt. Later, when Nebuchadnezzar was temporarily stopped, the prophet told him not to take advantage of the moment to revolt. Jehoiakim ignored him.

By 598 B.C., all Jeremiah's warnings came true as Nebuchadnezzar—probably aided by other nations around Israel—marched into Judah. On March 16, 597 B.C., Nebuchadnezzar took Jerusalem and appointed a new king, Zedekiah (zed-uh-KIE-uh). He looted treasures from Jerusalem, taking them back to Babylon.

Over the next few years, Nebuchadnezzar dealt first with the people of Elam (EE-luhm), a region in southern Persia (596 B.C.); crushed a rebellion at home (595); and marched against Syria in 594 B.C. It appears that he conducted a long siege against the Phoenician city of Tyre , which ended in about 587 B.C..

The capture of Jerusalem

In 589 B.C., Zedekiah, perhaps thinking Nebuchadnezzar was distracted and that his allies in Egypt would come to his aid, led a revolt against Babylonian rule. This proved a great mistake.

In the summer of 586 B.C., Nebuchadnezzar invaded Jerusalem, killing thousands of people and taking many more

Solomon, King of Israel, seated on throne, holding scepter. *Archive Photos. Reproduced by permission.*

Daniel and other prophets

Nebuchadnezzar is mentioned in the writings of two important Israelite prophets, Jeremiah (c. 650–c. 570 B.C.), and Daniel. Daniel was a young man taken into captivity by the Babylonians in 586 B.C.. He was still active, though clearly an old man, in 539 B.C., when the Persians took Babylon.

The term *prophet* is used broadly to describe a series of figures from Moses (see entry) to Malachi (MAL-uh-kie), the author of the last book in the Old Testament. Not all prophets had the same role. Some, like Moses and Samuel, were political leaders. More often, however, the prophets were outside the political power structure, and often at odds with it. This was the case with Elijah, one of the most important Old Testament figures, who was

constantly threatened by King Ahab and Queen Jezebel. Likewise, Jeremiah, who preached that Israel did not stand a chance against the Babylonians, was arrested and thrown into a deep well.

Some prophets spoke about a number of broad topics, as in the case of Isaiah; others, such as Jonah, had specific missions. Most were men, of course, but there was also Deborah. Though "prophet" usually suggests someone who can tell the future, in the Old Testament the term often meant someone capable of understanding and proclaiming God's will. Often prophets did both, as in the case of Daniel.

The Book of Daniel includes a number of interesting stories concerning Daniel and Nebuchadnezzar. One of the

as prisoners back to Babylon. The prisoners included Zedekiah, whom they transported in chains. Many of these people would become servants of the Babylonians, though not slaves in the strictest sense of the word.

Nebuchadnezzar also seized treasures from Solomon's temple and transported them to the temple of Marduk. This was the height of humiliation to the Israelites, who dated the beginning of the Captivity from the Babylonians' capture of Jerusalem.

The glory of Babylon

Under the forty-three-year reign of Nebuchadnezzar, the city of Babylon flourished. It covered about 4 square miles most fascinating, from the standpoint of ancient history, concerns Nebuchadnezzar's dream of a great statue. Actually, as explained in Daniel 2, Nebuchadnezzar did not remember his dream, so Daniel had to tell him both what he dreamed and what it meant.

According to Daniel, Nebuchadnezzar dreamed of a great statue made of different kinds of metal: a head of gold, chest and arms of silver, torso and thighs of bronze, legs of iron, and feet a mixture of iron and clay. Then a great stone came and knocked down the statue. The pieces of the statue blew away, and the stone became a great mountain. Daniel interpreted the stone as the kingdom of God, which would overcome the kingdoms of man. Those kingdoms were symbolized by the parts of the statue, each of which was less great than the one above it.

Biblical scholars have viewed the dream in terms of the empires that existed at that time and afterward: the gold was Babylonia, as Daniel said; the silver Persia; the bronze Alexander's Greek Empire; and the iron Rome. In each case, the metal was less valuable, just as the ruler of each had less absolute power than the one before him. But the metal was also stronger, just as each empire was a little more permanent in its influence. It would seem, also, that the iron and clay feet suggested the Roman Empire, divided in the late A.D. 300s into a strong eastern half and a weak western one.

(10.4 square kilometers), surrounded by a set of double walls, an outer wall 12 feet (3.7 meters) thick and an inner one 21 feet (6.4 meters) thick. Around the outside were a hundred towers, many of them 60 feet (18.3 meters) high, and beyond those a series of moats to further protect the city.

There were nine major gates to Babylon, the most famous of which was the Ishtar Gate (ISH-tahr) in the north. Covered in decorative figures and colored bricks, it was partially reconstructed in the 1920s and placed on display in Berlin's Pergamum Museum (PUHR-guh-muhm). Through the city ran the Euphrates River (yoo-FRAY-teez), across which Nebuchadnezzar erected a bridge some 400 feet (121.9 meters) long.

There was also a great ziggurat (ZIG-uh-raht), or temple tower, which stood about 300 feet (91.4 meters) high, as well as a huge temple to Marduk built by Nebuchadnezzar. In addition, some fifty temples (of which Nebuchadnezzar claimed to have built, or partially built, sixteen) dotted the city.

Then there were the fabulous Hanging Gardens, lush terraces covered with all manner of plant life, which Nebuchadnezzar supposedly built in order to satisfy Amyntis's longing for her mountain home. Whether or not this is true, the gardens certainly existed. If there were ever a Babylonian ruler with the power to command such a building project, it was Nebuchadnezzar.

The Greek historian Herodotus (see entry) visited Babylon years later, when it lay in ruins, but he still marveled at its glory. Perhaps he was the first to identify the Hanging Gardens as one of the ancient world's Seven Wonders.

The end of Nebuchadnezzar

Little is known about the last three decades of Nebuchadnezzar's life. Presumably, when he had finished conquering most of southwest Asia—he also apparently subdued Egypt in about 568 B.C.—he devoted himself to building projects in his home city.

The prophet Daniel [see sidebar] offered some insight into Nebuchadnezzar's later years. Chapter 4 of the Book of Daniel reports that the king temporarily went insane as a lesson from Yahweh, but it is possible that the ruler who actually suffered this attack of mental illness was Nabonidus (nab-oh-NIE-duhs; r. 555–539 B.C.).

Nebuchadnezzar died in October of 562 B.C. Daniel had prophesied that his kingdom would not long outlast him. In 539 B.C., as Daniel 5 so chillingly recounts, the Babylonian king Belshazzar (bel-SHAZZ-uhr) lost his kingdom and his life to the Persians.

Despite this inglorious end to his empire, Nebuchadnezzar would be remembered as perhaps the greatest of all Babylonian kings. The names of powerful Assyrian monarchs such as Tiglath-pileser, Sennacherib, and Ashurbanipal are chiefly of interest to historians, whereas Nebuchadnezzar's name—thanks in large part to the holy book of the people he conquered—is a household word. Given the long-standing conflict between the two nations, not to mention his obvious interest in making a name for himself, it would probably thrill the Babylonian king to know this fact.

For More Information

Books

Bolliger, Max. *Daniel*. Translated by Marion Koenig, illustrated by Edith Schindler. New York: Delacorte Press, 1970.

Frank, Penny. *King Nebuchadnezzar's Golden Statue*. Illustrated by Eric Ford. Belleville, MI: Lion Publishing, 1984.

Garfield, Leon and Michael Bragg. *The King in the Garden*. New York: Lothrop, Lee & Shepard, 1984.

Healy, Mark. *Nebuchadnezzar: Scourge of Zion*. Plates by Richard Hook. New York: Sterling, 1989.

Web Sites

"Ancient History Sourcebook: Greek Reports of Babylonia, Chaldea, and Assyria." http://www.fordham.edu/halsall/ancient/greek-babylon. html (accessed on July 7, 1999).

"Archaeology Explorer." http://www.iversonsoftware.com/business/ archaeology/Babylon.htm (accessed on July 7, 1999).

"The History of Plumbing (Babylonia)." *The Plumber.com*. http://www. theplumber.com/history.html (accessed on July 7, 1999).

"Inscription of Nebuchadnezzar." http://mcadams.posc.mu/edu/txt/ ASSYRIA/INSCRB00.HTM (accessed on July 7, 1999).

"Lunatic Leaders in Antiquity." http://www.xs4all.nl/~kvenjb/madantiq. htm (accessed on July 7, 1999).

Paul

Born c. A.D. 5
Died c. A.D. 67

Cilician missionary and religious leader

> I have labored and toiled and have often gone without sleep; I have known hunger and thirst and have often gone without food; I have been cold and naked. Besides everything else, I face daily the pressure of my concern for the churches.
>
> *2 Corinthians 11:27-29*

Other than Christ himself, no individual had as great a role in the development of Christianity as the apostle Paul. Christ brought his message of salvation to the twelve disciples and others around him in Judea but offered no practical program for organizing a church. Later it would be the job of Paul, who never met Christ, to present a series of instructions on the day-to-day operation of a Christian community. These he would outline in more than a dozen letters, or epistles, that form a large part of the New Testament.

Yet before he became a soldier for Christ, Paul was one of the Jewish scholars called Pharisees who had helped bring about Christ's crucifixion. He had no hand in that particular act, but he showed plenty of zeal for persecuting Christians. Therefore, when he decided to follow Christ, many did not believe his apparent conversion. Similarly, twenty centuries after his death, modern scholars still debate Paul's contribution to the faith. Did he help or hurt the cause of Christianity? Are his teachings in line with those of Christ? Those on both sides of the discussion are passionate about their positions.

A young Pharisee

Born by the name of Saul, Paul came from a Jewish family living in Tarsus, the principal city in the region of Cilicia (suh-LISH-uh). Tarsus is located in the southeastern part of Asia Minor, or modern Turkey. At the time of Paul's birth, Rome controlled the area. His family enjoyed Roman citizenship, which suggests their prominence.

As a young man, Paul studied the scriptures in Jerusalem under Gamaliel (guh-MAIL-ee-uhl), one of the foremost Jewish scholars of his day. As Pharisees, they had a strong interest in upholding the traditional faith. They were particularly disturbed by the spread of a strange cult based on the teachings of a carpenter named Jesus (Joshua in Hebrew). Paul, perhaps because he had been too young to participate in the plot to have Christ crucified, was especially ferocious in his persecution of Christ's followers.

The biblical Book of Acts tells about the stoning of the apostle Stephen, the first martyr. Stoning, killing someone by throwing stones at him or her, was every bit as gruesome as crucifixion. Yet Paul seems to have been an enthusiastic participant in the killing of Stephen. Afterward he decided to go north to the Syrian capital of Damascus (duh-MAS-kuhs) in order to find more Christians to persecute and kill.

Conversion experience

According to the Book of Acts, however, God had other plans for the Pharisee named Saul. As he was on the road to Damascus, probably in about A.D. 36, his eyes were assaulted by a bright light from heaven. The voice of God demanded that he stop persecuting Christians. At that point, his name was changed from Saul to Paul.

Blinded, he was forced to fast for three days. Then a Syrian Christian named Ananias (an-uh-NIE-uhs) laid hands on him, and he recovered his sight. Paul received his sight in more ways than one, according to the Bible. He finally understood that Jesus was the hoped-for Messiah and recognized that the prophecies of old had been fulfilled in Christ. Therefore he readily adopted the Christian faith. For this reason, when somebody has a sudden and striking change in a point of view, it is often called a "Damascus Road experience."

Not everybody believed that Paul's change of heart was real, however; when he learned of a plot to kill him, he had to escape from Damascus by being lowered over the city walls in a basket. He then went to Arabia, where he spent several years in the wilderness, probably gaining his first experience as a missionary.

Missionary journeys and epistles

Jesus had told his disciples to "go out into the world and preach the Gospel." That was precisely what Paul set out to do, acting with as much enthusiasm as he had in his former persecution of Christians. He believed that he was called to reach the Gentiles, or non-Jews, for Christ, and this belief brought him into a dispute with the disciples Peter and James. These disciples both believed that Gentiles had to become Jews before they could become Christians. Surprisingly, it was the former Pharisee who insisted that there was no need to embrace Judaism now that Christ had shown the true way of salvation.

Paul's view seems to have won out in the Council of Jerusalem, held in about A.D. 49. By that time, Paul had completed nearly five years of ministry in Syria and Cilicia and had embarked on the first of four missionary journeys. The journeys took him throughout the Mediterranean world, primarily to churches in Asia Minor and Greece. The locations of these churches can be found in the names of various epistles, such as the two letters to the church at Corinth in Greece, 1 and 2 Corinthians (koh-RIN-thee-uhnz), or the letter to the church as Ephesus in Asia Minor, Ephesians (eh-FEE-zhuhnz).

Paul wrote thirteen epistles in all, or fourteen if he is counted as the author of the Book of Hebrews, the authorship of which is disputed. The epistles were written to take the place of Paul himself, who could not always be present in the churches themselves because of the difficulties of travel in the ancient world—not to mention his later imprisonment. Usually the epistles were read aloud to the congregation.

Most of the epistles deal with specific problems. The Galatians (guh-LAY-shuhnz), for instance, were too concerned about abiding by religious law and failed to appreciate the gift

Ezana and Frumentius

The Book of Acts recounts that the apostle Philip led an "Ethiopian" official to convert to Christianity. In those days, the term referred to a number of nations, though it is quite possible the African came from the coastal land of Aksum. More than two centuries later, a Christian missionary from Syria would bring the Gospel to the Aksumite king, Ezana (AY-zah-nah; ruled A.D. 325–360).

There are somewhat conflicting stories, but it appears that a merchant named Meropius (meh-ROHP-ee-uhs), from Tyre in Phoenicia, was on his way to India. With him were two Syrian boys, whom he intended to provide with an education. The younger of the two, Aedesius (i-DEE-see-uhs), was a simple-minded lad, but the elder, Frumentius (froo-MEHN-shuhs), was quite bright. They happened to be shipwrecked off the coast of Aksum. Meropius was killed, and the two boys were taken as slaves to the palace of the Aksumite king, Ella Amida (el-AH AHM-ee-dah).

The king died soon afterward, having given the boys their freedom, but the widowed queen begged them—Frumentius in particular—to stay and help educate her infant son, Ezana. Frumentius agreed, and over the years that followed, he became a trusted advisor to the young prince.

Frumentius, who was a Christian, went on to receive an assignment as Bishop of Aksum. Meanwhile, Ezana grew up and was crowned king in A.D. 325. He became a conqueror, controlling an empire that stretched from southwest Arabia to Meröe in the west. In about A.D. 335, he embraced the Christian faith. He replaced pagan symbols on the coins of the nation with the cross. These coins were some of the first in the world to carry the symbol of Christianity.

Ezana and Frumentius began a tradition of Christianity in the nation of Ethiopia, as the area of Aksum came to be called, that would extend to the present day. Rumors persist that the fabled Ark of the Covenant found its final resting place there as well.

of divine grace that Paul stressed as one of the central ideas of Christianity. The Book of Philemon (fie-LEE-muhn), on the other hand, is concerned with the issue of a runaway slave named Onesimus (oh-NEHS-i-muhs), whom Paul had encouraged to return to his master. The letter urges the master, Philemon, to exercise kindness toward the slave.

Imprisonment and persecution

At the time he wrote Philemon, Paul was in prison. In A.D. 57, he had gotten into a scuffle with some orthodox Jews at the temple in Jerusalem. In the ensuing confusion, Roman soldiers had arrested him. He was imprisoned for two years and then appealed for a trial in Rome. On his way there, however, he was shipwrecked near the island of Malta. In about A.D. 60, he arrived in Sicily, where he found a thriving Christian community.

While imprisoned in Rome for the next two years, Paul was able to continue his missionary work on a local basis. He was released in A.D. 62, and on his way back east made his fourth and last missionary journey.

Paul had often been in trouble with the authorities and experienced other hardships. His earlier Roman imprisonment had been a relatively easy matter, more like house arrest. When he was arrested again in A.D. 67, probably by the Emperor Nero, he did not fare so well. This time he was confined in a dungeon, where he wrote his last epistle, 2 Timothy, in A.D. 67 or 68. Soon afterward, he was executed.

A controversial figure

Many of Paul's statements have been the subject of debate. Most controversial are his comments on the proper role of women, who he believed should submit to their husbands. He vigorously condemned homosexuality, which he placed on a par with incest. On a number of issues, he was what a modern person would describe as intolerant.

But of course Paul was not a modern person. In some ways, though, he was rather forward-looking. Despite his statements regarding the status of women, in many instances he treated them as equals. Furthermore, he said that "there is neither Jew nor Greek, slave nor free, male nor female, for you are all one in Christ Jesus" (Galatians 3:28). At the very least, this can be seen as a biblical condemnation of racism and sexism and has often been used for that purpose.

Paul also emphasized salvation by faith through grace. Not only did this give a practical dimension to many of Christ's statements regarding salvation, but nearly fifteen centuries after Paul's time, Paul's ideas would affect Martin Luther

(1483–1546). Luther would take his inspiration from the letter called Romans as he helped to forge the powerful revolution of faith known as the Reformation. Certainly there are legitimate critiques of Paul's effect on the course of Christianity, but one cannot deny that the effect itself has been immeasurable.

For More Information

Books

Becker, Jürgen. *Paul: Apostle to the Gentiles.* Translated by O. C. Dean, Jr. Louisville, KY: Westminster/John Knox Press, 1993.

Haughton, Rosemary. *Paul and the World's Most Famous Letters.* Nashville, TN: Abingdon Press, 1970.

Matthews, Leonard, reteller. *The Journeys of St. Paul.* Illustrated by Mark Bergin. Vero Beach, FL: Rourke Publications, 1984.

Rye, Jennifer. *The Story of the Christians.* Illustrated by Chris and Hilary Evans. New York: Cambridge University Press, 1986.

Tambasco, Anthony J. *In the Days of Paul: The Social World and Teaching of the Apostle.* New York: Paulist Press, 1991.

Tucker, Iva Jewel. *Paul, the Missionary.* Illustrated by Ron Hester. Nashville: Broadman Press, 1976.

Web Sites

"The Aksumite State." http://www.geocities.com/CollegePark/7139/aksum.htm (accessed on June 28, 1999).

"The Apostle Paul." http://www.geocities.com/Heartland/Pointe/5122/paulback.html (accessed on June 28, 1999).

"Civilizations In Africa: Axum." http://www.wsu.edu:8080/~dee/CIVAFRCA/AXUM.HTM (accessed on June 28, 1999).

"The Ecole Glossary: Frumentius of Ethiopia." *The Ecole Initiative.* http://cedar.evansville.edu/~ecoleweb/glossary/frumentius.html (accessed on June 28, 1999).

Hancock, Graham. "The Sign and the Seal (Continuation): Into Axum." *One World Magazine.* http://www.envirolink.org/oneworld/focus/ethiopia/ark3.html (accessed on June 28, 1999).

Pericles

Born 495 B.C.
Died 429 B.C.

Greek politician and general

The Athenian statesman Pericles was the very model of a politician, with all the good that word implies and some of the bad as well. Under his leadership, the people of Athens embarked on one of the most brilliant eras in all human history. It was the heart of the Athenian Golden Age, a time known as the Age of Pericles, when philosophy and the arts flourished as never before. Likewise, democracy—government by the people—experienced one of its proudest moments; but Pericles won his triumphs in part through foreign conquest and empire-building. In the end, like a hero from a Greek tragedy, his own mistakes would bring about his downfall.

A family tradition

Pericles (PAIR-uh-kleez) was born to one of the best families in Athens. His mother, Agariste (ag-uh-RIS-tee), came from the upper levels of the Athenian aristocracy, but her uncle Cleisthenes (KLISE-thuh-neez; c. 570–c. 500 B.C.) had established Athens's first democratic government in 507 B.C. Soon after Pericles's birth, the Persians invaded Greece. In 479 B.C., when he was sixteen, his father, Xanthippus (zan-TIP-us), led the Athenians to victory in the last important battle of the war, at Mycale (MI-kuh-lee).

Young Pericles studied under the Sophists as well as the philosophers Zeno and Anaxagoras (an-ak-SAG-uh-rus; c. 500–428 B.C.). The latter counted among his other pupils the playwright Euripides and possibly even Socrates. From these teachers, Pericles learned about logic, a system of reasoning, as well as rhetoric (RET-uh-rik), or the art of speaking and writing. These experiences helped foster his belief in education, his interest in philosophy and the arts, and his conviction that people—not the gods—controlled human destiny.

The Delian League and Sparta

With the Persian Wars over, Athens in 478 B.C. had established an alliance called the Delian (DEEL-ee-un) League. The Delian League brought together hundreds of city-states, originally for the purpose of protecting against any future invasion by Persia. It collected funds from various cities for this purpose, which it devoted to building warships and other projects to prepare for war. However, as time passed and the Persian threat faded, Athens came to use the League more and more for its own purposes.

Sparta, Athens's age-old rival, did not belong to the League. Even though they had joined forces in the war against Persia, the people of democratic Athens were eager to dissociate themselves from the Spartans, whose government was anything but democratic. In Sparta, the majority of the population were slaves, called helots (HEL-utz), and a minority of aristocrats ruled.

However, a group of Athenian aristocrats led by Cimon (SIE-mun; c. 510–c. 451 B.C.) favored continuing relations with Sparta. This became more and more distasteful to Athenians, particularly when Cimon sent troops to assist the Spartan aristocrats in suppressing a revolt of the helots in 462 B.C. This event helped lead to the rise of Pericles.

The rise of Pericles

In 463 B.C., thirty-two-year-old Pericles joined forces with Ephialtes (ef-ee-AL-teez) in the Athenian leadership.

Together they managed to ostracize (AHS-tru-size) Cimon, or force him to leave the city. Before Cimon's followers could recover, Pericles and Ephialtes instituted a number of reforms to reduce the power of the aristocrats and increase that of the poor.

Up to that point, Athenian leaders had not been paid, meaning that only the wealthy could afford to hold public office. Pericles and Ephialtes established pay for public officials, thus opening up offices to the poor. They did not do this simply because they had big hearts; they also knew that it would win the support of Athens's poor majority (which of course it did).

Next Pericles and Ephialtes turned on the Areopagus (ar-ee-AHP-uh-gus), the Athenian high court; this, too, they opened to people of all classes. This move proved too much for the aristocrats, who had Ephialtes assassinated, but this act paved the way for Pericles to take leadership.

The Athenian Empire

Athens had long controlled the treasury of the Delian League, to which all member cities contributed. Initially it ensured that all contracts for shipbuilding and other projects went to Athenians. Later, in 453 B.C., Pericles moved the treasury to Athens for "safekeeping."

By the time Pericles became principal leader of Athens in 460 B.C., the Delian League had become, in effect, the Athenian Empire. At first a few city-states tried to rebel against Athens's control, but Athenian military forces crushed those rebellions. Then Pericles went on to reclaim a number of cities that had fallen into the hands of Athens's enemies. To protect Athens's port at Piraeus (pie-REE-uhs) five miles away, Pericles built a defensive perimeter called the "Long Walls," stretching from the city to the sea.

Eventually Athens established colonies, and conquered territory as far away as southern Italy in the west and Thrace (modern Bulgaria) in the east. The Athenians did not see themselves merely as conquerors, however: they were spreading democracy, which to them was like a religion. Later their heavy-handedness would lead them to war with Sparta, but before that happened, Athens would enjoy its brightest hour.

The Age of Pericles

The war industry, combined with the Delian League's treasury, made Athens wealthy. The shrewd Pericles ensured his people's allegiance by sharing the wealth. In 453 B.C., he established pay for jurors, which made it possible for the poor to take part in the legal system just as his early reforms had opened up public offices to them. He also instituted a state-sponsored arts system, which ensured that everyone could attend the theater.

The latter move could be seen as a foreshadowing of the Roman Empire's policy of "bread and circuses," whereby it controlled the poor by putting them on the equivalent of welfare. Pericles's aims, however, were much more noble. He believed that Athens should be an example to all of Greece, which would seek to imitate its glory—and its democratic government.

The Athenian leader sought to give that glory a physical form, and he commissioned a number of building projects.

Ruins of the Parthenon, atop the Acropolis, Athens, Greece. *Photograph by Susan D. Rock. Reproduced by permission.*

Dozens of great structures came into being under Pericles's guidance. None was more spectacular than the magnificent Parthenon. The Parthenon, a temple to the goddess Athena, stood on the Acropolis overlooking the city. It would become as much a symbol of Greece as the Great Wall was of China.

Pericles's encouragement of the arts gave a great boost to the careers of playwrights such as Sophocles, Euripides, and Aristophanes. Philosophy flourished as well, thanks to the influence of this educated leader. The roster of influential figures in Periclean Athens, including Socrates and Herodotus (see entry) is long and glorious. Truly if any time deserved to be called a "golden age," it was this one.

Friends and enemies

Like many another great figure of ancient times, Pericles was not exactly a handsome man. He is said to have had a misshapen head. For that reason he always wore a magnificent war helmet, which of course also reinforced his image as a military leader.

He was as stingy at home as he was generous with public funds, in part because his wife and children had a longing for the finer things in life. This may have led to his divorce (his wife's name is not known) and to his children's later ill will toward their father.

In 445 B.C., however, Pericles met the woman who became the love of his life: Aspasia (uh-SPAY-zhuh; c. 470–410 B.C.). Aspasia was that rarest of figures in ancient Greece: a strong, outspoken woman. Athens excelled in many ways, but its treatment of women was not one of them. Athenians considered it scandalous when Aspasia opened a school of rhetoric. She even dared to speak her mind publicly, which earned her sharp rebuke from many, but she won the friendship of Socrates and the deep admiration of Pericles.

Because so many people wanted to live in his Athens, Pericles in 451 B.C. had established a law effectively preventing Athenian men from marrying outsiders. This greatly elevated the attraction of an Athenian bride, but it prevented him from marrying Aspasia. Nonetheless, they lived together and even had a son, whom they named after his father.

His relationship with Aspasia became one of the many issues that Pericles's enemies used against him; so, too, did the building of the Parthenon. Anyone who achieves as much as Pericles did is bound to have foes, but his enemies were not the ones who brought about his end. To a large extent, Pericles himself can be blamed for that.

The Peloponnesian War

Problems with Sparta had been simmering for a long time. No doubt the Spartans, with their miserable society based on warfare and slavery, were jealous of Athens's glory, and they hated and feared its democratic government. Meanwhile, Athens pursued a reckless foreign policy that led it ever closer to war.

The city of Corinth (KOHR-inth) to the northwest had allied itself with Sparta and maintained a less than democratic government ruled by aristocrats. Conditions were even worse in Corcyra (kohr-SIE-ruh), a colony whose citizens finally revolted against their Corinthian overlords. Athens supported the revolt, which led Corinth to demand help from Sparta against Athens. As tensions mounted, Athens in 431 B.C. refused to allow entrance to its harbor by ships from Megara (MEG-uh-ruh), a Spartan ally. This was the beginning of the Peloponnesian War [pel-uh-poh-NEE-zhun].

Fearing the strength of the Spartans' army, Pericles decided to take a defensive strategy, bringing all the people of Athens inside the city's walls. To prevent the Spartans from benefiting by taking control of nearby areas, he followed a "scorched-earth" policy, directing his navy to destroy much of the surrounding coast. He also encouraged the helots of Sparta to revolt. This revolt might have been a brilliant move if he had lived to follow it through.

End of a golden age

But he did not. The overcrowding of Athens created horrible sanitary conditions, which were not helped by the Athenians' habit of simply dumping their waste into the streets. This brought about a great epidemic, or plague. Pericles was one of its victims.

Before he died, however, he was said to have delivered a funeral oration, or speech, recorded by the historian Thucydides. In it, he remembered all those who had given their lives for the glory of Athens. He encouraged listeners to "reflect that it was by courage, sense of duty, and a keen feeling of honor in action that men were enabled to win all this."

The Golden Age died with Pericles: Athens lost the Peloponnesian War in 404 B.C. Among the victims of the hysteria that followed was his son. But the dream of Periclean Athens did not die. People throughout the ages continued to believe that one day there might be another city, and another land, as glorious as Athens in the Age of Pericles.

For More Information

Books

King, Perry Scott. *Pericles*. New York: Chelsea House Publishers, 1988.

Nardo, Don. *Democracy*. San Diego, CA: Lucent Books, 1994.

Nardo, Don. *The Age of Pericles*. San Diego, CA: Lucent Books, 1996.

Montgomery, Elizabeth Rider. *Toward Democracy: Great Documents in History*. New York: I. Washburn, 1967.

Poulton, Michael. *Pericles and the Ancient Greeks*. Illustrations by John James. Austin, TX: Raintree/Steck-Vaughn, 1993.

Web Sites

"Pericles' Funeral Oration." http://nimbus.temple.edu/~jsiegel/texts/pericles/pericles.htm (accessed on July 10, 1999).

"Plutarch, Pericles." http://www.acs.ucalgary.ca/~vandersp/Courses/texts/plutarch/plutperi.html (accessed on July 10, 1999).

"Temple of Pericles." http://sangha.net/messengers/pericles.htm (accessed on July 10, 1999).

Piankhi

Born 769 B.C.
Died 716 B.C.

Kushite king

Piankhi, king of Kush in Africa and conqueror of Egypt, paved the way for the Twenty-Fifth (Nubian) Dynasty of pharaoh. He was a remarkable figure in many respects, not least of which was his sincere devotion to his god, Amon. This alone distinguished him. Then, as now, rulers claimed to be godly men while pursuing their own interests, yet in Piankhi's case, his faith is clear from his actions. He was, in fact, a particularly rare combination, with religious passion on the one hand and gentleness and tolerance on the other. Even as he conquered in the name of Amon, he spared lives rather than taking them.

Also significant is Piankhi's heritage. Unlike many ancient figures who have been falsely identified as "black" [see sidebar], Piankhi truly was. (So, too, was Ezana of Aksum.) This does not prove anything about Piankhi's character, of course, but it shows that all peoples of the ancient world produced great rulers. Piankhi, judged in terms of how he treated a conquered people, was one of the greatest.

Without [Amon], no brave [man] has strength. He maketh strong the weak, so that many flee before the few, and one man overcometh a thousand.

from Piankhi's stela in Napata

Were they black?

In historical scholarship, race should never be a factor; however, due to conflicts arising from the movement known as Afrocentrism, it is necessary to point out that not everyone who lived on the African continent in ancient times was "black"—i.e., racially and ethnically related to the peoples who lived south of the Sahara Desert. The fact that a group of people comes from a certain continent does not determine their race: otherwise everyone living in America would be an Indian, and everyone in Europe would be white.

Thus neither Cleopatra (see entry) nor Hannibal (see entry), though they lived in North Africa, were "black." Cleopatra's ancestors were Greek, Hannibal's Phoenician. It is also questionable whether ancient Egyptians such as Imhotep (see entry), Hatshepsut (see entry), or Akhenaton (see entry) were what modern people would call "black" either: the Semitic roots of the Egyptian language suggest a closer ethnic relationship to the peoples of Mesopotamia and Arabia than to those of southern Africa.

This is not to say, however, that any of these people—except perhaps Cleopatra, a European—were "white." To guess at the appearance of Hannibal or Hatshepsut, one need only look at the peoples of the Middle East today, who share many facial features with Caucasians—but whose skin, hair, and eyes are dark.

In fact the terms "black" and "white" are meaningless. At best they describe physical features, and as the Rev. Martin Luther King, Jr. (1929–68) so eloquently observed, they have nothing to do with the actual character of the person, or with his or her abilities.

Kush and Egypt

Kush was the name for the kingdom that dominated Nubia (NOO-bee-uh), a region along the Nile River to the south of Egypt. It had long been linked with Upper Egypt (that is, the southern part of that country). Because it stood at Egypt's "back door," Egyptian pharaohs from that time onward had placed an emphasis on controlling Nubia. Senusret III (d. 1843 B.C.) built fortresses to protect against invasion from the south.

As the absolute power of the pharaohs began to decrease over time, Nubia began to enjoy greater political independence. This independence led to the establishment of the Kushite kingdom some time after 2000 B.C.., Egypt was also weakened, for a time at least, by the Hyksos (HIK-sohs) invasion in about 1670 B.C.., The Hyksos recognized Kush as a nation with equal to their own.

The Nineteenth Dynasty, which ended in about 1186 B.C., was the last strong line of native Egyptian pharaohs. Meanwhile Kush emerged as a strong political and religious entity, with its capital at Napata (NAH-puh-tuh) along the Nile in what is now the country of Sudan.

A strong Egyptian influence

Heavily influenced by Egypt's language, religion, and culture, Kush's relation to Egypt was like that of Macedon to Greece; thus Piankhi (pee-AHNG-kee) could be compared with Philip II. Like Philip, he did not see himself as a conqueror of a foreign land but as someone of a similar culture helping to restore the other nation—Egypt, in this case—to the right path.

The Egyptian influence on Kush was particularly strong in the area of religion. As Egypt faded (and along with it, the peoples' beliefs in the old deities), the Kushites embraced the old-time religion with even more enthusiasm. By the 700s B.C., the favorite god in Egypt was the relatively new deity, Ptah (TAH). Therefore, in the 700s B.C., the priests of Amon (AH-muhn) or Amon-Ra, once recognized as the supreme god, moved their headquarters south, to Napata.

The priests' action would have a great impact on Kushite society. Not only did the priests increase the peoples' zeal for Amon but they probably formed a strong bond with the leaders at Napata. One of these was Kashta (KAHSH-tuh), whose eighteen-year-old son Piankhi assumed the throne in 751 B.C.

Conflict with Tefnakhte

Historians know virtually nothing about Piankhi's early life or the first years of his reign. Thanks to an extraordinary stela, or pillar, later erected by the king in Napata, however, plenty is known about his invasion of Egypt.

What sparked the invasion was an attempt by Tefnakhte (tef-NAHK-tuh) to take over Egypt in about 730 B.C. At that time, leadership over the once-unified kingdom was splintered among many warring princes, among them Tefnakhte. As a Libyan, he was in more or less the same position with regard to Egypt as Piankhi—in other words, both came from cultures that bore a strong Egyptian influence. Piankhi opposed Tefnakhte primarily on religious grounds, because he viewed northern Egypt, Tefnakhte's base, as a place where Egyptian religion and culture had been allowed to decline.

Tefnakhte already controlled the Nile Delta and much of northern Egypt. When he laid siege to the city of Heracleopolis (hair-uh-klee-AHP-oh-lis) in the middle of the country, various Egyptian princes begged Piankhi to step in. He was not eager to make war, an unusual characteristic for an ancient monarch, especially one who—as later events would show—was certainly no coward.

Initially Piankhi sent in two armies but did not go himself. The armies scored a series of victories, but Piankhi became extremely displeased when he learned that they had allowed some of the enemy's forces to escape—including Tefnakhte himself. According to the Napata stela, when he heard this news, "His Majesty raged like a panther. 'Have they allowed survivors to remain from the armies of Lower Egypt? As I live and as . . . my father Amon favors me, I will fare downstream myself and I will overturn what [Tefnakhte] has done and will cause him to desist from fighting for all eternity.'"

Conquering Egypt

So Piankhi went to Egypt, but in a characteristic move that shows that he placed the highest importance on his spiritual life, he first stopped in Thebes (THEEBZ) to worship Amon at Karnak (KAHR-nak), a major temple site there.

Once this was done, he turned to the conquest of Egypt. First he sent a message to the ruler of Hermopolis (huhr-MAHP-oh-lis), a city allied with Tefnakhte: if the ruler would surrender to Piankhi's armies, then laying siege on the city, Piankhi would spare his life. Piankhi made good on his promise, another unusual act for an ancient king. When word of this decision spread, it encouraged other leaders to surrender as well.

Again and again, Piankhi demonstrated his capacity for mercy. At one point, he had an opportunity to kill Tefnakhte's son and chose not to. Had he done so, he would have been no worse than a hundred other ancient kings and emperors—for instance, Caesar Augustus, who had Cleopatra's son murdered. Instead, Piankhi let his conscience be his guide.

He was also a brilliant military commander. When he reached Memphis, Tefnakhte's headquarters in northern Egypt, Piankhi found a hole in the defenses of the otherwise heavily protected city. The Nile formed its eastern side. Because the defenders assumed an attack would come from the land, they had left that side unprotected. Therefore Piankhi ordered his men to steal all the boats in the harbor, which they used along with their own to cross over to the eastern walls. These they soon scaled and had entered the city before Tefnakhte's forces even had time to respond.

Giving glory to Amon

Having subdued Memphis, Piankhi had gained control of the entire country. He then went around the land, worshiping Amon and other deities at various sites. Everywhere he went as he made his way through Egypt, people were impressed by the glory of his court, particularly his crown (Nubia was a land rich in gold), as well as his mercy for the conquered.

Clearly he was on fire for his god without being a fanatic. In fact there is only one incident which suggests religious intolerance: when he had conquered Egypt and all its princes came to pay their respects to him, he refused to meet with some of them because they ate fish. Apparently his version of the Egyptian religion, like that of the Israelites, viewed certain foods as spiritually unclean.

Piankhi took an unusual approach, for an ancient ruler, from the beginning to the end of his conquests. At the end, instead of remaining to revel in the glories of Egypt, he returned to Napata and never ventured north again. He devoted his last years to building a new temple to Amon in Napata.

Despite his declaration at the beginning of the invasion, however, he did not "cause [Tefnakhte] to desist from fighting for all eternity." Though the Libyan prince pledged, according to the Napata stela, that "I will not disobey the King's command," in fact he later set his son on the Egyptian throne. It fell to Piankhi's brother Shabaka (SHAH-buh-kuh;

ruled 716–695 B.C.) to reassert Kushite authority in Egypt, which he did in 712 B.C.

Shabaka's invasion officially established the Twenty-Fifth Dynasty of Egypt, which ruled that nation until 667 B.C. During that time, the Nubian pharaohs continued Piankhi's tradition of sincere devotion to Amon. Amunirdis I (ah-moo-NEER-dis), Piankhi's and Shabaka's sister, held an important position as "god's wife of Amon" in the temple at Thebes.

For More Information

Books

Bianchi, Robert Steven. *The Nubians: People of the Ancient Nile.* Brookfield, CT: Millbrook Press, 1994.

Encyclopedia of World Biography, 2nd ed. Detroit: Gale, 1998.

Johnson, E. Harper. *Piankhy the Great.* New York: T. Nelson, 1962.

Russman, Edna. *Nubian Kingdoms.* New York: Franklin Watts, 1998.

Service, Pamela F. *The Ancient African Kingdom of Kush.* New York: Marshall Cavendish, 1998.

Spradling, Mary Mace. *In Black and White,* 3rd ed. Detroit: Gale, 1980.

Web Sites

"Amenirdas I." http://www.joslyn.org/permcol/ancient/pages/amen.html (accessed on July 7, 1999).

"Egypt: The Long Goodbye." http://www.ancientsites.com/~Raseneb_Amenemheb/gnosis/sais.htm (accessed on July 7, 1999).

"Twenty-Fifth Dynasty." *Egyptian Ministry of Tourism.* http://interoz.com/egypt/hdyn25.htm (accessed on July 5, 1999).

"Twenty-Fourth Dynasty." *Egyptian Ministry of Tourism.* http://interoz.com/egypt/hdyn24.htm (accessed on July 5, 1999).

Plato

Born 427 B.C.
Died 347 B.C.

Greek philosopher

He has been praised for his contributions to Christian thought and criticized as one who paved the way for Communism. Yet Plato knew of neither Christianity nor Soviet Communism: the former came into being more than three centuries after his death and the latter some nineteen centuries after that. His influence, however, has spread throughout the ages. One thing can be said of this Greek philosopher that can be said of only a few kings and conquerors: the world would be a different place if he had not lived.

A student of Socrates and teacher of Aristotle (see entry), Plato flourished in the twilight of Classical Greece. Socrates provided the foundation for Western thought, but Plato and Aristotle gave it form. What the two men offered were two sharply opposed systems of thought. It is hardly an exaggeration to say that all Western thinkers since that time have operated in the tradition either of Aristotle or of his brilliant teacher.

The Greek way of philosophy

The word *philosophy* means literally "love of learning." Philosophy itself is a discipline that seeks to reach a general

Until philosophers are kings, or the kings and princes of the world have the spirit and power of philosophy . . . cities will never have rest from their evils.

The Republic

The Library of Congress.

157

understanding of values and reality. It is difficult work, and—unless one publishes a book or gets a job teaching philosophy—there is no money in it.

Many people scorn philosophy as an impractical pursuit, yet there is no aspect of daily life, from TV commercials to clothes to popular expressions, that cannot ultimately be traced to the work of some great thinker. In their lifetimes, philosophers are practically invisible. Later, as their ideas take hold among a new generation, it is impossible not to see their effects.

Western philosophy had its birth in Greece in the mid–500s B.C. The first philosopher was Thales (THAY-leez; c. 62?–547 B.C.). Thales proposed that "everything is water"—in other words, he thought that the whole world is in a fluid state, like water.

Thales and those who followed him are often called pre-Socratic philosophers (soh-KRAT-ik). Socrates (SAHK-ruh-teez; c. 470–399 B.C.) revolutionized philosophy. Socrates became Plato's teacher, and through him had a profound effect on the future of the world.

A young man with promise

The most famous student of Socrates was born in Athens with the name Aristocles (uh-RIS-tuh-kleez) but came to be known as Plato (PLAY-toe; "wide") because of his broad shoulders. Plato's family was wealthy, and his father groomed him to become a political leader. But Plato lived at a time of great turmoil. As it turned out, life had another role in store for him.

It must have been a disappointment to Plato to see his city, once so great, begin to fade just as he came of age. In 404 B.C., an exhausted and demoralized Athens surrendered to Sparta, ending the Peloponnesian War. It was the beginning of hard times for Athens, as it came under the leadership of an oligarchy controlled by Sparta—not exactly the kind of environment that encouraged free spirits. With his aristocratic upbringing, Plato had an opportunity to join the oligarchy, but he chose not to. Instead, he became attracted to the teachings of Socrates.

Student of Socrates

At that time, the world of philosophy was dominated by a group called the Sophists (SAH-fistz). The Sophists were more interested in winning arguments than they were in the truth. Although the early Socrates is sometimes identified with the Sophists, he soon rose above them. Instead of contenting himself with trivial word-games and other pursuits typical of the Sophists, he encouraged people to question themselves and their world.

Naturally, this made Socrates few friends among the Sophists—and his habit of questioning the system in Athens earned him enemies in high places. Eventually they brought him to trial and executed him. Plato, who was with the great teacher at the time of his death, was profoundly affected by the event. It changed the whole course of his life. Having permanently set aside any plans for a career in politics, he became a wandering student and philosopher.

Years of wandering

As with many ancient figures, details about Plato's life are scanty, particularly because it was an Athenian practice not to mention one's living contemporaries in writing: thus Plato wrote extensively about Socrates, who was dead; but his own student Aristotle (AIR-i-stah-tuhl) barely mentioned Plato.

It appears that between 400 and 386 B.C., Plato wandered throughout the Mediterranean world. At age twenty-seven, just after the death of Socrates, he went to Megara (MEH-guh-rah), a seaport west of Athens, and lived with a friend there. Later he moved to Cyrene (sie-REEN), a Greek city in Libya. Apparently he then went to Egypt and studied mathematics and history with priests there.

His stay in Egypt, reported by the Roman statesman and writer Cicero, is the basis for the claim by Afrocentrists that Plato "stole" his ideas from Africa. No doubt he was greatly influenced by the wisdom of Egypt, a culture already more than 3,000 years old, but Plato was probably bright enough to come up with his ideas on his own.

In Athens and Sicily

In any case, Plato did not stay in Egypt long: by 395 B.C., at age thirty-two, he was back in Athens. In the following year, he took part in the Athenian revolt against Sparta. As that war wound down, in 387 B.C., he set out for Italy, where the Greeks had a number of colonies.

He visited several cities, then wound up in Sicily. There he met Dionysius the Elder (die-uh-NISH-uhs; c. 430–367 B.C.). Legend holds that after Plato criticized Dionysius's cruelty, the tyrant sold him into slavery, and that Plato's friend in Cyrene, the philosopher Anniceris (an-uh-SARE-uhs), had to buy him back.

The Academy

Supposedly Plato's friends raised a sum of money to pay back Anniceris. When Anniceris declined the funds, Plato used them to purchase a grove outside Athens called Academus (uh-KAD-uh-mehs). This, the first "academy," would last for nine centuries, until the Byzantine emperor Justinian I closed it as a pagan institution.

At the Academy, Plato taught his students a variety of subjects, from literature to mathematics to music to history. The Academy became something of a running joke because of the students' unusual clothing: caps, canes, and short gowns—clothing that, in a modified version, is still worn by scholars at graduation ceremonies, even in high schools.

Plato's writings

As with Socrates, Plato excelled at the spoken word. His greatest pupil, Aristotle, would later refer to the great teacher's lectures as his "unwritten doctrine." But he also wrote a great deal, first in the years of wandering and later at the Academy.

Most of these works took the form of a dialogue (DIE-uh-lawg), a type of conversation involving questions and answers. It was a method Socrates had used in his teaching, and so did Plato: in both teaching and writing, the use of dialogues caused the student or reader to actively participate.

In most of Plato's dialogues, Socrates occupied center stage. Plato started out with a desire to keep Socrates's memory alive in writing, and this he did, setting down ideas introduced by Socrates. Later, however, Plato increasingly brought in his own ideas; thus the Socrates of the *Republic,* written while he was at the Academy, is more Plato than Socrates.

The forms

It is difficult to sum up the ideas of such a wide-ranging thinker as Plato, but the foundation of the Platonic (pluh-TAHN-ik) philosophy was the idea of *forms*. Plato believed that when a person imagines a red object, for instance, they are calling up a specific form or idea; that is, that there is such a thing as "Red," which is greater and more "real" than any red objects in the physical world.

That physical world, in Plato's view, was far less important, and certainly less permanent, than the world of Ideas or forms. In later centuries, these notions would be meshed with Christian concepts. Thus many scholars saw a Platonic influence in a famous passage by the Apostle Paul (see entry): "For now we see through a glass, darkly; but then [in heaven] face to face." (1 Corinthians 13:12).

Certainly it is hard to imagine that Paul, as a well-educated man of his day, would *not* have come in contact with Plato's work. Many early Christians also agreed with Plato's emphasis on the mental or spiritual world over the physical world.

The quest for a philosopher-king

Out of these ideas about the fundamental nature of reality came certain views about government, most clearly expressed in Plato's greatest work, *The Republic*. There will always be people ruled by their bodies rather than by their minds, Plato believed. Therefore society should be controlled by those with the highest aims—those who are ruled by their minds, not their bodies. Thus he envisioned a class of philosophers who would also be kings, and kings who would also be philosophers.

In 367 B.C., it seemed he had his chance to put these ideas into practice when he went to tutor Dionysius the

Hypatia of Alexandria

One of the remarkable things about Plato was the fact that he treated women more or less as equals to men, a highly unusual idea in the Athens of his day. It is not surprising that the only known female philosopher of ancient times was a Neo-Platonist, Hypatia of Alexandria (hie-PAY-shuh; A.D. 370–415).

Hypatia became a teacher at the Neo-Platonic School in Alexandria. In A.D. 400 she was appointed director of the school. Though her writings did not survive, it was said that her lectures were lively, exciting events in which she wove together a number of subjects. She was also an inventor. Along with Synesius of Cyrene (suh-NEE-zhuhs; c. A.D. 370–413),

she apparently developed an astrolabe (as-truh-LABE), a device used for measuring the movement of bodies in the sky. They also worked together on several other inventions.

It was said that Hypatia was as beautiful and virtuous as she was wise. Not surprisingly, given her many good qualities—and the fact that she was a woman—she attracted enemies as well. One of these was powerful: Cyril (SEER-uhl, c. A.D. 375–444), Bishop of Alexandria. It is not clear how much influence Cyril had over the events leading to her death, but it is clear that in A.D. 415 she was brutally attacked and killed by a group of "Christians."

Younger, son of the tyrant who had once sold him into slavery. But Plato's experience was much like that of Confucius (see entry) with the Duke of Lü. Dionysius was more interested in drinking and revelry—pursuits of the body—than he was in learning. He readily believed a story by a jealous official that Plato's teaching was part of an Athenian plot to gain control of Sicily.

Plato packed up his things and returned to Athens, where he spent the remaining twenty years of his life teaching at the Academy. He would live on in part through Aristotle, the student whose system of thought was completely opposed to his, and through many Platonists and Neo-Platonists("new" Platonists) such as Hypatia [see sidebar]. His ideas would continue to hold appeal up to the present day. Various Platonist movements would rise and fall in the world of philosophy.

In the 1500s, the Englishman Sir Thomas More (1478–1535) wrote a book entitled *Utopia* (yoo-TOH-pee-uh), in which he envisioned an ideal state akin to Plato's Republic. "Utopia," Greek for "no place," became an English word for an ideal state. Many believed that the Russian Revolution of 1917, which established the Soviet system, would put in place a utopia. In fact what it established was a tyranny ruled by a group of educated Communist Party members. Some observers saw this as a terrifying outgrowth of Plato, but it is unfair to blame Plato for Soviet Communism. He was writing about politics in the Greek city-states. He could not possibly have imagined the effect his ideas would have on the world of the future.

For More Information

Books

Furan, Rodney. *Twelve Great Philosophers*. Mankato, MN: Oddo Publishing, 1968.

Nardo, Don. *The Trial of Socrates*. San Diego, CA: Lucent Books, 1997.

Pittenger, W. Norman. *Plato, His Life and Teachings*. New York: Franklin Watts, 1971.

Silverberg, Robert. *Socrates*. New York: Putnam, 1965.

Illustrated Introduction to Philosophy. New York: DK Publishing, Inc., 1998.

Turlington, Bayly. *Socrates, The Father of Western Philosophy*. New York: F. Watts, 1969.

Web Sites

Exploring Plato's Dialogues. http://plato.evansville.edu/ (accessed on July 9, 1999).

"Greek Philosophy: Plato." http://www.wsu.edu:8080/~dee/GREECE/PLATO.HTM (accessed on July 9, 1999).

"Greek Philosophy: Pre-Socratic Philosophy." http://www.wsu.edu:8080/~dee/GREECE/PRESOC.HTM (accessed on July 9, 1999).

"Hypatia of Alexandria." http://www.cosmopolis.com/people/hypatia.html (accessed on July 9, 1999).

"Hypatia of Alexandria (355–415)." http://www.mala.bc.ca/~mcneil/hypatia.htm (accessed on July 9, 1999).

"Hypatia of Alexandria—Ancient/Classical History." http://ancienthistory.tqn.com/library/weekly/aa033198.htm (accessed on July 9, 1999).

"Plato for the Young Inquirer." http://www-adm.pdx.edu/user/sinq/greekciv/philosophy/plato/candace.htm (accessed on July 9, 1999).

Sargon of Akkad

Born c. 2334 B.C.
Died 2279 B.C.

Mesopotamian king and conqueror

Though the name Sargon of Akkad is not as well known as those of other ancient conquerors such as Alexander the Great (see entry), it certainly deserves to be. One of the first historic figures outside of Egypt about whom reliable information has been found, Sargon was also the first empire-builder in history. Alexander, who lived nearly 2,000 years after Sargon, might never have conquered such a vast realm if there had not been rulers before him to inspire the dream of uniting many lands under one system.

A legendary figure

In Mesopotamia at the dawn of history, there was a good king named Urukagina of Lagash (perhaps pronounced "oo-ROOK-a-gee-nah"; LAY-gahsh). Records report that he "gave liberty to his people," but he was overthrown by Lugal-zaggisi (loo-guhl-ZAG-uh-see; 2300s B.C.). The latter destroyed the temple of the city's goddess, causing a poet of the day to write sadly: "For the city, alas, the treasures, my soul doth sigh .... O Lady of my city, desolated, when wilt thou return?" The people longed for someone to save them from Lugal-zaggisi; in fact there was already such a ruler in the city of Agade (uh-GAH-duh), capital of Akkad (AH-kahd).

Legend holds that Sargon came from the lower classes of society. His mother may have been a prostitute, and he was probably an illegitimate child. It is hard to separate myth from reality: a thousand years before Moses, it was said of Sargon that his mother placed him a boat made out of reeds, covered it with tar, and floated him down a river to where he was rescued.

Man of the people

Unlike Moses, however, Sargon's rescuer was not royalty, but someone of the lower classes himself, a simple gardener named Akki. Akki raised Sargon, and as the boy grew up, he tended gardens with his adopted father.

Perhaps they took care of the king's garden. Certainly those around Sargon must have realized he was a bright lad. As a young man he went to work in the royal house, as cup-bearer to Ur-Zababa (probably "uhr-ZAH-buh-buh"), king over the city-state of Kish. This was a highly important position in ancient times. It was the cup-bearer's job to ensure that no one poisoned the king's drinks. The cup-bearer had to be trusted and usually exerted great influence over the king.

Ur-Zababa was probably the king overthrown by Lugal-zaggisi. Apparently, while the latter was away conquering another town, Sargon raised an army and attacked Lugal-zaggisi's capital of Uruk. The defenders of Uruk put up a desperate fight, reinforced by armies from neighboring city-states, but Sargon's force was too strong. Meanwhile, it seems that Lugal-zaggisi returned and found his city under attack. Sargon captured him and brought him to the city of Nippur (ni-POOR) in chains. Now Sargon was undisputed ruler over the region.

King and conqueror

It appears that Sargon's victory marked the first time that the land had a Semitic (seh-MIT-ik) leader, someone from the language group that would include most of the later Mesopotamian kingdoms as well as Israel and the Arab world. Sargon went on to conquer territory, earning for himself the titles "King of Universal Dominion"—that is, ruler of all that

Liu Pang

Like Sargon of Akkad, Liu Pang (lee-OO BAHNG; sometimes spelled Liu Bang; 256–195 B.C.; ruled 206–195 B.C.) rose from humble origins to become ruler of a great empire. Later given the name Kao Tsu (gowd-ZOO), he founded the Han Dynasty, which would rule China for some four centuries. So great was the influence of the Han that, although the English name for the country comes from the earlier Ch'in Dynasty, the Chinese typically refer to themselves as "the Han people."

Born the son of peasants, Liu Pang grew up in a time of troubles as the Chou Dynasty (ZHOH) passed to the Ch'in. In 221 B.C. the Ch'in ruler Shih Huang Ti became China's first emperor. Liu went to work as a police officer. There were plenty of police under the Ch'in dictatorship. Liu Pang became one of many who longed to see the cruel empire overthrown.

Eventually he became leader of a rebel force; so too did Hsiang Yü (shee-AHNG yoo-EE; sometimes spelled Xiang Yu; 233–202 B.C.). The two rivals came from very different backgrounds: Hsiang Yü was a nobleman, and when he captured the capital city in 206 B.C., it seemed certain that he would become the new emperor. But in fact Liu Pang managed to overcome the forces of Hsiang Yü, and the latter became a tragic figure celebrated in the classic Chinese opera *Xiang Yu the Conqueror Bids Farewell to His Concubine.*

Liu Pang went on to found an empire that allowed the Chinese people considerably more freedom than the Ch'in Dynasty had. On the other hand, Liu Pang had no mercy on his enemies, and (perhaps because he knew about rebellion firsthand) he crushed any attempt to revolt against him. He was a friend to the peasants of China, lowering their taxes and strengthening the agricultural economy, but as an uneducated and possibly illiterate peasant himself, he had little use for scholars.

The followers of Confucius (see entry) would not come into favor until later, under the most famous Han emperor, Wu Ti. Another legacy of Liu Pang was the tradition of peasant-led uprisings. More than 2,100 years later, widespread discontent would help bring another peasant warlord, Mao Zedong—China's most influential leader of modern times—to power.

exists—and "the Great." He marched southward, taking cities as he went, then symbolically washed his weapons in the Persian Gulf. This would be a gesture used many times by ancient kings, most often meaning that their conquests were finished. In Sargon's case it was not true.

He added all of Sumer to his holdings, then began moving north and west all the way to what is now southern Turkey. Next, he marched eastward, making many conquests until he controlled a large part of Mesopotamia and lands beyond. It was later said that he sent armies to India, Egypt, and Ethiopia. It is unlikely he would have had much success in North Africa, because the extremely powerful pharaohs of the Old Kingdom were then in control.

It is certainly probable, however, that Akkad under Sargon had trade contacts with civilizations as far away as the Indus Valley; Oman (oh-MAHN) on the Arabian Peninsula; and possibly even Crete. To administer his vast empire, Sargon put Semitic officials in charge over cities far and wide. He also built a capital at Agade, not far from Kish. There, according to surviving records, he ruled a huge court: "5,400 men ate bread daily before him."

First great Mesopotamian ruler

Sargon built the first empire in history, but it did not last long. By 2150 B.C., the nomadic Gutians (GOO-tee-uhns) invaded from the mountains to the north. The torch of civilization passed to the city-state of Ur.

By then, Sargon's name had passed into legend. He became a favorite subject of poets and storytellers. Biblical scholars believe that he may have been Nimrod, mentioned in the Book of Genesis (10:8), "who grew up to be a mighty hunter before the Lord."

Throughout the ages, Sargon endured, symbolizing the dream of uniting all Mesopotamian peoples under a Semitic empire. The Assyrians came as close to doing so as anyone. Some 1,500 years after Sargon, when one of the their rulers assumed the throne, he did so with a name that announced him as a great conqueror: Sargon II (ruled 721–705 B.C.).

For More Information

Books

Durant, Will. *The Story of Civilization,* Volume I: *Our Oriental Heritage.* New York: Simon and Schuster, 1954, pp. 121-22.

Encyclopedia of World Biography. Detroit: Gale, 1998.

Kramer, Samuel Noah. *The Sumerians: Their History, Culture, and Character.* Chicago: University of Chicago Press, 1963, pp. 59-61.

Lewis, Brian. *The Sargon Legend: A Study of the Akkadian Text and the Tale of the Hero Who Was Exposed at Birth.* Cambridge, MA: American Schools of Oriental Research, 1980.

Pollard, Michael. *Empire Builders.* Ada, OK: Garrett Educational Corp., 1992.

Web Sites

"Akkad." *Information Please Almanac.* http://www.infoplease.com/ce5/CE001017.html (accessed on June 26, 1999).

"The Great Wind." http://www.okcom.net/~ggao/Asia/China/liupang1.html (accessed on June 26, 1999).

"The Legend of Sargon of Akkadê, c. 2300 BCE." *Ancient History Sourcebook.* http://www.fordham.edu/halsall/ancient/2300sargon1.html (accessed on June 26, 1999).

"Liu Bang." http://www.aohua.com/yule/poems/han/explain/he020001.txt (accessed on June 26, 1999).

"The Rise and Fall of Xiang Yu." http://www.sh.com/culture/legend/xiang.htm (accessed on June 26, 1999).

"Sargon—Did He Exist?" http://www.mazzaroth.com/ChapterFour/SargonDidHeExist.htm (accessed on June 26, 1999).

"Sumerian Civilization." http://www.republic.k12.mo.us/highschool/teachers/tstephen/meso-2.htm (accessed on June 26, 1999).

Scientists and Mathematicians

Hippocrates
Born c. 460 B.C.
Died c. 377 B.C.

Greek physician and anatomist

Hipparchus
Born 190 B.C.
Died 126 B.C.

Greek astronomer and mathematician

Euclid
Born c. 325 B.C.
Died c. 250 B.C.

Greek mathematician

Ptolemy
Born c. A.D. 100
Died A.D. 170

Greek astronomer

Archimedes
Born c. 287 B.C.
Died 212 B.C.

Greek mathematician, physicist, and inventor

Galen
Born c. A.D. 130
Died c. A.D. 200

Greek physician and anatomist

The work of ancient sculptors, writers, and even philosophers is as valuable today as it was in ancient times. Of course, many discoveries by ancient scientists and mathematicians have been overturned in light of later evidence. Yet Hippocrates, Euclid, Archimedes, Hipparchus, Ptolemy, Galen, and others—all Greeks, though the later ones lived in a world controlled by Rome—created the foundations of modern mathematics and science. Several of them are recognized as the "fathers" of their disciplines. All deserve to be honored for their roles in expanding humankind's understanding of the world.

Hippocrates

Born on the island of Cos (KAWS) off Asia Minor, Hippocrates (hih-PAHK-ruh-teez) came from a family of physicians. Later he taught at the medical school in Cos, one of the most prominent in the Greek world. Famous in his lifetime, he traveled around Greece and other lands, lecturing on his principles of medicine. He died in Larissa (luh-RIH-suh) on the eastern coast of Greece.

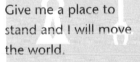

Give me a place to stand and I will move the world.

Archimedes, describing his lever and fulcrum

Hippocrates earned his reputation of "father of medicine" because he was the first doctor to identify the causes of disease in nature rather than claim the gods caused them. In the more than sixty books attributed to him (probably written by his followers), he established careful methods for medical treatment.

He believed that doctors should simply aid the body in healing itself, and he stressed diet, rest, and a clean environment. These are very modern concepts, but Hippocrates was less forward-thinking in his belief that diseases came from an imbalance of four "humors," or bodily fluids. One of these humors was blood. Medieval physicians' acceptance of this idea would lead to the ghastly practice of blood-letting—that is, of bleeding patients to "heal" them.

One of Hippocrates' greatest contributions to medicine was in the area of ethics, or moral behavior, on the part of a doctor. The Hippocratic Oath (hip-oh-KRAT-ik), probably written by his followers, instructs physicians to place the patient's well-being above all other concerns. Medical students today often swear to a version of the Hippocratic Oath, which can be found on display in many doctors' offices.

Hippocrates was the first doctor to identify the causes of disease in nature, not as a result of the gods' displeasure. *Corbis-Bettmann. Reproduced by permission.*

Euclid

Geometry is a branch of mathematics dealing with various shapes, their properties, and their measurements. Though not the "father of geometry," Euclid (YOO-klid) collected all the knowledge gathered by those before him and established a system that came to be known as Euclidean (yoo-KLID-ee-uhn) geometry. Beyond the fact that he founded a school of mathematics in Alexandria in about 300 B.C., however, little is known of Euclid's life.

Euclid's book *The Elements* discusses a variety of subjects related to geometry, in particular planes, or flat surfaces; irrational numbers; solid geometry, which deals with three-dimensional figures such as boxes; and number theory, which examines the properties of integers (IN-teh-jurz)—that is, all the positive and negative whole numbers, as well as zero.

The Elements, with its carefully written, understandable style, became a model for mathematical and scientific works over the next two millennia. Likewise Euclid's plane geometry was the *only* geometry until a number of mathematicians in the 1800s began developing non-Euclidean forms.

Archimedes

Born in the Greek town of Syracuse in Sicily, Archimedes (ahr-ki-MEE-deez) was related to one of that city's kings. It is said that while trying to weigh the gold in the king's crown, he discovered the principle of buoyancy (BOOY-uhn-see). The principle of buoyancy states that when an object is placed in water, it loses exactly as much weight as the weight of the water it has displaced. Supposedly Archimedes made his discovery in the bath and was so excited that he ran naked through the streets shouting *"Eureka!"* (I have found it.)

Physics (FIZ-iks) deals with the physical properties of objects and their interaction with one another, involving factors such as mass and acceleration. It is a pure science, not dealing with practical matters. Archimedes, on the other hand, put his discoveries to much practical use. Among his most important inventions was the Archimedes screw, a device for pumping water still used in many parts of the world. Through geometry, Archimedes proved that a lever, or bar, and a fulcrum (FUHL-krum), an object it rests against, can greatly increase the power of its operator. This led to his development of pulley systems and cranes.

His creations, most notably the catapult—which Rome later adopted as its own—aided Syracuse in a war against the Romans. He is also said to have developed a set of lenses which, using the light of the Sun, could set ships on fire at a distance. He may have been a little too successful in his wartime efforts: Archimedes was killed by a Roman soldier when Rome took Syracuse.

Archimedes working on a math problem.
Corbis-Bettmann. Reproduced by permission.

Known as the "father of experimental science," the use of models and trials to test scientific principles, Archimedes was also a mathematician. He came up with the first reliable figure for *pi* (PIE)—symbolized by the Greek letter π—which is used in calculating the area of a circle. Pi, typically rendered as 3.1416, is an irrational number, meaning that there is an apparently infinite amount of digits following the decimal point, with no repeating pattern. In his work with curved surfaces, Archimedes used a type of mathematics similar to calculus (KAL-kyoo-lus), which would only be developed some 2,000 years later.

Hipparchus

Hipparchus (hih-PAHR-kuhs), who probably lived in Asia Minor, wrote a number of works that have not survived, so most knowledge of him comes through Ptolemy [see below] and others. He created the first star catalogue, a map of the sky showing the position of the stars. He developed an early version of the astrolabe. He was the first to note what came to be known as the precession of the equinoxes (EEK-win-ahk-sez), a shift in the Earth's position relative to the rest of the galaxy.

Hipparchus calculated the length of a year at about 365.25 days, a great improvement on the figure derived earlier by Babylonian astronomers. He aided greatly in the understanding of eclipses, helping people to realize that these were not signs from the gods, but regularly occurring events. He also developed an accurate measurement of the distance between the Earth and the Moon.

As with Archimedes (see entry), Hipparchus had to develop a new type of math to aid him in his calculations. This became trigonometry (trig-oh-NAHM-eh-tree), the study of the properties of triangles and their applications. Finally, he became the first to establish a system of latitude, or north-south position, and longitude, or east-west position, to pinpoint locations on the Earth's surface.

Hipparchus, standing outside the Observatory at Alexandria, looking at the starry sky through one of his tools. *Archive Photos. Reproduced by permission.*

Ptolemy

Aristarchus (ahr-uh-STAHR-kuhs; c. 270 B.C.) had advanced the heliocentric (heel-ee-oh-SEN-trik) view of astronomy, holding that the Earth and other planets revolve around the Sun. Hipparchus (see entry), however, adopted a geocentric (jee-oh-SIN-trik) view, claiming that the Earth is fixed, and the Sun and other planets revolve around it. Unfortunately, the Alexandrian astronomer Ptolemy (TAHL-uh-mee), an influential follower of Hipparchus, accepted the geocentric view.

Ptolemy—not to be confused with the Greek ruler of Egypt and his descendants—developed a system of astronomy that would remain in use for some fourteen centuries. When science flourished in the Arab world during the Middle Ages, his book—known by its Arabic name, *Almagest*—became the bible of astronomy. Because of this, the geocentric view became the standard opinion until Nicholas Copernicus (kuh-PURN-i-kus; 1473–1543) disproved it.

**Greek astronomer Ptolemy
mistakenly believed that the
Sun and other planets
revolved around the Earth.**
Library of Congress.

Ptolemy also shared in Hipparchus's rejection of calculations made by Eratosthenes (ur-uh-TAHS-thuh-neez; c. 276–c. 194 B.C.) The latter, a librarian of Alexandria, had made a remarkably accurate measurement of the Earth's size. Because of Ptolemy's mistaken understanding, Christopher Columbus (1451–1506) would later drastically underestimate the westward distance from Europe to Asia; as it turned out, there was a whole New World in between.

Galen

Raised in the city of Pergamum (PUR-guh-mum) in Asia Minor, Galen studied at the medical school attached to the temple of Asclepias (ah-SLEE-pee-uhs), the Greek god of medicine. At age twenty, he journeyed to Alexandria and other cities, where he had an opportunity to study anatomy by working with skeletons. But medical students were forbidden to work on dead bodies for religious reasons.

Back in Pergamum, however, twenty-eight-year-old Galen began working as a physician for the gladiators there. This work gave him plenty of opportunity to study "blood and guts." In A.D. 161, Galen went to Rome, where he became well-known as a lecturer and wrote some of his many works, 120 of which survive. He also acted as physician to the emperor Marcus Aurelius (see entry). He served the two emperors who followed and probably died in Rome in about A.D. 200.

Although he could not use human bodies, Galen dissected a wide variety of animals and made a number of observations, some of which were not accurate when applied to the human system. He noted a difference between veins, which carry blood to the heart, and arteries, which carry blood from it. Unfortunately, Galen thought that the liver was the principal organ for pumping blood and that the arteries carried a "spirit" he called *pneuma*.

Yet Galen was also quite forward-looking in a number of his observations. He was the first to discover, as all weightlifters today know, that muscles work in pairs: as one expands, another contracts. He demonstrated that an injury to the spinal cord can cause paralysis (puhr-AL-i-sis), or the inability to move one's limbs. He recognized that urine flows from the kidney to the bladder.

His ideas about blood flow, along with his belief in the "humors," were among Galen's negative contributions to medieval medicine. But it was not Galen's fault that no serious anatomists appeared after his time and that his work therefore became scripture. Only with the discoveries of the British anatomist William Harvey (1578–1657) and others would scientists develop a more accurate understanding of how the body works.

Galen was the first to discover that muscles work in pairs: one expands, another contracts. *Archive Photos. Reproduced by permission.*

For More Information

Books

Bendick, Jeanne. *Archimedes and the Door of Science.* Warsaw, ND: Bethlehem Books, 1995.

Bryant-Mole, Karen. *Floating and Sinking.* Des Plaines, IL: Heinemann Interactive Library, 1998.

Gay, Kathlyn. *Science in Ancient Greece.* New York: Franklin Watts, 1998.

Goldberg, Herbert S. *Hippocrates, Father of Medicine.* New York: Franklin Watts, 1963.

Harris, Jacqueline L. *Science in Ancient Rome.* New York: Franklin Watts, 1998.

Lafferty, Peter. *Archimedes.* New York: Bookwright, 1991.

Nardo, Don. *Greek and Roman Science.* San Diego, CA: Lucent Books, 1998.

Web Sites

Archimedes. http://www.mcs.drexel.edu/~crorres/Archimedes/contents.html (accessed on July 11, 1999).

"Galen: A Biographical Sketch." http://web1.ea.pvt.k12.pa.us/medant/galbio.htm (accessed on July 11, 1999).

"Hipparchus of Rhodes." http://www-groups.dcs.st-and.ac.uk/~history/Mathematicians/Hipparchus.ht ml (accessed on July 11, 1999).

Hippocrates's Home Page. http://www.norfacad.pvt.k12.va.us/project/hippocra/hippocra.htm (accessed on July 11, 1999).

"Hippocrates: The Greek Miracle." http://web1.ea.pvt.k12.pa.us/medant/hippint.htm#history (accessed on July 11, 1999).

"Ptolemy, the Man." http://seds.lpl.arizona.edu/nineplanets/psc/theman.html (accessed on July 11, 1999).

Sculptors

Phidias

Born c. 490 B.C.
Died c. 430 B.C.

Polyclitus

Born 400s B.C.

Praxiteles

Born c. 390 B.C.
Died c. 330 B.C.

Greek sculptors

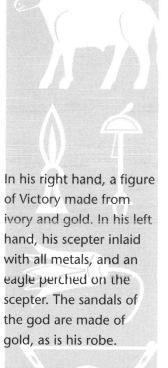

It is no secret that the artists of Greece were among the greatest in the ancient world. Among those greats, three names stand out: Phidias, Polyclitus, and Praxiteles. Phidias is the most famous of the three. Not only did his statue of Athena grace the Parthenon but his work appeared in two of the Seven Wonders of the World [see sidebar]. The work of Polyclitus, whose *Doryphoros* set a standard for human representation, also appeared at one of the Seven Wonders. The same was true of Praxiteles, whose *Aphrodite of Knidos* was a wonder unto itself.

In his right hand, a figure of Victory made from ivory and gold. In his left hand, his scepter inlaid with all metals, and an eagle perched on the scepter. The sandals of the god are made of gold, as is his robe.

Pausanias the Greek, A.D. 100s, describing the Statue of Zeus at Olympus by Phidias

Phidias (c. 490–c. 430 B.C.)

Born in Athens about 490 B.C., Phidias (FID-ee-uhs) came into a world shaped by war—a war with Persia, which Athens later won. It is known that his father's name was Charmides (KAHR-mi-deez), but beyond that there is little information on his early life. With his contemporaries Polyclitus and Myron (MIE-ruhn), he probably studied under Ageladas (aj-uh-LAHD-uhs), a prominent sculptor of the day.

Phidias designed the statue of the goddess Athena, which was placed in the Parthenon. *Corbis-Bettmann. Reproduced by permission.*

Phidias grew up in an Athens confident from its victories over Persia. He found himself in the right place at the right time. Up to then, his most notable works had been statues commemorating the Athenians' victory at Marathon. One of these, a statue of the goddess Athena atop the Acropolis in Athens, was nearly 50 feet (15.2 meters) tall. It was said that sailors far out at sea could glimpse the sun glinting off the bronze tip of Athena's spear.

With the official end of the war in 449 B.C., Athens under the great Pericles (see entry) (PAIR-uh-kleez) undertook a number of building projects. The greatest of these was the Parthenon (PAHR-thuh-nahn), for which Phidias designed a majestic statue of Athena—the *parthenos,* or maiden, for whom the city of Athens was named. This period, around 440 B.C., also saw the other greatest statue of Phidias's career, a gold and ivory statue of Zeus at Olympia [see sidebar].

Unfortunately, Phidias became entangled in a political dispute involving enemies of Pericles, who accused Phidias of stealing part of the gold set aside for Athena's statue. When he proved that he had done no such thing, removing and weighing the gold plates before witnesses, they claimed that he had carved pictures of himself and Pericles on Athena's shield. If true, this would have been a serious offense to the goddess; presumably it was not true, but the enemies of Pericles managed to make the charges stick. Pericles stuck by Phidias to the end, but the sculptor probably died in prison.

Polyclitus (400s B.C.)

It appears that Polyclitus (pah-lee-KLIE-tuhs) came from Sicyon (SIK-ee-ahn), a city-state on the Gulf of Corinth. In many ways, his career mirrors that of his classmate Phidias. Phidias created the gold and ivory statue of Zeus at Olympia; Polyclitus designed a similarly composed statue of Zeus's wife, the goddess Hera, in Argos (AHR-gohs). People said, in fact, that Polyclitus's statue was surpassed only by that of Phidias'.

Later, the two participated, along with two other sculptors, in a competition to create a statue of Artemis (AHR-teh-mis) for her temple at Ephesus [see sidebar]. According to legend, they were allowed to vote. Naturally, each of the sculptors named his own statue the best. But each—Polyclitus included, presumably—named Polyclitus's statue second-best; therefore he won the competition. In fact statues by all four stood in the temple.

Polyclitus seems to have been influenced by the philosopher and mathematician Pythagoras, who was especially concerned with the idea of proportion. Likewise Polyclitus believed that there should be a table of exact proportions (what he called the "canon") for the parts of the body, so that a sculptor could know with certainty, for instance, that a human figure's head should be a certain size in relation to its feet.

His *Doryphoros* (dohr-IF-ohr-ohs), or *Spear Bearer,* is practically an encyclopedia of the canon. The idea of a canon would persist in sculpture thereafter, though it would not necessarily be Polyclitus's canon. Thus in Byzantine times, for instance, people were routinely represented with extraordinarily long bodies, evidence that the artists of that age had lost the ability to "see" the human figure.

Praxiteles (c. 390–c. 330 B.C.)

First to overthrow the canon of Polyclitus was Praxiteles (prak-SIT-uh-leez), who lived about a century later. In his day, Greece was on the verge of its final glories under Alexander. The work of Praxiteles seems to suggest a somewhat more mature, perhaps less innocent, world. Whereas the figures of Polyclitus ripple with muscle, those of Praxiteles make a lack of physical exertion look attractive.

It appears that Praxiteles, too, had a work displayed in the Temple of Artemis at Ephesus, in this case a carved altar. Of the almost sixty works by Praxiteles mentioned by ancient writers, only four survive, and those in fragments. However, because of the many copies made by sculptors throughout the

The Seven Wonders of the Ancient World

The Greek historian Herodotus (see entry) in the 400s B.C. was the first to suggest a list of Seven Wonders of the Ancient World. More than a century later, the chief librarian in Alexandria finalized the list.

Of the Seven Wonders, there are two statues, two tombs, one temple, one lighthouse, and one set of gardens. Five of the seven are from the *Hellenic* world or from closely related cultures, though their locations are scattered over Asia Minor, Greece, and Egypt. In addition to the "Greek" Egyptian lighthouse, there is the purely Egyptian Great Pyramid, as well as the Babylonian Hanging Gardens. The lighthouse was the only structure with a practical, everyday use, and the Pyramid is the only one of the Seven Wonders still standing. The Seven Wonders were:

The Great Pyramid of Egypt: Completed in about 2550 B.C., the Great Pyramid of the pharaoh Cheops (KEE-ahpz) is as tall as a fifty-story building. It is 755 feet (230.1 meters) along a side, meaning that its base would cover ten football fields. It was almost 4,000 years before there would be a taller structure in the Middle East or Europe—the cathedral in Cologne, Germany (built in the 1200s), which is only slightly taller. The pyramid's size is particularly impressive because the people who built it were still living in the Stone Age; furthermore, they apparently did not know about the wheel, and they had only the most basic knowledge of mathematics.

The Hanging Gardens of Babylon: Legend holds that the great Babylonian king Nebuchadnezzar II in the 600s B.C. wanted to build a structure to make his wife happy. She came from the mountainous land of Media and was homesick in the flatlands of Mesopotamia. Therefore he ordered the building of a huge set of terraced structures containing all manner of lush plants watered by a complex network of streams. One Greek visitor described the Hanging Gardens as "a work of art of royal luxury."

The Temple of Artemis at Ephesus: Built in about 550 B.C. by Croesus, king of

Greek and Roman worlds, it is possible to know a fair amount about Praxiteles's work.

His *Hermes* (HEHR-meez) depicts the messenger god holding the infant Dionysus (die-oh-NIE-suhs), who would grow up to become the god of wine. The playful way that Hermes looks down at the baby, who reaches out for something,

Lydia, the temple to the goddess Artemis was located in southwestern Asia Minor. It contained statues by Phidias, Polyclitus, and others, as well as a carved altar by Praxiteles.

The Statue of Zeus at Olympia: Created by Phidias in about 440 B.C. for a temple at the site of the Olympic Games, the statue of Zeus was covered in gold and ivory. Seated, Zeus was 40 feet (12.2 meters) tall. The proportions of the building were such that if he had stood up, his head would have gone through the roof—which only increased the sense of his size.

The Mausoleum at Halicarnassus: Built in the mid-300s B.C., the structure was a tomb for the king Mausollos (MAWZ-uh-luhs), whose region in southwest Asia Minor was a vassal kingdom of the Persian Empire. At the time Mausollos moved his capital to Halicarnassus (hal-i-kahr-NAS-uhs), however, it had achieved a brief independence. The tomb was decorated with all manner of statues either life-size or larger, depicting humans, lions, horses, and other animals. As with the nearby temple of Artemis, a number of Greek sculptors contributed their efforts. Thanks to this structure, an aboveground tomb is called a *mausoleum* (mawz-uh-LEE-uhm).

The Colossus of Rhodes: The Colossus (kuh-LAHS-uhs) was an early example of a huge statue guarding a harbor. It inspired America's own Statue of Liberty. Completed in 282 B.C. to commemorate a military victory for the city-states of Rhodes, a Greek isle, the statue was some 110 feet (33.5 meters) tall. It stood for only fifty-four years before, like several of the Wonders, it was destroyed by an earthquake.

The Lighthouse of Alexandria: Last to be built, some time after 290 B.C., the lighthouse—sometimes called the Pharos Lighthouse (FAIR-ohs)—was also the last to be destroyed, by an earthquake in the A.D. 1300s. Using fire at night and a magnificent mirror, that reflected the sun's rays by day, the lighthouse guided ships safely into the harbor of the Egyptian city. It stood as tall as a forty-story building.

suggests that Praxiteles put a certain wittiness into his sculpture that is usually lacking from the works of Classical Greece.

Also notable is his *Lizard Slayer*, a statue of the god Apollo leaning against a tree, watching a lizard crawl up the trunk. This, too, is a visual joke about a legend involving the gods, in this case a myth concerning Apollo's defeat of a

dragon. Another of Praxiteles's statues, *Eros,* depicted the god of love, whom later artists would show as the chubby Cupid; in his treatment, Eros is a slender youth, lost in dreams.

Finally, there was the *Aphrodite of Knidos,* a nude statue of the goddess of love for which Praxiteles's lover Phryne (FRIE-nee) served as the model. It was so highly prized that, in exchange for the statue, a king offered to pay off the huge debts of the town that owned it; but the people of the town refused.

Praxiteles sculpted the highly-prized *Aphrodite of Knidos. Corbis-Bettman. Reproduced by permission.*

For More Information

Books

Boardman, J. *Greek Art and Architecture.* New York: Harry N. Abrams, 1967.

Corbett, P. E. *The Sculpture of the Parthenon.* Baltimore: Penguin Books, 1959.

Glubok, Shirley. *The Art of Ancient Greece.* Designed by Oscar Krauss. New York: Atheneum, 1963.

Kjellberg, Ernst and Gösta Säflund. *Greek and Roman Art: 3000 B.C. to A.D. 550.* Translated by Peter Fraser. New York: Thomas Y. Crowell, 1970.

Lullies, R. and M. Hirmer. *Greek Sculpture.* London: Thames & Hudson, 1957.

McLeish, Kenneth. *The Seven Wonders of the World.* New York: Cambridge University Press, 1985.

Paris, Pierre. *Manual of Ancient Sculpture.* Edited by Jane E. Harrison. New Rochelle, NY: Aristide D. Caratzas, 1984.

Silverberg, Robert. *The Seven Wonders of the Ancient World.* New York: Crowell-Collier Press, 1970.

Web Sites

"The Seven Wonders of the Ancient World." http://pharos.bu.edu/Egypt/Wonders/ (accessed on June 29, 1999).

"The Parthenon." *Great Buildings Online.* http://buildings.greatbuildings.com/The_Parthenon.html (July 2, 1999).

"Polyclitus (450?–420 B.C.)" http://www.mala.bc.ca/~mcneil/polyclit.htm (accessed on July 2, 1999).

"Praxiteles (ca. 350 B.C.)." http://www.mala.bc.ca/~mcneil/prax.htm (accessed on July 2, 1999).

Ch'in Shih Huang Ti

Born 259 B.C.
Died 210 B.C.

Chinese emperor

He was the first emperor of China, one of the most feared and hated men to ever lead that country. Yet the very name of China, in English, is taken from the short-lived dynasty that he established: Ch'in. Likewise the best-known symbol of China throughout the world, the Great Wall, was the brainchild of Ch'in Shih Huang Ti.

A prince with nerves of steel

For many centuries, China was caught up in periods of turmoil: first the Spring and Autumn Period, then the Warring States Period. From the many kingdoms that had fought for control of the land, six were left by the time a prince named Cheng (JUHNG) was born in the most powerful of those kingdoms, Qin or Ch'in.

Later historians claimed that Cheng was an illegitimate child and that he murdered his father in order to become king of Ch'in; whether or not this is so, he did take the throne at age thirteen. For the first nine years of his reign, he ruled with the supervision of his father's prime minister; but in 238 B.C., when he turned twenty-two, he assumed full control.

I suggest that the official histories, with the exception of the *Memoirs of Ch'in*, be all burnt, and that those who attempt to hide [their books] . . . be forced to bring them to the authorities to be burnt.

Li Ssü, prime minister of Ch'in Shih Huang Ti

Public Domain.

Around the same time, he uncovered a plot against him by his mother's lover and the prime minister: in a show of steely nerves that would later characterize his leadership of China, he had the lover executed and banished the ministers. In place of the prime minister, who later committed suicide, he appointed the scholar Li Ssü (LEE ZOO), who would do his bidding for many years to come.

Conquering all of China

Cheng then turned his attention to conquering the five kingdoms that might pose a threat to Ch'in. He conquered the weakest of them in 230 B.C. and then gradually picked them off. The crown prince of Yan, one of the kingdoms, tried to have him assassinated. It was a mark of the terror Cheng struck in his enemies' hearts that the king of Yan killed his own crown prince in the hope that it would please Cheng.

Cheng added Yan to his territories along with the others. By 221 B.C. he had conquered the entire country. He declared himself emperor of China and chose for himself the title *Huang Ti,* which means "august [aw-GUST; magnificent] emperor." It was not unlike the name given to Octavian when he became the first Roman emperor 190 years later. *Shih* meant "first." He identified himself as the first of all emperors. It was clear he expected his Ch'in Dynasty to last a long, long time.

Establishing his authority

Throughout his reign, Ch'in Shih Huang Ti devoted himself to tightening his grip over the country. He did this by remaking it in his own image. He reorganized the government and established a unified law system that provided extremely cruel punishments for even the slightest crimes. Shih Huang Ti had a fascination with standardizing things, or bringing them into a common system by setting standards for them: not only laws, but the currency, weights and measures, and even the style of writing Chinese characters.

He also standardized the state and local governments down to the level of city blocks, a remarkable feat of organization in an ancient kingdom—and a wonderful means for establishing his authority. He personally appointed every local official. He instituted his own form of "gun control," ordering that citizens give up their weapons. These were melted down and made into statues for his palace.

Shih Huang Ti had a habit of moving people around like a child playing with toy soldiers. He ordered the 120,000 wealthiest and most powerful families in the country to move to his capital, Xian or Sian (shee-AHN) in east central China. This made Xian look like a truly splendid city, and made it easier for him to watch out for anyone who might try to usurp him. He also moved the noble families of the five conquered kingdoms into southwest China, far from their former areas of influence. In 215 B.C., he sent groups north to help establish a human barrier against the nomadic Hsiung-Nu (SHAHNG-noo) or Huns. In 214 B.C. he moved large numbers of Ch'in people into the south when his generals conquered areas there.

The Great Wall and other building projects

The move into the north followed the recovery, by one of Shih Huang Ti's generals, of territories formerly lost to the Hsiung-Nu. Previous kingdoms had built walls to protect themselves against attack by the "barbarians." Shih Huang Ti ordered the repair and extension of these walls. From this command sprang the largest structure built by human hands, the Great Wall of China, which under Ch'in rule (it was later expanded) stretched some 1,500 miles (2,414 kilometers). Eventually it would be even longer. It remains the only man-made object visible from the Moon.

It was said that some 300,000 people worked on the Wall. Thousands died from sickness and starvation. No doubt such slave labor built another of the Ch'in Dynasty's great constructions, a system of three imperial highways. These highways, parts of which survive today, were 300 feet (91.4 meters) wide and stretched some 4,216 miles (6,785 kilometers) in all.

More slave laborers built a palace for Shih Huang Ti. The palace measured 1.5 million square feet (1.39 square meters)—that is, the size of 1,000 average single-family homes in modern-day America, let alone ancient China. Its entrances were equipped with magnets to detect secret weapons; after Shih Huang Ti's death, however, a rebellious general set the palace on fire. Supposedly, it burned for three months.

Aerial view of the Great Wall of China.
AP/Wide World Photos. Reproduced by permission.

One of the most amazing structures built by Shih Huang Ti, however, was his tomb, or mausoleum. It included a vast network of hallways. The builders used great quantities of mercury to create the illusion of moving rivers and seas inside the tomb. Millennia before the deadly traps seen in the movie *Raiders of the Lost Ark,* the builders of Shih Huang Ti's tomb designed the inner room so that anyone who tried to enter it would set off a rain of arrows that would kill them. The tomb, which also contains some 6,000 life-size soldiers and horses, was discovered in 1974. It is one of the greatest archaeological sites in the world.

Declaring war on the scholars

As fascinating as the achievements of Shih Huang Ti's rule were, however, it must be remembered that they were built at a vast cost in human life. Perhaps he could have mistreated the people and gotten away with it. But when Shih

Huang Ti had Li Ssü offend the writers of history—the scholars—they ensured that later generations would know the full extent of his cruelty.

In 213 B.C., some seventy scholars attended a banquet for the emperor's birthday. One scholar happened to remark, with some displeasure, that the Ch'in Dynasty had made a complete break with the past. This prompted Li Ssü—who might be compared with Joseph Goebbels (GUR-buhlz; 1897–1945; "minister of information" in Nazi Germany)—to make a truly frightening speech. He announced, "Now the empire is established and all laws come from one source." In other words, the scholars had neither the need nor the right to question anything.

Li Ssü then proposed that all books except ones concerning the Ch'in Dynasty, as well as works on nonpolitical subjects such as medicine, be burned. Anyone who did not give up their books would have their face branded with a hot iron and then be sent to work on the Great Wall for four years. As for those who discussed the past and compared the present system unfavorably with it, they would simply be executed.

Naturally, the emperor approved of all the measures Li Ssü had proposed. During the following year, when he suspected some 460 scholars of speaking against him, he ordered them buried alive.

A feared and hated emperor

Shih Huang Ti was what modern people would call a "micromanager." He had a habit of touring his empire, making sure that everything was in order. It was on one such tour, in northeastern China, that he became ill. Knowing he was about to die, he ordered that his eldest son should succeed him.

In a characteristic Shih Huang Ti touch, it was arranged that all his concubines who had failed to produce children would be buried alive with the emperor. So, too, were all the men who had worked on the tomb; thus, the logic went, nobody would know how to get in.

With the emperor barely cold in the ground, the tutor of Shih Huang Ti's second son changed the will so it said that the eldest son should commit suicide in order for the second son to take the throne. It hardly mattered in the long run who wore the crown of Ch'in: The dynasty's founder had left so many enemies that as soon as he was dead, revolt spread throughout China. The new emperor lasted only three years. Ultimately Liu Pang seized control.

For More Information

Books

Cotterell, Arthur. *Ancient China*. Photographed by Alan Hills and Geoff Brightling. New York: Knopf, 1994.

Guisso, R. W. L., et al. *The First Emperor of China*. New York: Carol Publishing Group, 1989.

Mann, Elizabeth. *The Great Wall*. New York: Mikaya Press, 1997.

McNeese, Tim. *The Great Wall of China*. San Diego, CA: Lucent Books, 1997.

Sabin, Louis. *Ancient China*. Mahwah, NJ: Troll Associates, 1985.

Web Sites

"Construction of the Great Wall Begins." http://www.northpark.edu/acad/history/WebChron/China/GreatWall.html (accessed on July 9, 1999).

"Discovering the Great Wall and Ming Tombs." http://zinnia.umfacad.maine.edu/~mshea/China/great.hmtl (accessed on July 9, 1999).

"EAWC: Ancient China." *Exploring Ancient World Cultures*. http://www.eawc.evansville.edu/chpage.htm (accessed on July 9, 1999).

"Shih Huang Ti." http://www.taisei.co.jp/cg_e/ancient_world/xian/axian.html (accessed on July 9, 1999).

Vergil

Born 70 B.C.
Died 19 B.C.

Roman poet

Among the poets of Rome, Vergil is usually considered the greatest: Rome's answer to Homer [see sidebar]. Indeed, Vergil's most famous work, the *Aeneid*, combines elements of Homer's two epics, the *Iliad* and the *Odyssey*. But it is much more than an imitation.

Just as the Romans thrived by borrowing from other cultures, so Vergil's work is almost an encyclopedia of all that went before it. His *Georgics* sums up the spirit of Rome, both its dark and bright sides. Together with the *Eclogues* the work paved the way for the literature of medieval times and the Renaissance. A host of everyday expressions have their origins in Vergil's writing, including "Mind over matter" and "Love conquers all."

Romans are usually known by short versions of their names: thus the full name of Vergil—sometimes rendered as "Virgil"—was Publius Vergilius Maro (POOB-lee-us vur-JIL-yuhs MAHR-oh). He was born on October 15, 70 B.C., near the ancient Etruscan town of Mantua (MAHN-tyu-ah), which is now part of Italy. At that time Mantua belonged to the Roman province of Cisalpine (siz-AL-pine) Gaul. It was a rural area,

Happy the man who has learned the causes of things, and has put under his feet all fears.

Georgics

Homer and Odysseus

Only a few writers in the history of Western literature enjoy a stature comparable with Homer's, yet people know almost nothing about the composer of the *Iliad* and the *Odyssey*. For centuries, many believed that he was not really one man but several. Later scholarship, however, suggests that there really was a man named Homer, who probably lived some time between 900 and 700 B.C. in the Ionian (ie-OHN-ee-un) colonies of Asia Minor.

Much more is known about the greatest of Homer's characters, Odysseus (oh-DIS-ee-us), hero of the *Odyssey,* sometimes known by his Latin name, Ulysses (yoo-LIS-eez). Odysseus was reluctant to join Agamemnon (ag-uh-MIM-nahn) and the others going away to the Trojan War. His wife, Penelope (pehn-EL-uh-pee), had just given birth to a son,

Telemachus (tel-IM-uh-kuhs). Odysseus wanted to stay and raise the boy. He tried to pretend he was crazy, but Agamemnon's messenger called his bluff, and he had to join the Greek forces.

Ten years later, with the war over, all the survivors went home, though not all lived happily ever after. Agamemnon, for one, was murdered by his wife's lover, and his son had to take revenge on the killer. A similar fate seemed to await Odysseus. Back at his palace, a number of young men, thinking Odysseus was dead, had gathered around Penelope. Telemachus, by then a young man, watched helplessly as they made advances toward his mother. Meanwhile, his father was lost at sea.

Homer writes that it took Odysseus a full ten years to return from Troy. It all

and despite his many visits to Rome, Vergil would be a country boy to the end of his days.

His father was a laborer, but his mother the daughter of his father's boss, a landlord. Thus Vergil's mother ensured the boy a better future than if he had merely been the son of peasants. He studied in Mantua and then attended the equivalent of high school in Rome, where he learned rhetoric (RET-uh-rik), or the art of speaking and writing. Later he went to Naples (NAY-pulz) in southern Italy, where he studied under the philosopher Siro.

Siro belonged to the Epicurean (ep-i-KYOOR-ee-un) school of philosophy, which had started in Greece. The Epicureans originally taught enjoyment of life's simple joys. Even-started because he had killed the one-eyed giant called Cyclops (SIE-klahps), who turned out to be the son of Poseidon, god of the seas. Poseidon cursed Odysseus, forcing him to wander throughout the Mediterranean.

Odysseus had all manner of misadventures at the hands of the witch Circe (SUR-say); the Sirens, with their deadly song; the cannibalistic Lestrygonians (les-tri-GOHN-ee-uns); and the beautiful Calypso (ku-LIP-soh), who held him prisoner. Eventually, however, he managed to return home, where he joined forces with Telemachus, killed the suitors, and was reunited with Penelope.

Many consider the *Odyssey* an even greater work than the *Iliad*, certainly it is a more mature one. The brave Achilles, hero of the *Iliad*, seems downright childish compared with Odysseus, whose hardships are those of an older and wiser man. Ultimately the theme of the *Odyssey* is one of wisdom and self-control, of learning how to get through life and to choose one's battles carefully.

The *Odyssey* has served as the model for a whole range of works dealing with long and perilous journeys, from Vergil's *Aeneid* to Dante's *Divine Comedy*, from Mark Twain's *Adventures of Huckleberry Finn* (1885) to the 1968 film *2001: A Space Odyssey*. James Joyce (1882–1941), one of the greatest writers of modern times, based his 1922 novel *Ulysses* on Homer's classic. Joyce described Odysseus as the only "complete" character—that is, one with a full set of flaws to balance his strengths—in all of literature.

tually this philosophy became corrupted to a pursuit of pure physical pleasure. To judge from Vergil's life, he embraced the "simple joys" part but never became an "epicurean" in the negative sense of the word.

The *Eclogues*

His family had originally planned for Vergil to pursue a career in law, but he was too shy for public speaking; therefore he returned to the family farm, where he began to write and study poetry. In 42 B.C., he started work on a set of poems called the *Eclogues* (EK-lawgz), or "Selections." His work was interrupted during the following year, when the Roman authorities seized his family's land to give it to war veterans.

**Vergil leading Dante
through Hell and Purgatory
in the story of the _Divina
Commedia_.** _Painting by
Delacroix. Corbis-Bettmann.
Reproduced by permission._

It was a troubled time for Rome, two years after the murder of Julius Caesar. Caesar's nephew Octavian (ahk-TAY-vee-un) had taken control, along with two other members of the Second Triumvirate. Vergil's friends suggested he go to Rome and ask Octavian to restore the farm. Apparently Vergil impressed Octavian, who would be known to history by his later title of Augustus Caesar. Augustus was a ruthless political leader, but he was also an admirer of the arts.

Although he had managed to rescue the family lands, Vergil moved to Naples, where he resumed work on the _Eclogues_. These consisted of ten poems of a style called _pastoral_ (PAS-tohr-uhl, from the same root as "pasture.") Pastoral literature, pioneered by the Greek poet Theocritus (thee-AHK-ri-tus; c. 310–250 B.C.), featured shepherds in a country setting. The language of the speakers in such poems was far more sophisticated than that of typical herdsmen, however.

The _Eclogues_ characterized Vergil's later work, most notably by referring to a whole array of ancient writings. Theocritus had set his pastorals in the Greek region of Arcadia (ar-KAY-dee-uh). For Vergil, Arcadia became not so much a place as a state of mind. Thus today, the word "arcadian" refers to a place of simple pleasures and quiet.

In spite of their peaceful setting, the _Eclogues_ contained more than a hint of the troubles in Rome—most notably the confiscation of lands by the state, a situation that had affected Vergil personally. His next work, the _Georgics_ (JOHR-jikz), or "Points of Farming," would build on this contrast of bright and dark.

The _Georgics_

With the publication of the _Eclogues_ in 37 B.C., Vergil attracted praise and admiration from many influential

Romans, most notably the statesman Maecenas (mi-SEE-nus; c. 70–8 B.C.). Maecenas took Vergil under his wing, both personally and financially, and suggested that he write a book on agriculture.

But Maecenas also had a political purpose in mind, one relating to the troubles in the countryside. He wanted Vergil to encourage Romans, many of whom had left their farms, to return to planting. The desertion of the countryside was one of the great problems throughout Roman history and would help bring about the fall of the empire centuries later. The *Georgics* turned out to be far more than a political advertisement.

The work consists of four books—actually long poems—that discuss in turn grain production, growing of trees and vineyards, raising animals, and beekeeping. Again, Vergil showed his command over all the classics of his day, bringing in themes from Homer and a number of other poets. Taking a cue from the *Works and Days* of Hesiod, for instance, he explained how humans had been forced to scratch out a living from the land. This theme is also discussed in the Israelites' Old Testament, though it is doubtful that Vergil had any exposure to the Book of Genesis.

As with the *Eclogues,* Vergil created a shadowy backdrop in the *Georgics,* suggesting that constant war would threaten the peaceful Roman countryside. For a Roman, such a viewpoint was not "politically correct." Roman citizens were always supposed to support their country's wars. In his final and greatest work, Vergil would continue this theme with even greater impact, weaving it into an epic that celebrated the founding of Rome.

The *Aeneid*

More honors followed the publication of the *Georgics* in 29 B.C.: Octavian, who had by then assumed full control of Rome, gave Vergil two country estates and a generous annual allowance. Two years later, Octavian would be crowned emperor. His friends suggested that Vergil compose an epic in his honor.

Vergil spent the last ten years of his life on the project, an epic that came to be known as the *Aeneid* (uh-NEE-ed). Its story picks up where Homer's *Iliad* (IL-ee-ed) leaves off, with the destruction of Troy. In many ways, it is the mirror image of the *Iliad* and *Odyssey* [AHD-i-see; see sidebar]. The Trojans, rather than the Greeks, are Vergil's heroes. Whereas the *Odyssey*—a tale of wandering—follows the *Iliad*'s story of conquest, Vergil reversed the order.

The *Aeneid* begins with the Aeneas (uh-NEE-uhs) leading a small group of Trojan pioneers who sail away to found a new Troy. The first half of the epic concerns their adventures as they wander through the Mediterranean. The latter half describes how they conquer the land that would one day become Rome.

The tale brings in a whole range of ancient ideas, from reincarnation to Stoic philosophy to Aristotle's (see entry) ideas about potentiality. Vergil suggests that the entire future of Rome was contained in the events of Aeneas's conquest, symbolized by a shield given to Aeneas by the gods that depicts all the major events of Roman history up to the rise of Octavian.

The death and legacy of Vergil

As always, there is a dark side to the *Aeneid,* suggesting the vast toll in human life that Roman conquests would take. Perhaps Octavian (who by then had become Caesar Augustus) missed this point, or perhaps he was broad-minded enough to appreciate it as literature in spite of its unpatriotic undertones. In any case, his influence helped to make it the most well-known of Roman classics. The *Aeneid* was required reading in schools throughout the empire.

By then Vergil was dead. In the tenth year of the project, he had left his home in Naples to conduct research in Greece and Asia Minor; however, he caught a fever in the Greek city of Megara (MEG-uh-ruh) and returned to Italy. On his deathbed, he ordered that the unfinished *Aeneid* be burned. Fortunately, Augustus overruled him, and after his death put two poets to work editing the poem.

Published in 17 B.C., the *Aeneid* was an instant and enormous success. Its influence never died out through the centuries that followed. So many copies were made that it, unlike many works of the Greeks, survived the fall of the empire and the centuries of darkness that followed.

As European culture began to revive again in the 1200s, Dante (DAHN-tay; 1265–1321) wrote his *Divine Comedy,* an epic in which the poet takes a journey through Hell, Purgatory, and Heaven. On this great odyssey, Dante chose as his guide the greatest poet of ancient Rome: Vergil.

For More Information

Books

Camps, W. A. *An Introduction to Vergil's "Aeneid."* New York: Oxford University Press, 1969.

Colum, Padraic. *The Trojan War and the Adventures of Odysseus.* Illustrated by Barry Moser. New York: Morrow, 1997.

Philip, Neil, reteller. *The Adventures of Odysseus.* Illustrated by Peter Malone. New York: Orchard Books, 1997.

Sutcliff, Rosemary. *The Wanderings of Odysseus: The Story of the Odyssey.* Illustrated by Alan Lee. New York: Delacorte Press, 1996.

Williams, R. D. *Virgil: His Poetry through the Ages.* London: British Library, 1982.

Web Sites

"Classical Studies Page." *Voice of the Shuttle.* http://humanitas.ucsb.edu/shuttle/classics.html (accessed on July 10, 1999).

"Homer's *Iliad* and *Odyssey.*" http://library.advanced.org/19300/data/homer.html (accessed on July 10, 1999).

"The Trojan War—History, Myth and Homer." http://www.geocities.com/Athens/Aegean/7545/Troy.html (accessed on July 10, 1999).

The Vergil Project. http://vergil.classics.upenn/edu/ (accessed on July 10, 1999).

Virgil.org. http://www.virgil.org/ (accessed on July 10, 1999).

Wu Ti

Born 156 B.C.
Died 87 B.C.

Chinese emperor

Wu Ti, whose given name was Liu Che, became the greatest emperor of the Han Dynasty, which ruled China for nearly 400 years beginning in 207 B.C. His reign would see enormous expansion in China's territories and the first Chinese contacts with Western civilizations. Under Wu Ti, Confucianism would finally triumph through his appointment of scholars to run the government. The power of the state would also greatly expand, thanks to careful maneuvering on the part of Wu Ti. He got the better of the feudal landlords who had long challenged the emperor's authority.

Taking the throne

Ancient Chinese emperors only received their official titles after their deaths. Thus the greatest of the Han (HAHN) rulers was known during his lifetime as Liu Che (lee-OO CHUH). A descendant of Liu Pang, he would be remembered as Wu Ti or Wudi (woo-DEE), meaning "the warlike emperor."

In 141 B.C., when he was fifteen years old, his father died, leaving Wu Ti as emperor. However, because of his age, he was overseen by his grandmother. He did not assume the full powers of the throne until she died in 135 B.C. By then, Wu Ti was twenty-one and eager to consolidate his power.

Establishing a civil service

Up to his time, emperors had relied on their chancellors, high government officials who held all the real power, but Wu Ti was not about to share power. In 135 B.C., at the outset of his reign, he began setting up a new system for running the government bureaucracy.

In order to do this, he brought in a number of Confucian (kuhn-FYOO-shuhn) scholars. By then Confucius (see entry) had been dead more than 300 years, but the school of thought he had established had continued. Confucianism taught principles of social harmony based on loyalty and obedience and placed a high value on education.

From an early time, the Chinese had believed that the emperor ruled according to authority given to him from on high, what they called the "Mandate of Heaven." It is doubtful that Wu Ti would have been Confucius's idea of a perfect ruler, but the emperor was able to use the concepts of the latter-day Confucianists (concepts that had changed somewhat since the time of the great teacher) in order to reinforce his authority as the "Son of Heaven."

In 135 B.C., Wu Ti decreed that local governments should recommend men of great ability, who could then take written examinations for official posts. This was the beginning of the Chinese civil service, and of its examination system, which would be formally adopted more than seven centuries later. Despite his interest in unrestrained power, Wu Ti produced positive results with the establishment of the examination system. The system rewarded only ability and thus offered an opportunity for advancement to all classes of society.

Consolidating his power

From the time of the Shang Dynasty (SHAHNG) some 1,500 years earlier, power in China had been uneasily divided between kings or emperors and noblemen. The latter exerted varying degrees of influence, depending on the strength of the ruler. Wu Ti decided he would break the nobles' power for good.

In 128 B.C., he declared that when a nobleman died, all his male heirs would divide the noble's lands and property equally. This had the effect of diluting the influence of any one noble house. From then on, Wu Ti was firmly in control.

Later, as he sent his troops on a variety of foreign expeditions, Wu Ti needed to increase his government's economic as well as political power. He did this by placing a variety of industries under the hand of the government and by taking control of the nation's money supply. Good or bad, this was a very modern approach to economics, not different in principle from socialism, a system practiced by many governments during the twentieth century.

Foreign wars

Wu Ti's consolidation of power at home was like the frame of a picture: the real focus of his reign lay in his pursuit of conquests abroad. Seldom would China ever be as large as it was under Wu Ti, who kept his soldiers busy in a series of wars from 133 to 97 B.C.

During his reign, Wu Ti brought a number of areas under Chinese control, including modern-day Vietnam and much of southeast Asia. Chinese troops took control of the northern part of Korea in 108 B.C. and added large parts of central Asia to the empire.

Unlike other conquerors, however, Wu Ti did not personally lead the troops, though in 111 B.C. he took part in a great show of military strength along the Great Wall. Leading thousands of soldiers with banners flapping in the breeze, he demonstrated that China was prepared to deal with foreign enemies.

The latter display was directed at the Hsiung Nu, a nomadic people living north of China. After nearly forty years of war, Wu Ti would drive out the Hsiung Nu. Some of them would wind up in Europe, where they became known as the Huns. There they would hasten the downfall of the Roman Empire six centuries later.

His battles with the Hsiung Nu gave Wu Ti an excuse for further expansion and an opportunity for the first Chinese contacts with other civilizations [see sidebar]. In 104 B.C., he sent troops into central Asia—what is now the former Soviet

Chang Chi'en

The name of Chang Chi'en or Zhang Qian (JAHNG chee-YEHN; d. 114 B.C.) is hardly a household word; yet in ancient times, he literally linked the East and the West and paved the way for journeyers such as Marco Polo. An official in the court of Wu Ti, he was sent westward in 138 B.C. on an important mission: to find allies in the emperor's war against the nomadic Hsiung Nu, or Huns.

Chang Chi'en's objective was to establish contact with the Yüeh Chih, another nomadic tribe driven to the west of China by the Hsiung Nu. The Yüeh Chih had wound up on the border of what is now Afghanistan, where they had subdued the Greco-Bactrian kingdom. The latter had absorbed elements of Greek culture left over from the conquests of Alexander, elements which they transmitted to the Yüeh Chih. Out of the Yüeh Chih, in turn, would emerge the Kushan Empire, under the leadership of Kanishka, which would further help to link the cultures of the ancient world.

But that all lay far in the future when Chang Chi'en made his way to the west. Captured by the Hsiung Nu, he lived among them for many years, and even had a Hsiung Nu wife and children. Eventually, however, he reached to Yüeh Chih territory.

Chang Chi'en failed in his immediate mission. The Yüeh Chih were happy where they were and had no interest in going back east to fight old enemies. But by making contact with those who had been in contact with the West, he helped to open up the world. Out of his journeys would come the great westward expansion of the Han Empire, and more important, the opening of the Silk Road. This route would eventually stretch from China all the way to Syria and would permit the flow of goods—and ideas—from East to West.

republics of Uzbekistan and Tajikistan—to secure a particular breed of horse known to the Chinese as "Heavenly Horses."

The world of Wu Ti

Wu Ti's interest in Heavenly Horses came from his adoption, in his latter days, of bizarre mystical beliefs. Influenced by magicians associated with the Taoist faith (DOW-ist), he became convinced that by riding one of those horses, he could make his way into Heaven. In his latter days, Wu Ti resembled an Egyptian pharaoh: not only was he obsessed with the idea of his own immortality, but he encouraged his people in the cult of emperor-worship. The Chinese, like the Egyptians, considered their rulers gods, but Wu Ti placed a particularly strong emphasis on this practice.

He also fostered a number of cultural pursuits, though here again, Wu Ti left the stamp of his personality. Among the prominent figures of his court was Ssu-ma Ch'ien (soo-MAH chee-YEN; c. 145–85 B.C.). Court historian and acknowledged "father of Chinese history," just as Herodotus (see entry) is credited as the father of Western history, Ssu-ma Ch'ien got into trouble with Wu Ti for defending a general who had surrendered to the Hsiung Nu. Wu Ti had him castrated. On a more positive note, Wu Ti ordered the establishment of the Chinese Music Bureau in 120 B.C. for the purpose of preserving and collecting folk songs.

Wu Ti's court was characterized by palace intrigue involving his various wives and sons. In 130 B.C., he became convinced that one of his daughters was using black magic against him. As a result he had her executed along with some 300 others. The plots only became worse in his later years. In 91 B.C. he forced the empress to commit suicide along with her son and heir.

Wu Ti left his country's economy in a shambles. He had established a pattern of infighting in the court that would later help to bring down the Han Dynasty. Nonetheless, his many conquests, as well as public works projects such as the building of a massive flood control system, made him one of China's most important rulers of ancient times.

For More Information

Books

Durant, Will. *The Story of Civilization,* Volume I: *Our Oriental Heritage.* New York: Simon and Schuster, 1954, pp. 698-701.

Nancarrow, Peter. *Early China and the Wall.* New York: Cambridge University Press, 1978.

Schafer, Edward H. and the Editors of Time-Life Books. *Ancient China.* New York: Time-Life Books, 1967.

Tompert, Ann. *The Jade Horse, the Cricket, and the Peach Stone.* Illustrated by Winston Trang. Honesdale, PA: Boyds Mill Press, 1996.

Web Sites

"The Early Han Dynasty." http://tqd.advanced.org/12255/library/dynasty/earlyHan.html (accessed on July 5, 1999).

"Empires Past: China: Han Dynasty." http://library.advanced.org/16325/c-han.html (accessed on July 5, 1999).

"The Former Han: 206 BC–25 AD." *Ancient China.* http://www.wsu.edu:8080/~dee/CHEMPIRE/FORMHAN.HTM (accessed on June 26, 1999).

"The Former or Western Han Dynasty: 202 BC–AD 9." http://www.northpark.edu/acad/history/WebChron/China/FormerHan.html (accessed on July 5, 1999).

"The Han Dynasty." http://deall.ohio-state.edu/jin3/c231/handouts/h8.htm (accessed on June 26, 1999).

Xerxes

Born c. 518 B.C.
Died 465 B.C.

Persian emperor

Xerxes was the third and last great ruler of the Persian Empire, after Cyrus and Darius, Xerxes's father. The first two built a glorious empire for Persia during the half-century beginning in about 550 B.C., but by the time Xerxes came to the throne in 486 B.C., that empire was beginning to break apart.

The reign of Xerxes saw rebellions among the empire's conquered peoples, first in Egypt and Babylonia and later in Greece. In spite of their greater numbers, the Persians would lose the Grecian conflict, thus helping to usher in the Athenian Golden Age. At home, Xerxes would play a less violent role in the history of another culture, that of the Israelites [see sidebar].

Cyrus and Darius

In 550 B.C., Cyrus the Great (SIE-ruhs; c. 585–529 B.C.; ruled 559–529 B.C.) established the Persian Empire. He went on to defeat the Lydians of Asia Minor in 546 B.C., and added the Ionian (ie-OH-nee-uhn) city-states of Greece to the empire. Seven years later, in 539 B.C., he conquered Babylonia. He also built an extensive network of roads and established the first significant postal system. Cyrus died in battle in 529 B.C. After a struggle for succession, a general named Darius (DARE-ee-uhs; 550–486 B.C.; ruled 522–486 B.C.) took the throne.

When they began conquering the world, the warlike Persians did not have a firmly established civilization of their own. Perhaps for that reason, Cyrus showed great tolerance toward the cultures of the people they subjected. He respected their religions as well and allowed the Israelites to begin returning to their land after a long period of captivity. Darius, however, was not so tolerant. He was a firm believer in Persia's own Zoroastrian (zohr-oh-AS-tree-uhn) faith and in its god Ahura-Mazda (ah-HOOR-uh MAHZ-duh). He expected others to come into line with it.

Like Cyrus before him, Darius (who also came to be called "the Great") was a mighty conqueror. He added parts of northern India to the empire and waged several campaigns in the west, where the Ionian Greeks had revolted in 499 B.C. Other Greeks, most notably the Athenians, joined their neighbors against him. The result was a major battle at Marathon in 490 B.C.. The Persians lost, and Darius planned to teach the Greeks a lesson, but he died while preparing to do so, in 486 B.C.

Cyrus the Great, founder of the Persian Empire. *Source unknown.*

Living up to his predecessors

Upon the death of Darius, he was succeeded by his son, Xerxes (ZUHRK-seez). Clearly Xerxes had a lot to live up to. The histories of Persia are largely silent about his early life, though its is safe to assume that he received the best education available at the time. The education of a future king would have included military training as well. Though he was not his father's first son, he was the first by the Queen Atossa (uh-TAHS-uh), daughter of Cyrus, a highly influential woman in the empire.

Esther

The biblical Book of Esther is the story of a young Jewish woman who became the wife of Xerxes—Ahasuerus (a-ha-SHARE-uhs) in Hebrew. Her beauty won his favor over hundreds of other girls, but on the advice of her uncle Mordecai (MOHR-deh-kie), she did not tell him she was a Jew.

An evil palace official named Haman (HAY-muhn) became angry at Mordecai when the latter did not bow down to him. Because of their religious faith, Jews refused to bow down to anyone but God. Haman decided that he would destroy all the Jews. But in an exciting and dramatic reversal that makes Esther one of the most fascinating books of the Bible, Haman was the one who ended up being destroyed, and Esther and her uncle Mordecai were honored. To this day, Jews celebrate the festival of Purim (POOR-im) to commemorate how God saved them from destruction.

Esther is typically treated as a religious document rather than as a historical one. There is no mention of Esther herself in the Persian records; however, this does not mean that the biblical account is untrue. In any case, the Book of Esther is an exciting tale, one that would hold up well against even the most suspenseful movie.

By the age of twenty, Xerxes already had an important responsibility, serving as governor over the province of Babylonia. To the Persians, and indeed to most peoples living in the wide expanse between Egypt and India, Babylon was the greatest city in the world. The only rival would have been Damascus, capital of Syria, which would become the capital of the Seleucid Empire that ruled over Persia two centuries later.

The historical records indicate that Xerxes oversaw the building of a palace in Babylon. The next significant mention of him came twelve years later, in November of 486 B.C., when Darius died and Xerxes became emperor of Persia.

Rebellions throughout the empire

The principal challenge of Darius's reign came from a series of revolts throughout the empire. First, there was an uprising in Egypt, which had started in the time of Darius and which Xerxes went to quash (suppress completely) in 485 B.C. He proved himself, according to the Greek historian Herodotus (see entry), by placing Egypt "under a much harder slavery than in the time of Darius." Then he went on to crush two revolts in Babylon.

The first of these began in the summer of 484 B.C., when a Babylonian leader murdered the Persian satrap (SA-trap), or governor, and declared himself king. He was killed two months later. In August of 482 B.C., another Babylonian proclaimed himself "King of Babylon and the Lands." By the following spring, 481 B.C., Xerxes had suppressed this revolt, but he did not stop there. He destroyed the great ziggurat, or temple tower, and tore down the Babylonians' temple to their god Marduk (mahr-DOOK). Thanks to Xerxes's harsh treatment, Babylon would never again be an important part of the Persian Empire.

Plotting war with Greece

Xerxes had crushed a rebellion in Africa and two in Asia; now he planned to do the same in Europe—specifically, in Greece, where his father had left some unfinished business. On his side he had traitors from the two principal city-states of Greece: Demaratus (deh-meh-RAH-tuhs), a former king of Sparta, and Hippias (HIP-ee-uhs), a tyrant kicked out by the people of Athens just before the establishment of democracy in that city.

The war with Greece could not have gone even as well as it did without plenty of help from the Greeks, including many who took the Persians' side in battle. Hippias and Demaratus both encouraged an invasion of Greece, as did Xerxes's cousin Mardonius (mahr-DOHN-ee-uhs). His uncle and advisor Artabanus (ahr-tuh-BANE-uhs), however, tried to talk Xerxes out of making the attack.

It is hard to assess Artabanus's intentions in light of what later happened, but at this point it seems he had the king's best interests at heart. Xerxes first grew angry, but then changed his mind and gave up on the invasion plan. According to Herodotus, however, that night he had a vision in which a ghost told him to go ahead with the attack. He changed his mind several times over the next few days, but the ghost kept coming back to him. Finally he decided to march westward.

Marching into Greece

The invasion of Greece was a huge effort, involving a military force of between 150,000 and 200,000 men. Herodotus wrote of the varied Persian army, which combined forty-six different nationalities from around the Persian Empire. Besides the Medes and Persians, there were Assyrians in brass helmets, Indians carrying bows made out of cane, Scythians armed with battle axes, and Thracians wearing coats

Xerxes watching ships battle. *Archive Photos. Reproduced by permission.*

of bright colors. Most magnificent of all, however, was the group called the Immortals, or the Ten Thousand, so named because whenever one of them fell in battle, he would be replaced by another to maintain their numbers. Along with this army was a navy of some 4,000 ships.

Though he was a Zoroastrian, Xerxes made a sacrifice to the Greek goddess Athena near the site of Troy. Perhaps he was hedging his bets; certainly there were a number of bad signs on the horizon. Twice the Persians tried to make a bridge of boats across the more than 2-mile-wide (3.2-kilometer-wide) Hellespont, and twice storms destroyed these bridges. On the third try, the army made it, but in all the crossing took a week. Another bad omen came in the form of a rumor, which spread throughout the army, that a mare had given birth to a hare—a sign, the Persians believed, that they would march into Greece like horses and run out like rabbits. It was around this time that Xerxes watched his troops march by and, according to Herodotus, began to weep. Artabanus asked him why he was crying, and Xerxes is said to have replied, "It came to my mind how pitifully short human life is—for all these thousands of men, not one will be alive in a hundred years' time."

Defeat and assassination

Though they defeated the Greeks at Thermopylae (thurh-MAHP-uh-lee) on August 28, 480 B.C., it was only at great cost. The Greeks, particularly the Spartans, were so noble in defeat that they seemed like the winners. On September 5, Xerxes burned the city of Athens, but this did little to help the Persians' cause. The Athenians had moved to the island of Salamis (SAH-luh-mis), where a few days later, the two forces met in one of the greatest naval battles of all time. Before the battle, Xerxes had ordered that his throne be placed atop a nearby mountain so that he could see his navy's victory; instead, he witnessed its complete defeat at the hands of the Greeks.

The omen about the rabbit came true: Xerxes led his men in a hasty retreat, a backbreaking march that took them to the Hellespont in forty-five days. There they boarded ships and sailed for home, though Xerxes spent a year in the city of Sardis in Asia Minor. Within a year, the Greeks had defeated the remaining Persian force under Mardonius.

Xerxes ruled for fourteen years after the defeat by the Greeks. In 465 B.C., he was assassinated by Artabanus. His son Artaxerxes (ahr-tag-ZUHRK-seez) succeeded him and slew Artabanus, but the glory days of the Persian Empire were largely past. In 338 B.C., Persia fell to a Greek invading force under Alexander.

For More Information

Books

Llywelyn, Morgan. *Xerxes*. New York: Chelsea House Publishers, 1987.

Meltzer, Milton. *Ten Queens: Portraits of Power*. Illustrated by Bethanne Anderson. New York: Dutton Children's Books, 1998.

Mindel, Nissan. *Complete Story of Purim: Compiled from the Book of Esther, Targum, Talmud and Midrash*. 3rd ed. Brooklyn, NY: Merkos L'inyonei Chinuch, 1949.

Neurath, Marie. *They Lived Like This in Ancient Persia*. Illustrated by John Ellis. New York: F. Watts, 1970.

Renault, Mary. *The Lion in the Gateway: The Heroic Battles of the Greeks and Persians at Marathon, Salamis and Thermopylae*. New York: Harper & Row, 1964.

Wolkstein, Diane. *Esther's Story*. Illustrated by Juan Wijngaard. New York: Morrow Junior Books, 1996.

Web Sites

"The Book of Esther." http://bibleinst.com/BibleSchool/OT-U-6E.htm (accessed on June 27, 1999).

Persian War Online. http://userwww.service.emory.edu/~jedgeco/history/persianwar.html (accessed on June 27, 1999).

"Purim." http://www.amfi.org/purim.htm (accessed on June 27, 1999).

"*Xerxes* [opera] by George Frideric Handel." *Canadian Opera Company*. http://www.coc.ca/99xerxes.htm (accessed on June 27, 1999).

Index

Boldface type indicates entries and their page numbers.

Illustrations are marked by (ill).